DEEP CUBA

The

Inside

Story

of an

American

Oceanographic

Expedition

DEEP CUBA

BILL BELLEVILLE

The University of Georgia Press Athens & London

Published by the University of Georgia Press

Athens, Georgia 30602

© 2002 by Bill Belleville

Designed by Kathi Dailey Morgan

Set in 10.5 on 14.5 Berkeley Old Style by Bookcomp, Inc.

Printed and bound by Maple-Vail

The paper in this book meets the guidelines for permanence
and durability of the Committee on Production Guidelines
for Book Longevity of the Council on Library Resources.

Printed in the United States of America

06 05 04 03 02 C 5 4 3 2 1

LIBRARY OF CONGRESS CATALOGING-IN-PUBLICATION DATA

Belleville, Bill, 1945–

Deep Cuba : the inside story of an American oceanographic
expedition / Bill Belleville.

p. cm.

Includes bibliographical references.

ISBN 0-8203-2417-5 (hardcover : alk. paper)

1. Oceanography—Research—Caribbean Sea.

2. Oceanography—Research—United States.

3. Belleville, Bill, 1945– —Journeys—Cuba. I. Title.

GC63.S48 B45 2002

551.46'35'072073—dc21   2002002856

BRITISH LIBRARY CATALOGING-IN-PUBLICATION DATA AVAILABLE

Map on page xx by Mary Estes.

To

Pedro Alcolado Menéndez

and

Rodolfo Claro Madruga

Good scientists and good men

Prying about in strange places

can either get on your nerves or be fun.

Archie Carr

The Windward Road

I have too deeply enjoyed the voyage,

not to recommend [it to] any naturalist,

although he must not expect to be so

fortunate in his companions as I have been.

Charles Darwin

Voyage of the Beagle

—

CONTENTS

PREFACE

I'm an itinerant environmental writer who often finds himself in strange overseas locales to tell a story—narratives that find their way into print, on film, even as "content" on the Internet. It is at once uncertain and challenging, stimulating and exciting. It is seldom dull.

Although shadowing marine biologists and archaeologists and anthropologists in the field generates more than its share of extreme adventure, I am not strictly an adventure travel writer. And while I care deeply about natural history and the people whose lives are bound by it, I am not strictly a nature writer, either. By aligning myself with neither genre, I have successfully skirted the high-profile loop that pigeonholing often provides. But I can't complain: my assignments have taken me to the Great Barrier Reef of Australia and the White Sea of Russia, throughout the Antilles and deep into the Amazon. I have gone not as a tourist but as a journalist trying to understand a bit about these local bioregions and what makes them tick. Since I am a veteran scuba diver, I also look for stories that allow me to use that skill in order to take my sensibilities underwater whenever possible.

One of these peripatetic jobs led me to Cuba in a sort of roundabout way. It did so by first taking me to the Galápagos Islands for a month. There, I worked on contract as the de facto field producer for the Discovery Channel's Web site, creating essay-style dispatches, shooting digital photos, and uploading the entire electronic package via laptop and satellite phone for posting online. My base was an oceanographic ship chartered from Harbor Branch Oceanographic Institution (HBOI) by Discovery itself. During that trip, I dove with biologists and filmmakers in sharky waters and watched over their shoulders as they went about the business of practicing their craft with an authentic savoir faire. I much enjoy the company of people who routinely risk their safety to practice their science or art; they often exude a good-natured, actualized confidence that bears little resemblance to the defensive posturing found back in the office cubicles of the civilized world. On the Galápagos trip, I met an evolutionary biologist by the name of John McCosker. He had an off-the-wall sense of humor as well as a sort of wry irreverence. Afterward, we kept in touch, looking for ways to reconnect on another expedition.

Four years passed. One day, out of the blue, I got a call from McCosker telling me about a plan Discovery had to charter an HBOI ship again—this time for a intense month-long cine-exploration of Cuba's coastal waters in the winter of 1997–98. I was ecstatic. Within the next few weeks, I found out all I could about the plan. And although I had done little recent work for the ever morphing Web site, I made arrangements with Discovery Channel Online to go along as field producer as I had in the Galápagos.

It seemed a good fit. As a longtime Floridian, I saw a large black void every time I visited Key West and tried to imagine what was going on just ninety miles away, near the shores of the gigantic land mass of Cuba and its 3,563 miles of coastline. Certainly, the information American newspapers and television offered was often repetitive—pack journalism fueling spot news had reduced Cuba to a one-dimensional banana republic and its leader to a cardboard cutout in fatigues and beard. And although there were thousands of more in-depth magazine articles, essays, and books about Cuba—many of them exceptionally good—nearly all dealt with politics or history. There was little or no sense of the real ecology of the place. If Cuba had a natural history, the average American was blissfully unaware of it.

For me, the six-week-long oceanographic expedition seemed almost mythic with possibilities. Adventure, intrigue, scientific mystery, and, of course, danger would likely play out, as they would during any expeditionary event. But there was an added bonus, a remarkable prize in the Crackerjack box: during the span of my life, Cuba had turned into a sort of Casablanca of the Caribbean—an off-limits, shrink-wrapped place that, at some unknown time in the future, faced imminent change.

Certainly, our high-tech gear and our sub would give us the chance to see this Cuban natural world in a way no major American expedition ever had. This alone would make our journey to Cuba more than a trophy experience; it might even ease us into the pages of history. Personally, the experience would go far beyond oceanography. It would also reveal—in moments at once surreal and profound—how science in a fragile and politically sensitive place would be translated into a corporate television documentary.

As I mulled over the construct of "nature programming," though, other concerns arose: there is a great distance between documentaries that only address natural history—with precious or predatory animals that evoke either warm fuzzies or squeamish fear, and which are far easier to produce and sell—and those that examine conservation, considered tedious, soapboxesque, or worse, politically volatile. Robert Lamb, founder of the London-based Television for the Environment, was stoic about this distance when he wrote in *Our Planet*: "If you've got the choice of going home in the evening and there's David Attenborough [going] on about amazing wildlife behavior or [there's] somebody droning on about how all the salmon are disappearing due to global warming off the coast of Canada, what are you going to watch?" I wonder how the eventual Cuba film would navigate the treacherous minefield between those two approaches.

To buoy myself, I read *Blue Meridian* by Peter Matthiessen, a modern classic McCosker had recommended. It was about the first expeditionary search in 1969 for graphic film footage of the great white shark—footage that would later become the documentary "Blue Water, White Death." Matthiessen had learned to dive specifically to go along on that quest. Ironically, several members of our Cuba cruise played key roles in that book—notably topside producer Jim Lipscomb and underwater producer Al Giddings. *Blue Meridian* was a great adventure, well told by a skilled writer objective enough not to have a stake in science or filmmaking. But there was a striking contrast between the straightforward melodrama of that earlier expedition and the mission of our trip. Clearly, the purpose of that three-decade-old voyage of discovery had little to do with science. As the subtitle of *Blue Meridian* declared, it was "The Search for the Great White Shark." As I got a quick look at our own expedition's "working treatment" of "Cuba: Forbidden Waters," the likely appearance of "a shark feeding frenzy" was part of the selling point. But our goals would be far more abstruse—and perhaps, more difficult for our filmmakers to package for mass consumption. There would be searches of jellyfish that emit low levels of bioluminescence, a hunt for sponges with drug potential, a collection of deep-sea fish to determine biodiversity, ecology, and distribution, and—of course—the taken-for-granted presumption that we would capture fish that were previously undescribed by science. We would poke about the edges of a two-mile-deep trench, visit the notorious Bay of Pigs underwater, and dive on seamounts rising mysteriously up from the abyss. There would be a search for sunken German U-boats and plunging blue holes and Spanish galleons. By the time we arrived in Havana at the journey's end, there was the promise that El Comandante himself—a former spearfisher who knew from personal underwater experience the coast we would be traveling—would come aboard. Indeed, Fidel's anticipated visit would be a prize the filmmakers coveted, a tacit admission of his importance to the salability of this tale.

Perhaps not surprisingly, the only widely distributed English-speaking marine documentary filmed in Cuba was made by Jacques-Yves Cousteau. It featured an adventurous look at the coastal waters and the Cubans in 1986—including an extensive on-camera interview with Castro—in a way that no one before or since had been able to pull off. But Cousteau's "Cuba: Waters of Destiny" was now dated; worse, it had also included some bogus aquarium footage of a Mediterranean fish, passed off as Cuban. And the

Calypso, despite the intrepid nature of its crew, was no modern oceano-graphic ship. At the very least, we would be carrying—in addition to our three-thousand-foot-deep diving submersible and sophisticated computerized gear—eight doctorate-level scientists (including two renowned Cubans), as well as one scholar of Latin American history. We were being touted as the first extensive American expedition to Cuba since the embargo—and given the technology of marine science before then, we were certainly the best equipped ever. How could we go wrong?

I stuffed my concerns and tried to comfort myself with the prospect of discovering firsthand how the great system of life revealed itself inside this void of the Caribbean. I hoped I might spend time with the Cubans who lived in this environment—indeed, who depended on it for their livelihood. Hemingway's Santiago from *The Old Man and the Sea* might still be here, tenaciously hand-lining and tragically proud of a marlin that, in some fashion, never quite got away. With that in mind, I packed my laptop, wet suit, regulator, and dive computer and headed my jeep down from my home in east central Florida to Fort Pierce, where the HBOI ship was scheduled to set sail the next day.

As I drove south, I thought of a keen observation the eclectic American musician Ry Cooder had made after recently traveling to Cuba to produce a CD of son music. Cooder's *Buena Vista Social Club* lifted vintage musicians from lifelong obscurity and introduced them to a world beyond the twelve-mile limit of Cuba. Although he was talking about music, Cooder could well have been referring to the anticipation I had for the Cuban sea and its people. *Utne Reader*, in an article entitled "Return of the Mambo Kings," quoted Cooder thusly: "Because of the isolation, because of the regionality of this stuff, the music seems to me to be more intact. There's no pollution in there; there's a lot of power. These people don't drive on freeways and make cellular phone calls or go to their lawyers. They sit and play. Day and night, day and night."

I slipped the *Buena Vista Social Club* CD into my jeep's player. As I did, Ibrahim Ferrer's strong, silky voice came to me from some dark Cuban place I could barely imagine, perhaps a backroom full of Cohiba cigar smoke and the smell of roast pork and maybe, from off in the distance, the sensual rhythm of the tropical surf.

ACKNOWLEDGMENTS

Thanks to Michael L. Smith, Senior Research Scientist with the Center for Marine Conservation, who provided valuable background information on Cuba, as did Georgina Bustamante, Marine Conservation Coordinator for the Caribbean Division of The Nature Conservancy.

A great deal of credit is due to both Jim Lipscomb and Al Giddings for having the ingenuity and verve to launch this expedition, and for their generosity in allowing me to come along.

For support during different phases of the manuscript: my good friend Mary Estes, Barbara Ras at UGA Press, and Grace Buonocore, my ever-diligent copyeditor. At Discovery Channel Online, I am indebted to Greg Henderson for weathering the storm.

Thanks to the crew aboard the R/V *Seward Johnson*, particularly those who went out of their way—Randy Wimberg and Karen Straus for being skilled diving buddies and good sports,

Dan Boggess and Sharky Martin for helping me when I needed it, and Vince Seiler, a captain in the most complete sense of the word.

Much thanks, too, to all the scientists for bearing up under my snooping, especially John McCosker and Richard Fagen for their patient and generous friendship. I am also much obliged to both for allowing me to review their personal journals of the voyage.

Finally, I am particularly indebted to chief expedition scientist Grant Gilmore, whose gentle and wise appreciation of the marine world and the culture of those bound by it greatly helped inform this work.

DEEP CUBA

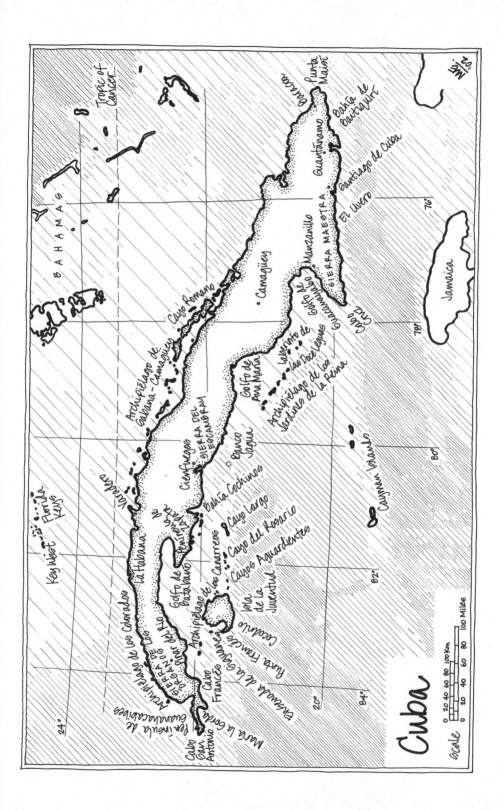

Cuba

scale
0 20 40 60 80 100 Km
0 20 40 60 80 100 Miles

Introduction

Dramatic sea voyages of discovery aren't special to the hyper-reality of the Information Age. After all, what was perhaps the prototypical maritime adventure had its first run somewhere in the eighth century B.C., when Odysseus took an especially slow boat home from the Trojan War in Homer's *Odyssey*. Along the way, he dodged Cyclops, sea monsters, and the near-irresistible call of Sirens. Homer was a gifted storyteller, and the sea was the stage set for his larger-than-life sagas. The world was flat, the ocean vast and uncharted, and sailors got lost a lot then, even in real life. Any long trip at sea could easily turn into a voyage of discovery. Survivors, blessed with the favor of the nautical gods, imbued their experience with the romance of the unknown. The great epic poems were imaginative art and allegory.

What of the truths hidden inside that great waterlogged cloak of the ocean? Aristotle, the founder of natural history, was among the first to report factually on aquatic critters like fishing frogs and nautiluses and eels in *Historia animalium* (344 B.C.), taking his astute gift for observation beyond the land. Fishes sleep, he discovered; so do mollusks and crustaceans. A nautilus is actually an octopus in disguise. Some fish hide under the sand and angle for prey with filaments on their mouth. Aristotle "discovered" 180 different marine species. And he didn't have to navigate the extended pitch and roll of the sea to do so.

It wasn't until Europeans started poking around in the New World for wealth to exploit that the real science of maritime voyages begin to acquire a life of its own. There were still sea monsters here—mostly at the known edges of maps—but increasingly, naturalists were signing on board with the explorers to keep track of the immense simmering resources swarming about them in the ocean, on islands, and on coastal shores.

Often, the voyages were merely the vehicle that took nascent biologists to the reaches of spectacularly unfamiliar topside flora and fauna of the newly established colonies. Sir Hans Sloane, invited to Jamaica as the personal physician of the governor, sailed there from Great Britain and returned to publish a natural history in 1707 that included more than eight hundred terrestrial species unknown to his compatriots. Sloane's success influenced Mark Catesby's voyages to the New World between 1712 and 1726 "to search after Plants, and other Productions of Nature." His watercolors—many from the Bahamas—became the basis for the first published, illustrated record of the British colonial biota in North America. Catesby's concern about the vital need for actual *pictures* of natural history foretold an image-driven world that would emerge a couple of centuries later. In *The Natural History of Carolina, Florida and the Bahamas* he wrote: "I may aver a clearer idea may be conceiv'd from the figures of Animals and Plants in their proper Color, than from the most exact Description without them."

By 1768, botanist Sir Joseph Banks funded and recruited a small scientific crew to join Captain James Cook aboard the HMS *Endeavour*, and they sailed off to verify the geographic myth of a great southern continent in the South Pacific. Later, Banks helped organize the infamous HMS *Bounty's* voyage, with the intention of gathering breadfruit from Tahiti to replant as a food source in the Caribbean.

When terrestrial biologist Charles Darwin boarded the HMS *Beagle* in 1831—fighting seasickness for nearly the entire five-year journey—he was baiting hooks to jerk animals out of the ocean and studying plankton within. Using Linnaeus's recently devised practice of taxonomy, he became one of the first to cull one newly "discovered" marine species from another, describing where each fit within the entire animal kingdom. Darwin even speculated on the origins of coral reefs, formulating theories that wouldn't be empirically proven for another century. And he made the astounding declaration that living fossils could be found in the depths, where they were protected from change that had long ago washed away their contemporaries back on land.

Between 1872 and 1876, the HMS *Challenger* circumnavigated the globe, probing ocean depths and surface currents and examining sea life trawled to the surface. Fitted with laboratories under the scientific direction of Charles Wyville Thomson, the *Challenger* was the forerunner of the modern oceanographic ship. The goals of the *Challenger* were both utilitarian and theoretic: one major chore was to survey the seabed in preparation for laying telegraphic cable; another was to see if Darwin's living fossils did indeed exist. By the time it drew back into port, the *Challenger* had also taken 492 soundings of the earth's seas, giving the terrestrial world its first hint that the oceans covered a terrain of mountains, trenches, and crevices as elaborate as anything back on land.

While Europe militarists feuded over who would commandeer the strategic tropical waters of the New World, scientists—like Felipe Poey in Cuba and Jean Louis Rodolphe Agassiz in Brazil—were diligently cataloging entire inventories of local sea creatures, largely from specimens fishermen dredged up from the ocean depths.

As the twentieth century dawned, ocean science underwent its own sea change: in California, the Scripps newspaper dynasty funded the Scripps Institution of Oceanography in 1903 in La Jolla, and back in the Northeast, the Rockefeller family founded the Woods Hole Oceanographic Institution in 1930 at Cape Cod. Both would become distinguished for their explorations of the deep, using fleets of research vessels—later augmented with submersibles, remotely controlled vehicles, and high-tech sea-probing instruments that functioned as the eyes of scientists.

By the 1920s, the intrepid scientist William Beebe of the New York Zo-ological Society became the first American biologist to wear a hard hat and to observe sea creatures in situ. Beebe snapped crude black-and-white photos, while assistant Ruth Rose took the image capturing one step further: using water-insoluble oil paints, she actually sat on the shallow ocean bottom and painted the reefs, rocks, and fish on canvas. Beebe later stretched those shallow depth limits by descending in a tethered, steel pressurized sphere, a bathysphere, to 2,800 feet off the coast of Bermuda in 1934.

Voyages of discovery began to acquire a second dimension, one that took natural sensibilities downward, instead of merely across an often desolate blue surface. Certainly, humans had long dreamed of bringing a tether of air into the sea for ages. Indeed, Aristotle told of *iebes*—caul-drons—dropped mouth first into the ocean so that sponge divers could dip up inside for a quick breath as early as the fourth century B.C. Rudimen-tary subs had been around in one form or another since 1620, and work-ing hard hats connected by air-pumping hoses had been first invented in 1837. French biologist Henri Milne-Edwards, professor of zoology at the Sorbonne, wore a breathing helmet to study marine life in the Straits of Messina in 1844. But such gear was unwieldy, dangerous, and expensive. And, instead of being used for the understanding of the aquatic environ-ment, it was most often employed for military stealth and the salvage of wrecked treasure ships.

But when modern scientists like Beebe got a glimpse of the subaquatic world firsthand, it became increasingly clear that there was no substitute for actually being there. Trawls, traditionally used to collect underwater specimens when dragged from the sterns of ships, couldn't begin to define the ever shifting, deep universe lit only by the muted glow of biolumines-cence. "No wonder that but a meager haul results from our slow-drawn, silken nets," wrote Beebe in *Half Mile Down*, "when almost all the organ-ism which came within my range of vision showed ability to dart and twist and turn, their lights passing, crossing and re-crossing in bewilder-ing mazes."

Unquestionably, our well-outfitted expedition to Cuba would have the chance to blaze new trails both over and under the waters swashing at the edges of that island-nation. And it would offer a flesh-and-blood perspective of daily expedition life, one that would turn out to have more than its share of uncommon moments—some heroic, some poetic, and some even approaching caricature.

As scientists began to develop a thirst for undersea exploration in the twentieth century, so too did the visual artists—who were egged on by the producers of entertainment. Their own sea change arrived midcentury with the invention of the aqualung, as well as the development of reliable subsea housings for still and movie cameras. Not only could the average diver stay underwater for an extended length of time, but he or she could bring back images of that exotic world for those who would otherwise never experience it. Within this era, enterprising storytellers wearing tanks of compressed air began stringing these images together to create films the rest of us knew as documentaries.

French naval officer Jacques-Yves Cousteau, co-inventor of the aqualung, was a pioneer of these cinematic undersea stories. The overwhelming success of his premier 1944 four-reel motion picture *Epaves* ("Sunken Ships") in Paris convinced him that the public had a yearning for this new unseen world. In short order, he bought and outfitted a ship with an air compressor and aqualungs, recruited a hardy crew of Gallic divers, and planned to explore the global oceanic mysteries through the viewfinder of an underwater camera housing. In 1951, Cousteau launched the *Calypso* on its premier voyage in the nearby Red Sea, an event that would lead to an entire lifetime of underwater filmmaking. "[The Red Sea] was virtually unexplored, transparent, and not too far away," Cousteau explained candidly in his book *The Living Sea*. "It had the reputation of being a nice hot bathtub full of sharks, and it was a coral sea." The impact was profound, creating a template that other filmmakers still imitate today.

To add a richer dimension to this storytelling, Cousteau considered bringing along academically trained natural science professionals who would help viewers better understand what they were seeing. "We sought out scientists who would like to use divers and submarine photography" to help tell the story of the sea, he explained. Yet the captain admitted to being apprehensive about how fully useful these strange cerebral academics might be: "To us, a scientist was an inscrutable type with a sad, doctrinal face and a stiff collar."

To Cousteau's surprise, he began to find academics like Jacques Bourcart, a professor of marine geology at the Sorbonne, who were articulate, robust, and camera-friendly. "Scientists, with their clutter of instruments, specimen jars and chemicals, had a great deal to teach us; and they, in turn, appreciated our direct knowledge of animal behavior and the morphology of a bottom they had never seen." Suddenly, there was a window to the undersea world, and it started right at the glass surface of the average family's television screen. Just when everyone seemed to think the last frontier was outer space, cine-science was proving otherwise. The ocean, which covered 70 percent of all the earth's surface, was *innerspace*, with the sea bottom materializing as a place more bizarre and unknown than some craters on the moon.

As the public's fascination with the sea grew in giant strides, so too did that of corporations hoping to profit from minerals and drugs on the ocean floor. Economics of such industry coupled with the new recreation of "sport diving" drove the development of better gear and technology. Clunky, corrugated double-hosed regulators were streamlined and made more reliable; inflatable buoyancy compensator vests allowed individuals to assume the full benefit of weightlessness. Between the 1950s and the mid-1970s, more than fifty scientific submersibles were built, each of them a one-of-a-kind inner space capsule that seemed lifted out of a Jules Verne novel.

As scientists acquired their own funding and exploration gear, commercial underwater filmmaking seemed circuslike in comparison with their more serious aims. For purists, it was an outright compromise in which only the most melodramatic adventure and photogenic discoveries could be pursued. Indeed, action was often rehearsed or replicated to match a "treatment" with a marketable expectation, and sometimes reality was altered altogether. As for original discovery, it was often shelved in favor of endless remakes of the salable formula of clear water, sharks, and coral— with sunken treasure galleons as the premium addendum.

Whenever filmmakers, writers, or photographers found their way onto a true scientific expedition, it became more as expendable tag-alongs than as co-partners. Serious scientists participated at their own risk, with the knowledge that the end result was a product for which an audience survey was far more important than approval by a panel of academic peers. Oceanographers were struggling to prove that their work—however novel—was science, and not art.

In an odd way, ocean documentaries began to serve the same educational purpose as zoos: they generated broad public empathy for the sea and the animals living in it. But if anyone cared to look closely, they found this was not exactly reality. Special underwater lighting made coral seem brighter than the human eye could imagine; the chumming of fish often made schools seem far more abundant and healthier than in real life; and countless days of patient observation edited into ten seconds made little miracles seem commonplace.

Nonetheless, such films were the main link to the underwater world for most of us land-bound, air-breathing mammals. And their graphic drama did much to raise our consciousness for the vast marine environment that lay just beyond the edges of the shore. Certainly, films entertained and engaged—and even had the power to inspire.

And then the paradigm shifted again. Universities and government agencies funding oceanographic research refocused their priorities: there were more than enough specimens in the world to study without going out and finding new ones. As for field research, well, the earth was mapped and known and the dragons at the edge of the map excised. Great oceanographic voyages now examined physics and hydrography and climate change, usually ignoring the organisms these factors influenced. It was time now for molecular research, bench work back in the lab that would reveal secrets from DNA and other tiny mysteries—none larger than a diatom—that bore into the infinitesimal core of the universe. Voyages of discovery would be a stroll from one electronic microscope to another.

From the perspective of the federal government, if there was any serious fieldwork left to be done, it would be in space; politics of the growing aerospace industry demanded it. In 1983, then president Ronald Reagan leveraged the fear of the Russian "Evil Empire" and proposed a plan to arm outer space with his $35 billion Star Wars program. Rocket launches were highly visible tools—they were seen on TV news in great blasts of smoke and fire!—and thus easier to peddle to taxpayers as worthwhile public expenditures. During that same year, American oceanographers received $124 million in federal funding for research. A search for a sea squirt, despite its biomedical potential to cure disease, lacked the vote-grabbing celebrity of a booster rocket.

Back in the parallel universe of marine filmmaking, the imitators of Cousteau's original formula were gaining stature in the open market. Cable television, encouraged by earlier nature programming successes, took private sector advertising money and swam with it. There was no longer just one modest educational television outlet or random network specials available for underwater documentaries—there were many, and they were in business to make profits. Of them all, the most successful by far was Discovery Communications, which created its own empire of action-themed channels (Discovery Channel, The Learning Channel, Animal Planet, the Travel Channel, and so on) that could be sent anyplace in the world via a satellite dish.

Soon, with its own retail stores and multimedia marketing, Discovery became iconic in the realm of "nature" filmmaking. As an entertainment conglomerate, the Discovery Channel didn't have to beg to tag along on expeditions. It could sponsor its own, as it did when it chartered an HBOI ship and sub at the rate of $10,000 a day during a month-long cruise to the Galápagos Islands in 1995.

In many ways, this Cuba was as unknown as the Galápagos, but for vastly different reasons. Indeed, the working title of the documentary treatment, "Cuba: Forbidden Waters," was implicit.

During the Cold War, the United States had placed an embargo on the country with its "Trading with the Enemies" act, which prohibited Americans from leaving any money—from investment to tourist dollars—in Cuba. As a result, Cuba's major trading partner vanished virtually overnight. Its lack of prosperity, and the absence of Americans—who once treated Cuba as a sybaritic neocolonial suburb—had helped keep the largest island in the entire Caribbean unspoiled in a way conservation laws elsewhere had not.

Barred from spending money there, Americans went to the Bahamas and the Caymans and the Turks and Caicos, cloning their own versions of Miami Beach on local soil over the past four decades. Ironically, these Americanized tourist resorts—which cut out great swaths of the fragile coastal zone—also became the biggest threats to the mangrove wetlands, seagrass pastures, and coral reefs in the region. Even though Cuba had its share of such development—most of it on the northern coast outside Havana—it was not even close to what the rest of the Antilles were experiencing. There was hope that the marine environment in Cuba was as time-stuck as the shark-finned autos—*cacharros*, old crocks—that still cruised the streets of Havana.

Fidel Castro—who has touted Cuba as "an environmental haven"—would have the world believe that the higher values of socialism have protected natural lands and waters. True, there are six Biosphere Reserves and eighty-one national parks and preserves, including fifty-one marine protected areas. Together, they cover 6,562 square miles, or 17 percent of the island. Government rules keep the lobster fishery sustainable, live coral cannot be harvested for sale, and a no-spearfishing law prohibits divers from javelining the larger mature fish. But protection is always easier in an economic vacuum. Would this so-called ethic be enough to resist the "prosperity" that boatloads of American investment dollars might ultimately promise? Some analysts, like Wake Forest professor Charles Logino Sr., author of *Retirement Migration in America*, are startlingly blunt in their predictions. Says Logino: "Baby boomers, to retire in the next decade, will be searching south of the border for cheaper housing and labor. A land rush in Cuba will follow soon after the U.S. embargo is lifted, and a tourism retiree boom will take place, picking up where Fulgencio Batista left off over 30 years ago."

Was Logino an alarmist? To get a better idea of where Batista did leave off, I took a stroll back into history, reading the dated reports of apolitical *Miami Herald* columnist Jack Kofoed as he guilelessly reminisced about Cuba in *The Florida Story* in the late 1950s, just as Castro was coming to power: "It's not stretching the truth to call Cuba . . . Florida's suburbs, though scenery, customs and language are different. I saw it from the visitor's point of view for many years—Havana's gay, wicked excitement. It will be that way again. Cuba needs not only American sugar buyers, but holiday seekers, too."

If this neocolonialism resumed—if Cuba again became an accessible "suburb" of Florida—sensitive wetlands would fall victim to the same malaise of dredge-and-fill destruction that has nearly ruined the once pristine Florida Keys and its reefs. Caribbean tourism experts predict that a million cruise ship passengers and a million hotel guests—all from the United States—will arrive in the first year after the embargo is dropped. Agribusiness investors say that normalized trade with Cuba would reclaim the winter vegetable market lost to Florida. Fertile soils, generous rainfall, and tropical weather—not to mention cheap labor—make the island a natural competitor for a big chunk of the $1.6 billion worth of crops Florida grows yearly, including citrus, tomatoes, and sugar. Cane growers, widely blamed for much of the destruction of the Everglades via their fertilizers and pesticides, would be eager to flee Florida for a more welcoming, less restrictive climate.

And what would happen to the fishing villages that depended on a healthy marine environment when agricultural runoff and coastal zone manipulation affected the nearshore waters? Our impending visit to this natural environment would have an urgent poignancy if we could record the condition of an unsullied and wild place *before* change washed over it. Scientifically, our scouring of the Cuban coast might even provide valuable baseline data—a snapshot of biota against which future impacts could be measured.

I spoke with Michael L. Smith, a biologist with the Center for Marine Conservation in Washington, D.C. Smith has quietly led small CMC-sponsored missions to Cuba for years, most recently a specimen-collecting trip to the Golfo de Batabanó. Other American nongovernmental organizations have done likewise—including Reef Relief of Key West and the Nature Conservancy. All have avoided the limelight to keep their work from becoming politicized. Smith told me that biodiversity of land and sea is concentrated in the Southern Hemisphere, while institutions and resources for studying it are usually situated in the north. "Cuba is the extreme case," Smith said, "the single most important country in the Caribbean because of its sheer size." Although exchange of information between scientists of the two countries is far better now than it was at the end of the height of the Cold War, Cuba is diplomatically excluded from any regional management plan because of the artificially imposed political boundaries.

Unlike the smaller expeditions, we would be covering substantial ground—traversing the entire southern Cuban coast. And after we left, we would be very public about what we had been doing by broadcasting it to the entire world.

Whatever "Cuba: Forbidden Waters" would turn out to be, the voyage offered me the chance to satisfy my own curiosity about Cuba's seas, as well as the people they sustained. If you traced the origin of that curiosity, you would end up plying the same emotions that have seduced other writers who fell in love with Cuba. Certainly, Ernest Hemingway, who did some of his best work here, was enchanted with its narrative potential for mano-a-mano naturalism. And while one might make a case for that allure being woven into a gringo domination of the resource—shooting sharks and killing billfish from his *Pilar*—Papa's action-driven stories had a far more complex beneath-the-surface sensibility to them, if one was willing to wade through the blood and machismo. And they spoke, often elegantly, to the spirit of an island in which reality is shaped and tested by the waters that surround it.

As I plunged into the literature of the region, I also began to understand more fully the surreal and complex relationship that Latin American writers also had with the sea. It was especially true for those who spent a lot of time either on islands or on the coastal mainland—from Chilean Pablo Neruda and Nicaraguan Rubén Darío to the great Cuban writers like José Lezama Lima and Nicolás Guillén. For them, the ocean effortlessly slipped from the tangible ebb and flow of its moon-driven tides into a great magical reality. The island of Cuba, as poet Guillén once wrote, "was a long green lizard with eyes of stone and water." Novelist and poet Lima sank headfirst into his metaphor of a "starfish in a dream disappearing into giant leaves of chlorophyll circulating visibly."

Still, the more I learned about Cuba and the expedition, the more I began to wonder how much of the natural world special to this island would ultimately be revealed. In my concern, I was reminded of Louis Agassiz's nineteenth-century warning about new discovery not being in the simple description of yet one more new animal or fish but in the understanding of what that species taught us. "When less was known of animals and plants, the discovery of new species was the great object," he wrote way back in 1867. "We should look rather for the distribution and limitations of different genera and families, their relations to each other and to the physical conditions under which they live."

Although the word was unfamiliar then, Agassiz's plea was for *ecology*, for the comparing of environmental habitats and the placement of each animal within. I realized how much more difficult a story like that would be to tell, because it could not be told without addressing the much broader question of cultural ecology—of how we all fit into the endless puzzle of life, how we both shape it and are shaped by it. And for this off-limits Cuba—frozen in time because of its lack of prosperity—it was a question that begged reportage of real-world politics to help explain it. Certainly, the veteran filmmakers on this project had the skills to address such matters. But would a politically sensitive corporation like Discovery allow this, particularly given the vociferous anti-Castro sentiments of Cuban exiles?

I also wondered if cameras would make the expedition more meaningful and the discoveries more real—or just make it *seem* that way to the folks back home. As writer Umberto Eco has so wisely observed, our contemporary world often relies on the virtual reality of thrice-removed tale-telling to capture events, a predicament in which we have come to expect the media to validate reality for us. But we *were* the media, and as such, we would bring with us a certain Oz-like power to the venue. With no one to call us on it, we could pull the levers and strings from behind a curtain to manipulate reality. Cyclops, Sirens, and sea monsters might all emerge, but only if we really wanted them to.

Fort Pierce,

Florida

1

Tuesday, December 2

Fort Pierce, Florida

The "campus" of Harbor Branch Oceanographic Institution (HBOI) sprawls at the edge of the Indian River Lagoon at Fort Pierce, on Florida's east coast. To reach it, I turn at a modest HBOI sign on U.S. 1 and drive up to a checkpoint, where a uniformed guard deliberates before letting me through. "Extra security today," he says, half in apology. "The *Seward*'s going to Cuba."

He directs me to the dock, through a well-landscaped series of roads, bermed at the edges with neatly manicured tropical foliage. It seems as if I am entering some sort of affluent neighborhood, the walled and insular kind typical to gentrified Florida. If your only reference for "marine research" is the romance of Steinbeck's Cannery Row, then the organized linear neatness of the place will be disconcerting.

It is early December now, rainy and overcast but still warm in the tepid way Florida can be between winter cold fronts. Although I had spent a month on the research vessel (R/V) *Seward Johnson* in the Galápagos once, I had flown to Guayquil, Ecuador, meeting the ship finally on the island of Santa Cruz. This is the first time I have been on campus. As I get deeper inside, I see a U-shaped, concrete-walled canal with the serifs of its mouth poking into the lagoon, well disguised with mangrove jetties. At dock is the R/V *Seward Johnson* just as I remember it, a low-slung white ship with the bow and steering house reminiscent of an oversized Coast Guard cutter. Aft, the entire flat stern is given over to the care and launching of the deep-diving sub, with an immense A-frame crane cocked and ready for action. I notice that the *Johnson-Sea-Link* (JSL), which usually sits on a cradle under the crane, is missing.

Elsewhere on this five-hundred-acre site, there is also a museum, a cavernous workshop where submersibles have been built virtually from scratch, classrooms, offices, and a tony gift shop with a biodiversity of species—octopuses, fish, penguins, manatees—portrayed either as four-teen-karat-gold jewelry or as cuddly "Teeny Weeny Beanie" toys. A bro-chure description makes the philanthropic mission of HBOI sound like an old *Star Trek* line: "The scientists and engineers of Harbor Branch Oceano-graphic Institution are like latter-day pioneers. They plumb the watery depths in search of new life forms, methods to clean up pollution, find better ways to produce food, and even organic compounds that may hold the keys to eradicating cancer, AIDS and other diseases." I figure all they left out was to go where no man has gone before, and to scuffle with the Klingons.

Despite the comic-book hyperbole, HBOI does devote considerable time and energy to biomedicine, aquaculture, dolphin conservation, and other marine research and education. There's a full-time staff of 280, of which about 12 percent are doctorate-level scientists. The rest are tech-nicians, engineers, mariners, and other "support " personnel. Surely the operation of a fleet of three ships, two subs, and two remotely operated submersibles—all with highly sensitive electronic gear in great jeopardy from the sea salts—requires constant tinkering.

While HBOI's work of plumbing the watery depths in search of new life forms is funded by an annual $35 million budget, a big chunk comes from hiring out its vessels and subs—including the crew—for research, usually by universities and marine foundations. Filmmaking rentals are something new, but in an era when grants for ocean research are diminishing, HBOI can't much complain. The institution, low key and virtually unknown outside certain scientific circles since its founding in 1972 with the Johnson Science Laboratory here, is the new kid on the block when compared with its more famous counterparts, Scripps and Woods Hole. But, like the others, it has its eye on the day when some obscure sponge or sea squirt it collects from the netherworld of the abyss turns into a billion-dollar biomedical windfall.

For now, HBOI does seem to be working diligently to right some out-of-whack environmental wrongs in its own backyard: clam and shrimp and finfish hatcheries and technical workshops help retrain fishermen who have outlived their place and time in modern Florida. Nearshore waters like the Indian River Lagoon, once easy pickings for the free-roaming independent fishermen, are now under siege from development-related impacts. Declining harvests and tighter laws reserve sport fish like speckled trout and red drum for recreational anglers, and even the algae-gumming mullet—as part of the food chain for those fish—has been taken out of the commercial loop. As a result, the picturesque waterfronts with nets and wooden traps and fishermen as raw as a fresh oyster are being displaced with condos and fancy marinas and a clubby, self-conscious sort of affluence. Prosperity, at least the short-term kind, has transmuted much of Florida's coast and its southerly Keys in this way, affecting both ecology and culture in the process. By all accounts, Cuba will likely tell the flip side of that story, and I am eager to see how that tale takes form.

I park my jeep near where the 204-foot-long ship is berthed and board across a short gangplank. On deck, I run into a couple of guys I spent time with in the Galápagos, seaman Sharky Martin and sub pilot Phil Santos; like most of the seventeen-person crew, they are hardy, congenial folks well suited to spending about half their life at sea, and it is reassuring to see them again. Al Giddings's underwater film crew flew in a few days ago from Montana to finish supervising the final installation of bright exterior HMIs—supercharged twelve-hundred-watt lights that are each four times the power of a tungsten—and interior cameras aboard the sub; their topside counterparts followed soon after. The three out-of-town scientists—ichthyologists Dick Robins from Kansas and McCosker from San Francisco, as well as political scientist Richard Fagen from Lopez Island, Washington—arrived yesterday. And all the participating HBOI staff live nearby. I am the last one to board.

Yesterday, a series of phone calls from my home to HBOI set my priorities: permission to scuba dive from an oceanographic ship requires some hoop-jumping—from a detailed report showing extensive dive experience to a physician's certificate saying I am fit enough so as not to die in the process. Poor communication delayed my approval, and I'll have to intercede somehow. There will also be a pretrip meeting for film and ship's crew.

I clank up the metal stairs to the bridge, where the meeting has already begun. A man named Roger Dooley is running down a checklist of sites we tentatively plan to visit along the southern coast. Dooley emphasizes the historic role of Cuba in the development of the New World. There are 1,280 known wrecks at least four centuries old scattered on the bottom around the island—some 500 off Havana alone. (Thousands more still undiscovered may exist; indeed, the optimistic *Potter's Treasure Guide* estimates that there may be as many as 13,000.) With tenacious scuba divers and the sub scrutinizing the depths, chasing after this goby and that jelly, who knows what archaeological treasures we might stumble on along the way?

Dooley, although born in the United States to Cuban parents, lived in Cuba from 1957 to 1997 and graduated from the Cuban Academy of Sciences with a specialty in marine archaeology. A veteran scuba diver who has also worked in the dive tourism business there, Dooley knows the waters of Cuba well; with Giddings and chief scientist Grant Gilmore, he helped identify the prospective "stops" along our route. Unlike feature films, which have a script and directors and actors, documentaries like this work from a loose treatment, shooting as much film and video as possible to catch every available story line of science and adventure as it journalistically unfolds. Later, an image-rich script is written from the best available story, and the footage is edited down to a fraction of its original volume. Certainly, any shoot list may change over morning coffee, with filmmakers and scientists trying to be flexible enough to accommodate whatever the weather and impending reality dish up for them. It is not a business for those left-brained types who want every detail of their life nailed down in advance. Often, a scribbled map on a napkin will decide what the day will bring—and of course, that is part of the true discovery of such a trip.

Dooley, who has dual citizenship in the United States and Cuba, appears to be in the midst of some immigration hell in which he "can't risk leaving the country" and won't be traveling along with us as planned. It is a predicament that clearly disappoints him. As I will later discover, the practical experience that would allow him to put us atop certain underwater sites will be sorely missed. Although there is a natural trial-and-error component to any expedition, a shipboard guide who knows local waters can better evaluate options when dead ends arise from the sea.

As I look around on the bridge, I recognize several friendly faces from the Galápagos cruise, including Captain Vince Seiler, who gives me a broad smile. McCosker nods, and Giddings waves. There are also three scientists here from HBOI I have not yet met—sponge expert Shirley Pomponi, and Edie Widder and Tammy Frank, both bioluminescence specialists. Like the other biologists, they are "hitchhiking." (As Frank later tells me: "It's a chance to do research without having to pay for it.") Pomponi, widely regarded among marine scientists for her biomedical work on sponges, was unknown to the filmmakers. She was allowed to come along at the last minute because chief sub pilot Don Liberatore is her husband and he had a spare bunk in his room. This is, after all, December, and Christmas will be spent somewhere in Cuban waters. Ironically, Pomponi will turn out to be one of the key "characters" in the documentary. (Back at HBOI, a sponge collected on an earlier cruise, *Discodermia dissoluta*, had been shown to contain an anticancer compound, Discodermolide. As a result, a pharmaceutical agreement had been signed with the Swiss drug maker Novartis Pharma AG, and millions of dollars were suddenly at stake. Thanks to the addition of Pomponi, biomedicine—the poster child of the argument for assigning economic value to the sea—will become a subtheme of our expedition.)

When Dooley finishes his briefing, Giddings gives us a spirited pep talk about how sensational the trip and the eventual film will turn out to be. "It's a Pandora's Box anywhere you go underwater around that island," he says. "We could find *anything* there!"

Giddings, a robust veteran of Hollywood feature films as well as environmental documentaries, comes across as a sort of good-natured, gung-ho high school football coach, one who won't settle for anything but a complete win, on his own terms. Not surprisingly, Giddings—despite winning Emmys for several underwater natural history docs—is best known for his subsurface work on high-profile features like *The Abyss*, *The Deep*, assorted James Bond films, and *Titanic*. By comparison, co-producer Lipscomb is soft spoken and thoughtful, more than willing to let a story play itself out. A beanstalk of a man with a master's degree in creative writing from Iowa, Lipscomb also seems far more literate and genteel. With thirty-odd films to his credit, he's won as many awards as Giddings, and just under the surface, he is every bit as tenacious. In the early 1960s, he helped pioneer the more candid, character-driven filmmaking approach known as cinema verité. Many of his television docs ("Tall Ships," "Carrier") use the ocean as a backdrop, and he is clearly as comfortable as Giddings spending weeks at sea.

Both men will also act as the key shooters for their own segments, Giddings using custom-designed video cameras—with lenses ground to his specifications—below water and Lipscomb using his standard format camera above. During the trip, the two filmmakers will play off each other like some Odd Couple at Sea. Lipscomb, in reflective moments, will recite lyrics from his favorite poets, like John Masefield and Samuel Taylor Coleridge. Giddings, by contrast, will tell stories about movie stars he has worked with, the wet T-shirt scene he once filmed with Jacqueline Bisset in *The Deep* off Bermuda still a cherished snapshot in his mind. It is almost a caricature that the more fastidious Lipscomb lives in Manhattan and the rough-hewn Giddings on a ranch in Montana.

As a character study, Giddings will be more dynamic to watch. I have seen him before in action, and—even now at sixty—he is nothing if not a natural athlete, a big-boned, vigorous man who moves with a sort of effortless grace, whether climbing down from ship to bucking dive boat or hovering motionless underwater at one hundred feet with a Betacam housed inside a console the size of a large desktop computer. One scientist has already dubbed him the "Alpha filmmaker." Giddings, who badly injured his inner ears during a decompression accident while filming on the deep wreck of the *Andrea Doria* a few years ago, is also about half deaf; yet he wears no hearing aids—which is exasperating to those who must communicate with him.

Giddings's demands on his film crew, as well as himself, are routinely harsh. On his shoots, all work long hours, diving in conditions that are often unsafe, shooting video until the last breath of air is sucked from a tank. Marine biologists who scout remote underwater locales in pursuit of their science are often quite fearless; Giddings and his crew seem even more so, often straying into the realm of recklessness. Certainly, when you are diving in the midst of them, it is important to remember your own limitations—as well as to monitor constantly the ever changing sea and your place in it—because it's clear no one else will.

During Giddings's pep talk, I have begun to notice a corpulent, bespectacled middle-aged newcomer who seems entirely out of place among these field-tested veterans. He is dressed in the gaudy colors affected by Florida tourists and, wielding a flash camera, is pacing anxiously about in nervous birdlike motions. Just as I am beginning to think he may really be a gift shop visitor who somehow blundered onto the meeting—perhaps a German tourist who spent way too much time at the coffee bar—he introduces himself. He is the in-house Discovery Channel producer assigned to the project, a corporate staffer whose high-strung nature presents a startling contrast to the casual aplomb of the independent contract producers and crew.

The corporate producer takes the floor to explain how much he would really *love* to be going along on an expedition to Cuba with folks like ourselves. "If you only knew how *envious* I am!" He repeats this, rephrasing it several times. But the effect, instead of being charming, seems patronizing and insincere. I can't imagine a less likely candidate for adventure. When we encounter a crisis at the end of the cruise that requires good common sense, the producer will intervene by satellite phone, making capricious demands that infuriate nearly everyone aboard.

After the bridge meeting, I stop by the marine operations office to make sure I am approved to dive. Confirmation in hand, I head back to the *Seward* to unpack in the matchbox-sized, two-person room below the main deck I will share with McCosker for the next six weeks. Tucked away inside cabinets are full survival suits for each of us, life preservers, and even emergency breathing canisters that provide five minutes' worth of air— enough, ideally, to get you out of any smoke-filled cabin and up above deck, if it should come to that.

Trained as an evolutionary biologist, McCosker has studied venomous sea snakes and eels, great white sharks, penguins, and the primitive fish known as the coelacanth. As a scuba diver, he seems undaunted by depths and currents and has "discovered" dozens of fish previously unknown to science—chasing them down, squirting them with tranquilizer, and collecting them by hand in clear plastic bags. Formerly director of San Francisco's Steinhart Aquarium, McCosker now holds the Research Chair at the California Academy of Sciences, which means he can indulge his love of adventure by going along on expeditions whenever he can find funding. While clever at word play and very bright, McCosker is also irreverent, restless, and sometimes self-absorbed. When pushed on an issue he cares not to deal with—or thinks is boring—he often uses humor to cloak his feelings or quickly changes the subject. On a lark, McCosker served as "consultant" to *Jaws 3-D*, the film in which a great white leaps from the sea, roaring like a lion.

Inside our room, there are two bunks, two narrow closets, a single desk, and a bookshelf. Everything is built in, boat-style, to save space and eliminate those special moments when furniture crashes over during particularly rough seas. We share a bath with a room on the other side, which is occupied by two of the ship's crew. Cramped and spartan by cruise ship standards, our rooms are clean and air-conditioned—which makes them luxurious for oceanographic work. (Indeed, others share four-person "worker bee" rooms, with extra bunks replacing the desk and counter space.) I notice that McCosker has already set up his fly-tying vise on the desk; containers of fur and feather and hooks are piled nearby. On overseas expeditions, when the work of science is done, McCosker often wanders off with his fly rod, and I expect Cuba won't be any different. ("If Fidel comes aboard," says McCosker, only half joking, "we can invite him to go bonefishing.") On the desk I stack a couple of plastic boxes of flies I have already tied and add a few books to our small library on the shelf. We have both packed copies of the photo fish identification guide by Paul Humann. Otherwise, our shelf covers everything from technical studies of marine biology to the Carl Hiaasen novel *Lucky You*.

There is nothing now to do except wait for the ship to depart. McCosker and I change into our shorts, put on neoprene dive boots, and, with our fly rods, head out for the edge of the lagoon. We each are armed with several hand-tied saltwater flies—little menaces McCosker has assembled on his vise, binding dyed yellow and green deer hair with a pinch of Flashabo to a hook with a set of metal "eyes." The Flashabo has a shimmering fiber-optic-like effect, and once underwater, it will capture the light and do wildly seductive things with it, becoming a Homeric Siren to any fish within sight. "My version of a 'Crazy Charlie,'" says McCosker, referring to the fly design.

We walk down a road paralleling the canal, past a "No Trespassing/ Private Residence" sign, and duck inside a portal of mangroves that opens to the brackish river. Hulking a few hundred yards away at the edge of the shore is what appears to be a massive bomb shelter. McCosker tells me it is the home of the namesake of our ship, Seward Johnson Sr., an avid sailor, industrialist, and philanthropist. "He was always worried his family would be kidnapped because he was kidnapped as a child," says McCosker, without a trace of irony. Heavily fortified, with secret passageways, the home now is used to host visiting scientists. Sturdy enough to withstand a mortar attack, the house is styled after a ship, with teak decks, slanted walls, and a bridge overlooking the channel. The swimming pool is covered by a hemisphere of the earth with latitude-longitude lines as structural supports to hold up the screen. Ocean visionaries have long been known for their quirky and expressive approach to reality; subsequently, real-life personas often have more in common with Verne's Captain Nemo than with midstream Americana. After all, normal folks don't run around custom-building little submarines—wonderful oddball gadgetry all welded and molded and screwed together—in which men and women risk their lives to explore the underside of the sea. A fortified home with secret chambers perched on the edge of a lagoon is just another day at the office.

Out in the Indian River Lagoon, McCosker and I wade off in different directions, false casting our lines back and forth overhead until they each build up enough momentum to carry our bantamweight flies to the water with authority. It is late afternoon by now, and the low sun finally breaks through the clouds just above the fringe of mangroves on the western shore. I am waist-deep in the lagoon; the bottom beneath my feet is soft sand and sea grass, the sort of place that should make fish very happy. In the distance, brown pelicans dive for food, and large silver-sided mullet jump, fracturing a surface that in the gentle, low light seems like a blue mirror-lake in a kid's giant train set. The Spanish first mapped this place as Laguna de Ais—for the pre-Columbian nation that lived on its banks. Only later did the British rename it the "Indian River"—perhaps in memory of the Ais, whom their Spanish predecessors long ago decimated.

After each cast, I "strip" the sinking line back to me by pulling it with my left hand through an organic notch I have created by loosely grasping the rod with my right. After ten minutes of casting and retrieving, the line suddenly stops abruptly, as if the fly is caught on the bottom. Within seconds, a snook jumps from the water, shakes at the hook like a tiny marlin, and then falls back down into a powerful swim. I let him run, and in reward, he performs another jump, showing me his distinct black lateral line and—at the last moment—turning his head toward me so that his eye seems to glow in the afternoon light. When he tires, I finally pull him in, and with a quick snap of my hand, I release the hook. He zips away like a slim torpedo.

It was our chief scientist, Grant Gilmore, who, fresh out of grad school, helped launch research in this lagoon in 1971 on behalf of HBOI. By 1975, thousands of marine specimens had been collected from the Indian River—proving it to be the most biologically diverse estuary in all of North America. Today, while Harbor Branch uses the deep-diving subs to understand the ocean abyss better, they still scrutinize similar shallow-water lagoon systems throughout the wider Caribbean Basin. Cuba is the last remaining piece of that puzzle, and biologists are understandably eager to see how it will fit together with the rest of the known mosaic.

McCosker packs up and leaves early. I continue fishing until it is fully dark, pulling in a small barracuda and watching in excitement as a large school of something—redfish?—churn the water as they move toward me. At the last minute, they stop en masse and quickly scatter in an explosion of copper-colored fins and tails. At the horizon, a sliver of a new moon rises, and a bright star that is Venus glows, as if the watchful eye of my released snook has become celestial. Tomorrow, we will leave for Cuba.

Friday, December 5
Fort Pierce, Florida

Our departure has been delayed for two days, first by more camera outfitting problems, and then later, when we were under way, by an odd clanking in one of our diesel engines. The engine glitch brought us back to a Fort Pierce marina for repairs after we were well at sea, several miles off the Florida coast. The return was wise, though, as any stranding in Cuban waters could prove costly. Hardware, even the commonplace sort, is notoriously unavailable; specialized nuts and bolts for an oceanographic ship like ours are out of the question.

During our delay, McCosker and I hike around a fenced enclosure to a sandy shore and, wading out to our waist, resume fly-fishing. An osprey glides overhead, while a kingfisher darts about near the water. A West Indian manatee surfaces just yards away, prop scars from go-fast Florida boaters crisscrossed on his back. Nearby, I notice that a homeless person has built a crude shelter back at the edge of the scraggy woods. It begins to rain, and since we are having no luck, we stow our rods, put on our rain gear, and trudge several miles into town. McCosker figures we need some floating line, handy for casting surface flies in Cuba. After stopping at three fishing shops, we finally find the right weight and type of line. A store clerk, interested in where we are planing to fish and taking note of McCosker's HBOI shirt, asks about our impending trip. "The Bahamas," McCosker tells him, not wanting to draw undue attention to our real destination. It is a wise move: there is no stronger reaction to Castro's Cuba than among exiles in Florida. Lives of otherwise apolitical people—including academics and musicians—have been threatened for simply appearing on the same agenda with Cuban nationals here. In 1976, a Cuban jetliner with seventy-three people on board was blown up in a plot allegedly hatched by exile Orlando Bosch; after serving eleven years in a Venezuelan prison, he was paroled to Miami, where he was welcomed as a hero. More recently, innocent tourists in Havana have been killed by bombs placed by anti-Castro militants. Certainly, there is a very real concern for our safety on this trip, but not because of anything El Comandante might have in store.

Back aboard ship, the politics of concern turns into a surreal comic opera. The Discovery producer, whom we apparently will not be free of until we finally cast off later today, has called an impromptu meeting with Giddings, Lipscomb, and me. We assemble at a table in the mess. I have already filed the first installation of a series of essays I will be sending back to the Discovery Channel's Web site during the expedition. The site link, designed to look like a color magazine page, is entitled "Cuba: Forbidden Waters"—a tagline the Web editors simply plucked from the name of the actual documentary treatment. Nonetheless, the producer is livid, having dropped all pretense of envy. The transformation is almost cartoonish, shifting in the blink of an eye. "Why do YOU PEOPLE always have to see the negative? . . . Why forbidden? . . . Why not *enchanted?* Why not *marvels* of the sea?"

Giddings seems stalwart and nonplussed. I wonder how much he has really heard. Lipscomb, on the other hand, raises his eyebrows and flashes me a fatalistic look. I sense he feels this is a discussion outside the range of logic. Since I am not a filmmaker and have the least to lose, I try to make the obvious point that the reason we are going to Cuba is precisely because it is off-limits—*forbidden* to Americans—and we aren't sure what will be found here. The producer is undeterred. "It's that 'forbidden' word. It's so negative. Why not a more positive word?" The producer pushes strongly for "Cuba: Enchanted Waters."

To calm him down, a new treatment is printed out and rushed to him after the meeting; its title is "Cuba's Marine Marvels." (Oddly, he eventually buys into the notion of the treacherous depths the sub will probe as *forbidden*. And the doc title will eventually become "Cuba: Forbidden Depths.")

Back in my stateroom, I tell McCosker the story of our meeting and of the new temporary title. He gives me a wry look. "How about 'Captain Marvel Goes to Cuba'?" he asks. Soon, we are finally under way, steaming from the dock one last time, headed for the Jewel of the Antilles. Dinner is being served up in the mess, and we clang up the metal stairs, holding on to the railing against the new pitch and roll of the sea.

"Forbidden roast beef tonight," says McCosker, eyeing the meat that chief steward Jay Grant is slicing from behind a metal counter.

"With Marvelous french fries on the side," I say.

"I got a better title," says McCosker as we sit to eat. "How about 'Forbidden Thought'?"

Saturday, December 6

The Bahamas

I am up at dawn this morning, just in time to see the ancient coral reef of Abaco Island moving past the starboard gunwale of our ship at a twelve-knot clip. Abaco is as flat and low as a road-kill snake, crusted with dark green and interrupted only once with the pinpoint of a lighthouse, a protruding sliver of vertebrae.

Deeper into the Bahamas we go, threading our way through the channels between Eleuthera and New Providence, Cat Island and Little San Salvador. The ocean is slate gray under a heavy cloud cover, broken only by the churning white of the ship's wake.

The initial crossing over the deep Florida Straits took us through six- and eight-foot seas with ten-foot swells. The Gulf Stream, a warm water current equal in volume to a thousand Mississippi Rivers, pushes through the geographic bottleneck between the cape of Florida, Cuba, and the shallow banks of the Bahamas here, headed northward. As it does, it muscles its way into the yawning chute of the straits. Last night, before I fell asleep, I bounced about in slow motion on the top bunk, the swash of the ocean pounding just on the other side of the bulkhead. It was like being in a cradle rocked by a nanny on a bad coffee jag.

Before we leave Bahamian waters and head for the eastern cape of Cuba, Captain Vince Seiler navigates our big white oceanographic ship into the lee of Cat Island and cuts the throttle. We are in blue oceanic water—at least four thousand feet worth—barely a mile off the shore of the remote Bahamian out island, teetering just above the Tropic of Cancer. The late afternoon sun is sinking fast on the horizon, and its departure streaks the smoky cumulus pink, then orange, and finally a burnt sienna that glows like the hot fire of charcoal.

It is an appropriate natural fanfare, a soundless roll of the timpani, for the first real event of the voyage: the *Johnson-Sea-Link II* submersible, which sits tethered to the stern deck like a giant mechanical wingless insect, will be dropped into the water for a test dive. There has not been a sub on the deck of the *Seward* since 1995—the year the Discovery Channel last chartered the HBOI submersible to film "Galápagos: Beyond Darwin." Indeed, there are crew members now aboard who have never launched or recovered a sub at sea before. This deployment and recovery will wet check the JSL as well as help test their own skills.

The event not only rousts sub technicians and ship's crew; it also brings out both topside and underwater filmmakers to record it all on tape. By the time I wander out onto the deck, I find the entire contingent of scientists here as well. With pilot Santos and sub engineering tech Dan Boggess inside, the sub will be lifted up off the deck with the **A**-frame crane and set down into the ocean. There, bobbing like a gigantic cork on a fishing line, it will blow ballast and sink just under the surface. After more arcane gadgetry is tweaked—including three microcameras mounted inside the pilot sphere—the *Sea Link* will be retrieved and returned to its cradle on deck.

There is no science in this, except the electronic kind, but it is a physical drama nonetheless. Giddings turns on three HMIs, and the stern suddenly turns into a movie set. Shoulder-mounted cameras roll, and strobes flash, and all of a sudden, out here off the remote shore of a far-flung Bahamian island, we have created a rare, white moment apart from the drab, half-gray world that has surrounded us over the past three days. The scene is hot-wired not just with bright light but with an odd, bewildered expectation, a hyperreality several times removed from the moment. Sub tech Jim Sullivan, who was aboard when we practiced the same blend of marine science and cinematography two years ago in the Galápagos, leans next to me on the railing. "It's sort of like déjà vu and amnesia at the same time," says Sullivan, dry as always. "Like falling off a bike."

As for the adventurous pursuit of natural science, there will be plenty of that to come. It will begin Monday morning as we steam into the historic harbor of Santiago, over the ghost ships of the Spanish-American War. There, we will be officially greeted by Cuban authorities at the dock. Two military observers, as well as two top Cuban scientists with the Instituto de Oceanología—Pedro Alcolado Menéndez and Rodolfo Claro Madruga— are expected to join us for the expedition. With them aboard, our month-long route will then take us westerly along the southern coast toward the Yucatán Channel, where we will hook around the far westerly tip of Cabo San Antonio, heading finally eastward to Havana and its Malecón at journey's end.

Even with permission to work in this country, we are still on tricky, sensitive ground—what Giddings calls a "breath-hold." Some of this has to do with the way well-appointed oceanographic ships are treated throughout developing and needy countries of Latin America. For instance, at the end of the 1995 Discovery Channel–sponsored cruise to Ecuador, local officials there made an attempt to impound the *Seward* in order to confiscate many of the rare marine specimens and photos to bolster their own sorely underfunded scientific efforts. By doing so, though, they ended up destroying many fish that had not yet been described.

But Cuba has its own special concerns. After all, large American-sponsored missions that have landed there in the past have been anything but benign. Although the U.S. State Department was forthright and reasonably prompt in granting approval, the government of Cuba dragged its feet right up to the very moment when we boarded the *Seward*, weighing the odds of what a ship full of divers and sophisticated scientific gear might really mean to the sovereignty of its country. In fact, despite the enormous investment already made in chartering the *Seward* and lining up the film crew—and despite the fact that Castro had "invited" Giddings to his country—the final sign-off by the Cuban government came within only seventy-two hours of the castoff. Political scientist Fagen, a former Guggenheim Fellow astute in Latin America affairs, has told me the reason for the indeterminable delay: "It was that damn submarine," he said. "And the *Seward Johnson* with all its high-tech gear looked like a fucking spy ship. It went all the way to Fidel. The tough nut to crack was not U.S. permission—it was getting permission from Cuba. They were worried we would use the JSL to spy on them."

Despite the now-departed producer's corporate fit over the use of *forbidden*, Cuba is by law the "enemy" of the United States, and science and journalism are all that can be legally practiced inside its borders by Americans at this time. The result of our trip will be more than the tangibles we encounter beneath Cuba's seas and along its coast. In the best of worlds, our expedition will be fish diplomacy in its highest form, an affirmation of liquid ecology that links the marine biodiversity of Cuba to that of Florida and the eastern United States.

Up on the bridge, chief scientist Gilmore is watching the sea through the window panels. A hulking, bearded figure, Gilmore is congenial, gentle, and low-key, with an easy manner that hides a keen intellect and a deep sense of caring. A tropical ichthyologist and fish ecologist, he has studied shallow-water mangrove systems and collected deepwater fish from Harbor Branch subs around the Caribbean—nearly everywhere, in fact, but Cuba. "There's still hope in Cuba to see what it all used to look like in the Caribbean," says Gilmore. "That's why biologists are so anxious to get in here. It's a time machine." He has tried twice before to organize quietly pure science expeditions to Cuba on his own earlier in the 1990s, but both were short-circuited—one for the political fallout that resulted after two "Brothers to the Rescue" planes were shot down over Cuba in 1996, and the other for lack of funding.

Once, during a meal in the mess on the Discovery-funded Galápagos cruise in 1995, Gilmore sat across from Giddings, and the always inquisitive filmmaker asked Gilmore: "What could we possibly do as an encore to this Galápagos expedition?" Realizing Giddings had a better chance of using his connections to get a trip to Cuba funded, Gilmore pitched the idea to him. The proposal was more relevant and appropriate than

Gilmore could have guessed. After all, Giddings had first visited Cuba in 1978 to film an underwater segment of "American Sportsman"; he returned again in 1981–82 to do one part of a five-part series called "Ocean Quest." Castro, an outdoorsman himself, admired the work of the spirited, outgoing filmmaker—perhaps appreciating his stubborn cowboy independence, which was not dissimilar from his own self-concept. The men had quickly become friends. Gilmore's Cuba idea resonated strongly with Giddings, and back in the States, Giddings enlisted Lipscomb, another Discovery veteran, in the concept. Together, they obtained Discovery sanction and funding, which allowed them to charter the Harbor Branch ship and crew at the discounted rate of ten thousand dollars a day.

And now, here we finally are, cutting steadily through the black waters toward Cuba at twelve knots per hour.

For Gilmore, Cuba has come to mean much more than curiosity about a rare local environment. Of all the American scientists aboard, he is perhaps the most intimate with the Cubans as a people. He grew up on the Florida Gulf Coast, near Ybor City with its strong Cuban flavor, and remains close to Cuban friends and college roommates from those days. Cuban national Claro has spent time with Gilmore and his family during visits to the United States. Near Gilmore's home in Vero Beach, the full impact of Cuban waters becomes real when he sometimes takes a long walk along the Atlantic shore. "Occasionally, I run across homemade rafts washed up on the beach. I've found them with high-heeled shoes, silk scarves, children's toys. Most are from Cuba." The same prevailing currents that bring us those rafts—and the *balseros* who ride them—bring us a soup of marine critters. "Florida is more influenced by the fauna of Cuba than it is by that of North America," he says.

Most fish and invertebrates begin their lives as tiny eggs, at the mercy of prevailing currents. The longer the larvae take to metamorphose from their free-floating stage, the longer the distance they will travel. Spiny lobsters arrive thusly off the Florida coast, as do many species of game fish—grouper, snapper, tarpon. Ecologically, the southeastern United States is downstream from Cuba, inextricably connected. For now, this is all good, Gilmore tells me. But if the health of the coastal habitat of Cuba diminishes, so too will its supply of new fish and shellfish. And if the local natural systems become loaded with sediments and pollution, the currents that bring both *balseros* and lobster our way will suffer likewise. Scientifically, we all have a stake in the marine health of Cuba—whether we like it or not. Examining that connection will be part of what this exploration is all about. "Ecology," says Gilmore, resigned as only a biologist can be, "does what it wants, regardless of politics. We're all interconnected—there's no embargo on fish larvae . . . or pollution."

Into the blackness of night goes our ship, passing beyond Long Island and Deadman's Cay, aiming to sluice through the deep trough inside the shallow Bahamas Banks at Crooked Island Passage. We are still within satellite television range of American TV. I walk down the metal stairs and past the conference room, where off-duty crew members are watching a Chuck Norris shoot-'em-up on the television. In the weeks ahead, videocassettes will replace live transmissions, but the action movies will get far more play than any other. The bloodier, the better.

2

The Windward
Passage and
Santiago de Cuba

Sunday, December 7

The Windward Passage

The key players cram into Giddings's stateroom this evening for a briefing on what we might expect after we arrive in Santiago de Cuba. We are still somewhere off the windward coast of the island, not yet around the eastern horn, and the weather is brisk. Giddings, with his hair slicked back, is wearing hiking boots, jeans, and a black T-shirt; McCosker, rail thin and barefooted, is in a parrot shirt and shorts; Gilmore, in sweatshirt and khakis, looks like a grown-up Boy Scout; Lipscomb, sitting on the floor, hands on his angular legs, reading glasses hanging from a noose around his neck, seems the most professorial of the bunch.

We've just received an alarming message: since Cuba and the United States have no official diplomatic relationship, we have relied on different "Interest Sections" and neutral embassies in our respective countries to communicate. The fax machine up on the bridge has just spit out a missive from the Swiss Embassy in Havana, informing us that official permission to visit certain sites on our itinerary has not yet been granted. These locales are described in the fax as "Forbidden Zones," which—given the loaded discussion with the in-house producer a few days ago—seems to be great irony. Since Castro had assured the filmmakers that his country would be wide open to them, there are groans of disappointment.

Prominent among these "Forbidden Zones" is Playa Girón, at the mouth of the infamous Bahía de Cochinos, the Bay of Pigs, far to the west. Gilmore says this area is a major spawning site and nursery for many fish, the larvae of which are carried westerly by prevailing currents across the Gulf of Batabanó. Here, they either settle out to become adult fish or continue to drift westward to the Gulf of Mexico and the United States. This subregion is especially intact because Castro, who has a vacation villa on the offshore island of Cayo Piedras, has closed the bay as well as the nearby Gulf of Cazones for any use by other Cubans—from subsistence fishing to research. "Their own scientists would love to get in here," says Gilmore. Even for those sympathetic to Cuba's lonely fight against the United States, there is the suggestion that El Comandante has mixed highly personal emotions with political reaffirmations: the consensus among insiders is that Castro, an avid sport fisherman, simply wants the local waters to himself. There is hope that we might be able to renegotiate access when the Cuban observers and scientists join us in Santiago.

McCosker, a filmmaking veteran, emphasizes that our Cuban scientists, Alcolado and Claro—who are highly regarded in the larger community of marine studies for their work in the Caribbean—should be engaged in the expedition and film as much as possible when they come aboard. "They should be *players*, and not just passive observers," he says. Giddings quickly agrees. "Yes, we should sit down and say: 'How can we all do this together?'"

We also learn from the Swiss fax that one of our official "government observers" will be Ariel Ricardo Amores, an old friend of Giddings's. Ricardo, although listed on the manifest as a naval observer, actually works for the Cuban Ministry of Economics, functions as a counsel when in the United States, and, for some reason no one seems able to explain, lives part-time in Los Angeles. "Holy smokes," says Giddings. "I'm speechless. This is great for us! I was afraid we'd get some droid functionary." Fagen, the seasoned analyst, describes Ricardo as "straightforward, with a lot of political courage."

Giddings, elated with tomorrow's landfall in Santiago as well as the inclusion of Ricardo, inexplicably launches into a pipe dream about how thrilling it would be if Fidel visits and scuba dives with us or rides aboard the deep-diving submersible. Lipscomb visibly tenses, awash with concern. "Absolutely, positively, NOT," he says emphatically. "What if he dies? What if he has a heart attack in the sub? The guy is seventy-two years old. Anything could happen! They'd never let us leave. For Christ sakes, they'd kill US!" Lipscomb and Giddings continue to debate the merits of Castro's impending subsurface death. Fagen wonders to himself: "Is this a serious discussion? I think so." The rest of us, realizing that the meeting has for all practical purposes come to an end, file out of the room.

Down on the stern, McCosker busies himself tying together a series of large blue rubber Tuffy garbage cans. Our personal scuba gear will be stored in individual containers between dives to keep it from turning into a confusing pile of neoprene and hoses and gauges, which under the tropical sun would soon acquire the unmistakable scent of wet dog. The lid of each can is inscribed in black Magic Marker with the name of the diver whose gear is inside. The ship, which once had an active "dive locker" to accommodate such gear, has stripped its scuba support down to bare necessities—a compressor and a decompression chamber. It might seem as if HBOI would rather use the ship as a platform for the JSL, as it presents just one large underwater problem to worry about instead scads of individual ones. Or as Fagen writes in his journal: "They hate scuba ops because of liability and control problems: Half a dozen, half-assed scientists-divers swimming around, running out of air."

But that is not the complete story. In the past several years, the *Seward*—originally commissioned to tend a submersible equipped with a lockout chamber for scuba divers—has evolved into a physical oceanographic survey vessel. As such, it has become more accustomed to dragging survey instruments and trawls than serving as a platform, either for sub or divers. Gilmore tells me HBOI is in the process of phasing out "Man in the Sea" programs because they are too costly, and grant support for them is drying up nationally. ("Ivory tower scientists who run federal oceanographic programs from Washington don't believe 'true science' can be gained from a human presence below the waves," he says.) The lone anomaly is the continuing search for biomedical "miracle drugs" from the sea—an exercise with potential for a hard-cash payback.

Later, after dinner, a member of Giddings's team hired at the last minute to replace his rebreather specialist gathers the scuba diving scientists downstairs in the dry lab for a briefing on his technology. Rebreathers, first invented by the military two decades ago for covert operations, leave little or no exhaust bubbles because much of the exhaled gas is scrubbed by circulating through a canister filled with a form of soda lime. The oxygen left can then be "recirculated" to the diver. The mission of the expedition can certainly be met without rebreathers, but including them adds more bells and whistles to the high-tech nature of the theme.

The rebreather techie is a strapping, self-important guy in his forties, with a ponytail. Glib and facile, he makes the elaborate, sensitive technology sound safe and perfectly reliable. Rebreathers allow users to dive deeper with fewer decompression stops and to stay down longer, and with most of the exhaled bubbles being recycled, they cause less noise to frighten critters—thus, better stealth to film or capture fish. Decompression sickness, known as the "bends," is, in theory, less a problem than with scuba. Even those relaxed divers who can efficiently control their breathing seldom have more than an hour underwater on scuba at moderate depths of sixty feet. Rebreathing turns the average dive into three to four hours, says the techie, and can even expand it to eight to ten hours—not to mention greatly extending the depth range. Such complex systems can cost up to twenty-five thousand dollars each and demand the use of a PC-like dive computer as well as tedious postdive maintenance. In reality, most are used mainly for technical navy diving and in cave-diving expeditions in which a continuous air supply is the core issue. Scuba accidents often happen when a diver runs out of air, and a rebreather could surely help remedy that. On the other hand, the *cause* of those accidents is usually diver error—panic or the failure to pay close attention to remaining air supplies. A rebreather that is not monitored closely could cause oxygen toxicity, carbon dioxide overload, and even hypoxia—oxygen deficiency. All could lead to unconsciousness and death.

McCosker is unconvinced of the ease and safety of use. Later he confides to me that the guy's salesmanship was too loquacious and the technology still too suspect, especially in that there is no time on the tight schedule for training in the rebreather use. "I don't even want my gear in the same barrel as his—it'll probably get bent just by association."

Monday, December 8
Santiago de Cuba

We enter the narrow mouth of the natural harbor of Bahía de Santiago de Cuba early this morning, American and Cuban flags flying at the top of the bridge of the R/V *Seward Johnson*. Morro Castle, a turreted stone fortress of moats and dungeons first built in 1664, sits silently atop a rocky bluff, its cannon bereft of thunder. Rising behind it is the Sierra Maestra, a cloud-shrouded wilderness, so remote that anti-Batista guerrillas hid out here for years. Santiago is often described as the "cradle of rum and revolution." Santiagans have long resisted the colonial rule in Havana, defying the power structure of wealthy, sugar-growing dons whenever they could. Castro lived as a boy in the nearby village of Birán, and his own resistance fermented in Santiago, beginning with his education at the Jesuit Dolores College. Later, he accepted the surrender of Batista's army here in 1959.

In the classic *A Naturalist in Cuba*, published in 1945, American expatriate Thomas Barbour wrote of approaching Santiago from the sea: "As you come close to the shore, you will see the Farallones rising like great steps, one above the other, along the face of the mountains, for here the land is really high. You sail past Guantánamo Bay without even dreaming of its existence so perfectly hidden is the harbor."

Off to the west is the island's tallest peak, the 6,448-foot-high Pico Turquino. The mountain crest falls from the clouds into the sea, cascading into the 23,600-foot-deep abyss of the Cayman Trench, down to where the Sierra Maestra really begins. Our research submersible will scramble about the edges of that abyss in a few days, take some underwater photographs, and maybe collect some scientific specimens, fish that don't swim too fast or invertebrates that crawl slowly or not at all. For now, we have diplomatic business to conduct: Santiago is our first landfall, our official port of entry into Cuba. We are the first American ship in more than forty years to put ashore here. Santiagans, we have been told, are expecting our arrival and are very excited about it.

Last night, the *Seward Johnson* ran for hours along the vast unlit northeastern cape of Cuba with only the beam from a single lighthouse to break the numbing darkness. I went up on the stern deck and stood there alone, gripping the railing in the chop of the six- to eight-foot seas for my first glimpse of Cuba. In the darkness, all I could make out was the outline of a land mass that seemed to go on forever, fuzzy mountains finally dissolving into the sea level of the flat eastern cape of Punta Maisí. I understood better why Columbus—who named this island "Juana" when he first sighted it on October 27, 1492—thought it was part of a peninsula of Asia, perhaps Malay. Before landing, he sent a message ashore to the local emperor, which must have perplexed the native Taino who received it. In his journal, the great navigator wrote of his "discovery": "[It is] wonderfully beautiful countryside . . . not flat but diversified by hill and vale, the most lovely scene in the world."

Humid tropical rain forests feed the rivers along the northeastern chunk of the coast, sending them surging down out of the aged volcanic mountains in a froth of whitewater. The last living Cuban ivory-billed woodpecker was sighted somewhere in this tangle of rock and woods in 1986; although a subsequent hunt for the cryptic bird by an international team turned up nothing, eyewitness reports of the woodpecker still persist. Although I saw no lights, I knew the town of Baracoa was here somewhere, nestled between the mountains and the sea. Locals, territorial and proud, argue that Columbus first made landfall at Baracoa rather than farther west, at Gibara. Baracoans have staked their claim with an age-weathered, three-foot-high cross—Cruz de la Parra—which they say Columbus himself left behind. It is now protected inside a glass case, a condition that might be said of the entire country itself.

As our arrival in Santiago nears, the excitement aboard is tangible. Even the ship's crew—which routinely travels from Brazil to the North Atlantic to coastal Africa—lines the rails, wielding Instamatics and plastic disposable cameras for this special moment in history. Cook Jay Grant and his assistant come out in their white aprons, queuing up with fellow crew, filmmakers, and scientists along the starboard side. We idle here just inside the mouth of the natural embayment and wait for a Cuban "harbor pilot" who will guide us some eight miles upstream to Santiago.

Fagen edges up next to me on the rail and asks me to snap his photo. Morro is in the background, its ancient lime rock and fossilized coral block walls looming ominously from atop the easterly edge of the narrow mouth. A newly retired professor of political science from Stanford University, Fagen is along to help us maneuver through the delicate political roadmap a scientific expedition to an "off-limits" destination like Cuba requires. The author of fifteen scholarly books on Latin America, he taught in Mexico as a visiting professor and in Chile during the Allende government. Fagen, along with Taima Hervas, Lipscomb's associate producer, is the most fluent of all the gringos aboard. Last night at dinner in the mess, we talked of Cuban movies—*Fresa y Chocolate* by the late filmmaker Tomás Gutiérrez Alea being a shared favorite. Fagen told me that Alea's *Memorias del Subdesarrollo*, which made the *New York Times'* list of the year's top ten films back in the late 1960s, is still a classic. Alea used a satirical sense of humor to question the revolution, the bourgeoisie, and the bureaucracy of Cuba. Given the repressive censorship of the regime, I wonder how he got away with it. The realities of Cuba, Fagen reminds me, are far more complex and mysterious than the Crayola-rendered sketch of the country fed to us by the American media. Fagen also proudly told me he has been a frequent enough visitor to Cuba over the past thirty years to warrant his own FBI file. "I got a look at it through the Freedom of Information Act," he says, shaking his head. "It reads: 'Richard Fagen, we have reason to believe, is a known visitor to Cuba.'" Fagen is literate, funny, and unabashedly enthusiastic about being along on the trip.

Despite his knowledge of the place, Fagen is as eager as any of us to make our own historic landfall. "Look at how well fortified this harbor is," he says, clearly impressed. Fagen reminds me that the English pirate Henry Morgan once made his assault on colonial Cuba here, followed by an assortment of other less successful buccaneers. "It would have been impossible to sail in here like this . . . without getting hot oil poured on you." Indeed, the old castle on the bluff now holds a Museum of Piracy inside its walls, including confiscated blunderbusses, muskets, and cutlasses. In case the full definition of piracy isn't lost on visitors, it also includes a room devoted to "Operation Mongoose," the CIA's not-so-covert war on the Castro regime.

A boxy boat in faded carnival colors with a bicycle on its stern and the large letters PILOT stenciled on its side zooms out toward us. It brings us the harbor pilot, who will commandeer the precarious navigation from the harbor mouth upriver to Santiago—guiding us around shoals and wrecks as other pilots have done for centuries before him. Diógenes González is the pilot's name—I take this as a hopeful sign, perhaps symbolizing some metaphoric lineage to the ancient Greek who searched for practical good as a means to truth. Crisply uniformed in khaki, Diógenes takes his place on our bridge. Our officers have changed out of their T-shirts and jeans into their own brown uniforms. The world is watching through a tiny knothole in the fence, and so, it is time for us all to look smart, at least for today.

In we go, beyond Morro Castle and the rusted-out power plant and the low-tech fisherman floating in an inner tube with a line tied to his toe. Diógenes seems searching not as much for truth as for the meandering channel, which unquestionably holds a certain practical good. Tarpon roll in a flash of silvery fins, gulping air. Rustic Caribbean-style homes of wood and tin edge up next to the water, laundry flapping from windows and rooftops. We pass a four-story building with the words "Frank País" clearly visible from hundreds of yards away. The building, says Fagen, is likely a school. País, a revolutionary hero who was tracked down and killed by Batista's secret police in 1957, also has his own park nearby, in which he forever exists as statuary, far larger than life, cradling an M-15 carbine.

Ten years ago, this harbor would have been full of Russian freighters, Fagen tells me. Today, during this "Special Period," when the Soviet Union has collapsed and support has vanished, it is nearly empty. Beneath us, the water is mud brown—but it is without the rainbow of oil slicks that bustling harbors often endure. Finally, we reach the squat glass-and-steel port authority building, an odd contrast to the colonial city of brick arches and lattice, balconies and cupolas that rises steadily behind it on the foothills. Except for a rusting Vietnamese freighter moored nearby, the massive concrete docks are deserted, helping to give the city a feeling of shabby abandon. Noticeably absent are the throngs of curious Cubans we have expected to greet us. At 10 A.M., it is as hot as any summer day in Florida, and I realize we are squarely in the tropics now.

Cuban officials dressed variously in guayaberas, military fatigues, and light khakis finally stroll out on the dock and march aboard, sitting solemnly around the richly grained wooden table in the mess hall. Customs and Immigration has come to us. At the table, each man takes turns examining our passports, which lie before them in a pile. Cook Grant brings out a platter of cold cuts and homemade blueberry bread and coffee and sets them down, a peace offering. We are entering a country that has thumbed its nose at the United States since 1959, its own president outlasting nine of ours, surviving numerous attempts on his life and at least one major invasion orchestrated by our government. And now, here we are, the neighborhood bullies, hats in hand, asking politely if we can climb up into the little kids' treehouse, the one we've been stoning for forty years.

One Cuban official, slight, balding, and gaunt, quizzes Captain Seiler at length about the ship's speed, its height and width and length, even its place of registry, even though all this information has been provided in writing prior to our landing. Cameras roll, and soundman Ray Day holds a long-handled mike just above the table. The process is interminably long, with each official firmly clutching a rubber stamp and then, as his turn comes, hovering over a Cuban visa with it for ten and twenty seconds at a time—as if he might come to his senses and reconsider the approval. Later, Seiler is good-natured about it all, attributing the wait to Latin American officiousness, an ancient love of pomp squeezed down into a theatrical moment that is pumped for all it is worth. By the time it is all done, we each have a single "Permiso de Entrada" card added to our passport; when we leave at the end, it will be collected by Cuban officials. As is the custom with U.S. citizens, there will be no record of our entry left behind in our actual passports.

Also aboard now are Claro and Alcolado, as well as the government observers. Both Cuban scientists come across personally as modest and ardent—devoted to both biology and their country's government. Both have also written scores of scientific papers on the waters of Cuba and the Caribbean, Claro on fish and Alcolado on sponges and other invertebrates. They travel routinely out of Cuba for scientific symposia; with their vast experience and education, they could—if so inclined—defect and work elsewhere in the region. Both men are also good humored, affable, and curious, which contrasts sharply with the politically reactive media argument that all Cubans wallow in gloom, in want of happy-faced American-bred materialism. Although Claro and Alcolado will fit seamlessly into the expeditionary roster, it is clear during some welcome-aboard filming that neither seems particularly comfortable playing to the camera. Despite their vast scientific knowledge of the Caribbean, I wonder how much they will truly be engaged in the ultimate documentary. Compounding this dilemma is that neither has received the extensive medical checklist forms that would allow them to scuba dive from the ship. In a preexpeditionary memo to his colleagues, Gilmore has also stressed that Alcolado—as the only Cuban among the two sponge experts aboard—should be able to use valuable submersible time to hunt for the soft animals he studies in the phylum Porifera at every opportunity. Although both Giddings and Lipscomb whole-heartedly agree, other dynamics will soon come into play.

With our temporary visas, all but the few crew members on duty leave the ship with the notion of exploring Santiago. McCosker and I do the same. Within blocks of the ship, we find nearly the entire shore contingent, including filmmakers, ship engineering techs, and a couple of scientists, packed into the alfresco bar in the vintage Hotel Casa Grande. There are more than a dozen museums scattered around the city, not to mention scads of historic plazas shaded with tamarind trees and flowered with hibiscus and bougainvillea. And that great revolutionary icon José buried somewhere here in the Cementerio Santa Ifigenia, along with more contemporary revolutionaries. But the Casa Grande and its cold *cervezas* have a tight grip on our expeditionary colleagues from the *Seward Johnson*, and it is clear most of them won't make it beyond its tether. Before Batista beat a hasty retreat with suitcases full of millions of dollars, affluent Cubans used to sit here on the veranda and watch the richly textured flow of life in the street and the adjacent Parque Céspedes. And so now do we, using our first landfall to knock back cold Hatuey beers and smoke Cuban cigars, prerecorded son playing in the background.

When American naturalist Barbour visited the Casa Grande in the early twentieth century and poked about in the giant ficus trees of the park, he encountered one rare anole; in the arbored patio of a nearby hotel, he actually discovered a brand new one, *Anolis greyi*.

Anxious to make our own cultural discoveries, McCosker and I strike out into the city. We hike for blocks, up through the hills of this historic port, past the handwritten inscription of Che admonishing the people to resist repression, over the trolley tracks with no trolley, the narrow, colonial streets with sputtering Russian Ladas and Chinese bicycles and horse-drawn carts and carriages that are really for transportation and not just for show. The mountains of Cuba's eastern Oriente Province that surround us are geologically young compared with the Central and Occidental Ranges to the west. Stirred by a tectonic whisper somewhere deep below, the Oriente still promises to continue rising up from the sea. In some places, the mountains grow at the rate of one meter every three thousand years. Smaller tremors are common here in the east; and in 1942, a massive earthquake shook the timbers of Santiago to its core. As naturalist Alfonso Silva Lee observes in *Natural Cuba*: "Cuban mountains still tremble now and then, complying to rhythms of the planet's deep pressures."

McCosker reminds me of Steinbeck's Doc, updated and refined, but still with a child's impulsive curiosity about all living things. That curiosity goes beyond the ocean, extending into the cultural fricassee bubbling around us on these narrow colonial streets. At the Casa de Venus, two chubby Cuban teenagers with heavy makeup sit in chairs next to a statue of Venus de Milo under a chandelier in an open-air lobby, separated from the street by a low faux Roman stone railing. With no hesitation, McCosker climbs over the railing and asks one girl in Spanish if she minds if I take a photograph of them, together with the statue. The girl counters that she would be happier if he were to come upstairs with her, Casa de Venus being the sort of place where such activities routinely take place. McCosker politely declines and asks for a picture again. The girl says okay, calls him a fag, then sits in his lap for a souvenir photo.

Back out in the streets, the Santiagans swarm about us in a vibrant, high-energy throng. We dodge a battered motorcycle and sidecar, which seems as vintage as the 1950s-era American cars we will later find in Havana. The contraption appears to be carrying an entire family, dad at the wheel, mom just behind him, and three kids in the sidecar. When the kids see us, they wave excitedly. We must be an odd novelty here; white and pale and dressed in shorts and T-shirts, we could be British or more likely Canadians, strange anglicized ducks of some sort. After we stop a passerby for directions, he recognizes us for what we are. "Norteamericanos!" he says, with a smile and a thumbs up.

At a shop, McCosker buys a wooden cane with a hollow handle; I purchase a map of the island, a bamboo mug with a likeness of Che burned into it, and a package of brightly colored Cuban stamps. Detailed maps like this are nearly impossible to find back in the United States; it will prove to be of great utility for me as we travel gradually westward along the coast, providing me with the geographic knowledge of where we are at any given time. And the allure of Che and the stamps is inescapable, for vastly different reasons: Martí fought for Cuban independence against the Spanish; Che, against Batista. In my college days, back when idealism was often inseparable from some fuzzy and smug adolescent rebellion against authority, posters of Che hung in many American dorm rooms. Death and revolt and blood—which we only knew on TV or in books—had little to do with that poster. Che was more the romantic symbol of striking out on our own, of thinking outside the lines for the first time in our lives. For the young people of our generation, Che was an updated Kerouacian beat fantasy in which a vague sort of claim on socialism seemed more fun than going to the office every day in a cardboard-flat, coat-and-tie world. Afterward, most of us grew up, went to work, got over Che. But here, along with Martí, he was still iconic, less a symbol of what Cuba really was than what it once wanted to be.

The stamps I have bought are wonderful little portraitures of Cuban critters, perhaps even a promise of what is to come: among them are a long-billed toucan, a tricolor heron, leatherback and hawksbill sea turtles, a cocoa damselfish, a butterfly fish. But there are also several long-gone critters, which may exist here as fossils. These are labeled "animales prehistóricos"—one is a giant sloth the size of a tree (*Megalocnus rodens*), and another looks something like a triceratops, except with one horn instead of three (*Monoclonius*). In *Natural Cuba*, Silva Lee explains that the sloth originated in South America near the end of the era of the dinosaurs, some 68 million years ago. Later, it found its way to some of the larger islands of the Antilles. This is no small thing: while birds and insects can fly and smaller critters can float on driftwood and seagrass mats, it's no easy chore for larger animals to reach islands from the mainland. Could it have shuffled across land bridges created during the last Ice Age, when the sea was 300 to 400 feet lower than it is today? However it arrived, sloth remains—indeed, entire skeletons—are often found in Cuban caves.

The triceratops is more suspect. By Silva Lee's argument, Cuba did not arise from the sea until 42 million years ago—allowing for a considerable gap between dinosaur extinction and island creation. But geologists specializing in the history of the earth as it is revealed in rocks report that they have dated some formations here to the Cretaceous and even into the Jurassic periods. If true, that would make Cuba far more ancient than its Antillean counterparts, with chunks of its terrain dating from 208 million years ago. It would certainly be old enough to allow most any Jurassic refugee to lumber about over land bridges that are now long submerged.

Whatever the science, the local culture has its own unique twist on history: just outside Santiago, there exists a sort of bizarre Dino World, El Valle Prehistório, in which massive concrete replicas of the vanished dinosaurs of earth are forever frozen in a kitschy larger-than-life diorama. Why not a triceratops stamp?

Vendors appear here and there, sitting on the sidewalk, their backs to the walls of the colonial buildings, using razor-sharp machetes to carve things from wood and coconut. These are finely detailed things, refined with smaller knives, and they take on the form of horses and parrots and fish, some to be finished with a bright coat of paint. These curios are only a few pesos each, but there seem to be no tourists at all on the streets of Santiago, and certainly, none of the locals are buying. From our vantage point high in this city on a mountain foothill, we can look down over the crumbling red-tile roofs below us, see the hanging balconies, Moorish balustrades, forged iron railings. Cacti grow from the roofs, cultivated because here—in this most Caribbean-African of Cuban cities—there is a superstition that they will protect the dwellers from the evil eye. Indeed, Santiago is a stronghold not just of revolution but also of Santería, the faith that co-opts African gods and Catholic sacraments and magic.

This Santiago, cupped inside the hills, is sweltering even in midwinter; by the time we reach the Plaza Martí, both McCosker and I are soaked with sweat. At the edge of the small plaza is a bust of Martí himself, and in the middle stands a monolithic column tipped with a fat red cone. Although its origins are unclear, it is heavy-handed enough to qualify as Soviet art. San Juan Hill, farther up the steeply inclined streets by another couple of miles, had been our tacit goal, but it is clear we don't have enough time to make it and return before the *Seward Johnson* departs at 4 P.M. Teddy Roosevelt's charge up the hill in 1898 has been traditionally credited for breaking Spain's resistance, forcing the Spanish fleet to flee the harbor of Santiago. (The more complete story, though, is that scrappy Cuban nationals fought valiantly against Spain and its powerful colonial sugar dons long before the Americans ever showed up.) Although we abandon our own charge on the hill this afternoon, we will ironically come face to face with one of the grandest of those Spanish ships in a couple of days, hidden under a hundred feet of water.

Back we go to the harbor over the sloping streets, a down-ramp relief after the aerobic, breath-sucking stride that took us up. Despite the draconian view the American media has given us of Cuba as a place of despair and anger, the people we pass seem friendly, energetic, alive. Even within the crush of pedestrians, nobody is pushy or rude or threatening, not even the sleek, bare-midriffed young woman who puts a forefinger gently on my chest and offers to become my dearest friend for the next hour or so. Soon, a street corner with a vista open to the sea reveals the harbor and with it our spanking white American ship. We dodge horse-drawn carriages to cross the waterfront boulevard separating the old city from the long concrete pier. At the ship, there are still no curious, on-lookers; we climb back up the gangplank, so anonymous we have hardly existed at all for locals.

Soon, all are aboard, and we are headed back out of the bay under the steady gaze of Diógenes. He guides us to the *boca*, at Morro Castle, where the pilot boat speeds out to retrieve him in a fury of clatter and fumes. And now, we are on our own. Captain Seiler steers us to sea under the bronze light of a setting sun. Down in the mess, we have our first communal meal with our new Cuban friends, a feast of broiled scallops. Jay Grant, a big husky guy, is an unordinary cook who—understanding how an exemplary meal can uplift the spirits of those away from family and friends for weeks at sea—takes the notion of chow far beyond the bare meat-and-potato essentials. During our voyage, Grant will buy local fish and lobster and, sparing no butter or other fats, deliver it as authentic haute cuisine. Expeditionary days are often long and, in the Tropics, exhausting and dehydrating. But HBOI scientists joke that instead of losing weight, as they normally do in the field, they accumulate poundage on the *Seward*. Grant stops by my table, pats his not inconsiderable gut, and warns of the culinary danger: "Body by Jay," he says to the lean McCosker. "You're next, buddy." After dinner, most of us walk out to the stern for some fresh air. The more southerly latitude and the protective lee shore have mitigated the chill we felt during our crossing in the Bahamas. The night air is exhilarating, sweetly scented with sea breeze and a hint of tropical wildness, wafting out from the darkened coast. It is a heady moment. We are at anchor now under a starry Cuban sky, and beneath the hull of the ship, the tropical waters shimmer like mercury, a liquid mirror of promises, whatever I want it to be.

There is fish collecting to be done tonight—but it doesn't require scuba or a sub or even a trawl. Ariel Ricardo joins several of us at the starboard railing, where McCosker and Gilmore have baited a downrigger and its two-thousand-foot-long wire line with frozen bait at the end, hoping to entice something big and hungry to the hook—perhaps a deep-dwelling six-gilled shark. Ricardo is slightly more distant than the other Cubans; with a patina of Americanization, he is more stylishly dressed in designer jeans and tassel loafers and sport shirt. On first read, I imagine him to be more defensive, but he quickly drops his officious role and joins in the spirit of the evening. Looking around for a something to do, he grabs a long-handled net and sweeps it through the water carefully. Slender fish flit at the surface, attracted by our lights. From my vantage point several yards above the water, I guess most of them to be Atlantic needlefish, but thicker ones are also splashing there too, and I have no idea what they are. Soon, Ricardo has captured one in the net and swings it onto the deck.

McCosker unfolds the mesh and gingerly turns the little critter over in his hand. As he does, its pectorals open and shut like lacy wings, and its dorsal and upper body gleam with a bright metallic blue, so blue it seems unreal—more like an artificial lure than a fish. "Volador," says Ricardo, excitedly, flying fish, and so it is. Into the collection bucket it goes, the very first specimen of our expedition, a whimsical gem of a fish harvested by a whimsical gem of a moment, out here with no diplomatic bone to pick, except maybe who catches the first fish or how many countless Cuban *estrellas* there are burning like flare tips in the black sky overhead.

It is still early in the trip to congratulate ourselves for any scientific successes. But certainly, the carefully navigated mediation of ocean diplomacy has already worked some magic, creating a fable-come-true of a flying fish tinted the color of the sky and a ship guided into a forbidden harbor by a man named for the search of truth. As I climb into my bunk tonight, I am as optimistic as I have ever been about the expedition.

3

Bahía de Baitiquirí
and El Uvero

Tuesday, December 9

Bahía de Baitiquirí

Overnight, we have backtracked, steaming ninety miles *east* of Santiago, circling wide to avoid the restricted boundaries of Guantánamo, until we finally anchor off the remote Bahía de Baitiqurí. The mouth of the bay that U.S. servicemen and women word-squeeze as "Gitmo" is back on the other side of the cape we have just rounded. Gitmo has never been on our list of sites; its assumed familiarity via American occupation breeches the notion of unexamined mystery. Too, since we are now flying under both U.S. and Cuban flags, we are not solely an American vessel; we simply would not be able to enter without a great deal of official hurdle jumping, this time on the part of the U.S. military. Gitmo functions in a sort of upside-down Gulliveresque world; it would need an entire documentary just to explain its own existence.

The Sierra Maestra looms ashore, rising from the bottom of the abysmal Cayman Trench under us, the second deepest sea-bottom gulch in the Western Hemisphere. The steep coastline nearby marks the uppermost portion of that rise, with only the most ambitious of its igneous peaks poking through the low cumulus. Without the cover of the sea, this range would be higher than Everest.

As the mist over the morning terrain gradually dissolves, it reveals a series of limestone terraces stair-stepping away from the shore, ancient Pleistocene scarps embedded with the yaw of a prehistoric sea. There is no beach, only a bulkheadlike ridge of gray rock, backgrounded with a narrow deserted road. Here in the rain shadow of the mountains, the tropical landscape of the southeast is nearly always dry, the foliage stunted, composed mostly of cacti and scrub. After a quick breakfast, I climb up to the captain's bridge and unfold the local charts. On them, a lone river mapped as Río Macambo squiggles its way downhill to the sea. As I look out the windows toward shore, I see a fissure of green in this otherwise xeric terrain, a verdant fold created by the moisture of what is left of the Macambo's dry-season flow. It is a good primer in how geology influences the plants and animals that must live atop it. Indeed, there are some five hundred rivers in Cuba, but most are short, shallow, and largely unnavigable—raging in the May-to-November rainy season but nearly dry otherwise. At breakfast, Gilmore told me he wished we had a geologist along to provide clues as to how the biological secrets of the deepwater terrain might also be suggested by the surface rock.

As I study a map of the Gitmo reservation, it is clear that a century of U.S. occupation has resulted in an anglicizing of place-names. *Playas* along the Caribbean shore of this sovereign U.S. territory are described not in Spanish, nor even in the original Taino—which flavors much of Cuban geography—but in English: they are "beaches" here, and they are named Blue and Hidden, Windmill and Kittery. Gitmo is the only other natural harbor cut into this southeasterly slab of bedrock, and I can only guess at how it must have sheltered earlier sailors, from *cayuco*-paddling Taino to the conquistadores.

Our country's role in the destiny of Cuba has not been a noble one. After the United States tried unsuccessfully to "buy" Cuba from Spain,

U.S. Marines landed here to intercede in Cuba's War of Independence (the Spanish-American War). After Spain was ousted, the United States performed a political sleight of hand: instead of handing the country over to the Cubans, it set up its own military government. Pressured to leave, it agreed to do so in 1901—but only if Cuba would sign the Platt Treaty, giving the United States a perpetual lease to Gitmo, a strategic presence on forty-five square miles of land. After Santiago, it was the only good natural harbor along the volcanic southeastern coast. Neocolonial American investment, protected by the presence of its own military force, flourished earlier in the century. Today, the Platt Treaty, and the naval base it justifies, seem obsolete. The treaty seems especially so in an era in which jerry-rigged imperialism is not as blindly accepted as it once was. Yet here Gitmo remains, enfenced with barbed wire and land mines—sort of a Berlin Wall of the Caribbean, a dandy metaphor for the relations between the United States and Cuba. Since Cuba poses no military threat to America, and because there are certainly plenty of other U.S. bases in the region, there is little reason to keep Gitmo active. Except of course, to torment Castro, at which it fully succeeds.

Oddly, Gitmo's environment has been well studied—although few North Americans are aware of the results. A "Rapid Ecological Assessment" commissioned by the U.S. Navy of its base reveals this natural bay to be exceptionally rich in wildlife, including populations of Antillean manatees and bottle-nosed dolphin, as well as peregrine falcons, brown pelicans, and the snail kite. Other rare U.S. songbirds overwinter around Gitmo, including the Cape May warbler and the black-throated blue warbler, as well as sixty-two other migratory birds. Unaffected by politics and the embargo, all freely roam between continent and island. But the assessment (performed on contract by the international office of the Nature Conservancy) will also show a dramatic lapse in environmental stewardship by the navy: road and facility building have led to the loss of 90 percent of local cactus and scrub palm communities, natural habitats that nurture Cuban birds found nowhere else on earth. Over the decades, large populations of feral cats and dogs—descendants of Fluffies and Fidos once owned by military personnel—now threaten native critters, such as the endemic Cuban pygmy owl. And the don't-ask, don't-tell mentality of the

U.S. military apparently extends to garbage: tons of discarded machinery, bales of wire, and other debris are simply dumped around Gitmo Bay in great heaps, leaking God-knows-what into the groundwater and wetlands. Surely, an expeditionary visit here would be fraught with complex storytelling peril.

Although we are barely a thousand feet offshore, the graphlike colored lines on the subsurface sonar on the bridge show our ship to be smack above fourteen hundred feet of water. Seaward of our position, the line plummets entirely off the screen, headed for the four-mile-deep canyon. The trench gouges out the ocean bottom between the southern coast of Cuba and Jamaica. As such, it marks the boundary between the tectonic plates of the Caribbean and North America, its intimations reflected in the geologically tortured westerly shoreline of this island mass. It all began some 150 million years ago when the free-floating Caribbean plate— drifting northeastward at the rate of ten centimeters a year—smashed into the slower-moving North American plate, moving up and over it like a Humvee might do after colliding with a Honda Civic. Here, in the lee of the Sierra Maestra, with a new Cuban winter sun rising from somewhere near Punta Maisí, we are in a fine place to launch our first series of sub dives.

Down on the main deck, everyone gathers for the routine start-of-day briefing in the conference room. Although small, the room, with its richly finished rectangular wooden table and upholstered chairs and its drop ceiling to hide the wires and pipes, is another perk of the *Seward*. Only the portholes—and the never ending roll of the sea—give this away as part of a ship, and not a corporate board enclave somewhere back on the well-coifed HBOI campus. Enclosed only by a waist-high partition on two sides, the meeting space opens into the adjacent mess, allowing crew to crowd around outside its perimeter. On the wall is a large candid black-and-white photograph of Seward Johnson Sr., brim of his sailor's hat turned down, shading his face and his white goatee, boats and docks a blur in the background. Also on the wall is a plaque from the Kennedy Space Center thanking the *Seward* and the JSL for helping to recover the largest intact chunk of the fated *Challenger* space shuttle— the piece that illustrated the O-ring failure. Crew and scientists push in at the edge of the partition, balancing coffee cups. McCosker casually informs me that the sub's five-inch-thick acrylic pilot sphere has a hairline crack in it. Instead of diving to its 3,000-foot limit, it must bottom out at two-thirds of that. Oceanic pressures are awesome forces to be reckoned with—each "atmosphere" of 33 feet adds another 14.7 pounds per square inch (psi) of pressure. A crack that might withstand 911 psi at 2,000 feet might not hold up too well at 1,352 psi at 3,000. "Forbidden Crack," says McCosker.

Giddings, in denim shirt and jeans, leads the meeting. The dive plan for today's mission is inscribed in blue on a white chalkboard, along with names of the crew assigned to each role—the pilot of the JSL, the engineer operating the crane lifting the sub, even the "swimmer" who must plunge into the water at the critical moment of ascent and attach a thick cable from the A-frame crane to the top of the JSL. Launch time is 0800. Maximum sub depth is fifteen hundred feet. Giddings will ride in the front of the JSL, next to chief pilot Liberatore; Gilmore and assistant pilot Hugo Marrero, in the cramped rear compartment. Objectives are also listed:

1. Launch JSL over target
2. Descend to bottom
3. Run all Camera systems
4. Run transect up wall
5. Deploy Rotenone [a biodegradable chemical used to stun fish], if possible
6. Recover u/w [specimens].

All of which sounds like a routine dive, except that Giddings is in the catbird seat up front, and chief scientist Gilmore is squashed back in the rear, only a tiny port from which to watch the drama of the depths unfolding around him. The bubblelike pilot sphere, which allows nearly a 360-degree vista, normally would have a scientist spotting a fish or bottom-dwelling invertebrate and then directing the pilot to capture it. Instead, Liberatore—trained as an engineer—will, by default, be the one both to select and to collect the critters. This is not entirely specious: with twenty years of piloting experience, Liberatore has seen enough deep-sea life to have a fair idea of what is worth collecting and what is not. Next to him, Giddings will fiddle with his cameras. There will be another JSL dive this afternoon and a third this evening, both with front-riding scientists. But it is auspicious that the virgin plunge of the JSL into Cuban waters is driven by images and not biology.

A loud buzzer alerts us to the impending sub dive, and we file out quickly to the stern. Film is rolling, and boom mikes are swinging about. Chief engineer John Terry, a roly-poly navy vet whose expressive range vaults the entire spectrum of glum, takes his post at a starboard metal platform a few feet above deck. From here, he will manipulate controls that move the massive hydraulic **A**-frame crane to lift the sub up and into the sea. Like the other half dozen crew members who are on the stern, Terry is wearing a life vest for that moment when a rogue wave washes over the deck or a surge plummets the less surefooted into the sea.

The **A**-frame folds itself back, lifts the thirteen-ton JSL up and over the stern, and then places it gently into the sea. A thick cable, the last remaining tether, is popped from the sub's top with a loud *whoooosh* of compressed air, and the JSL sinks slowly under the turquoise tropical water. Since the sub is facing us, I can see Liberatore and Giddings through the clear acrylic sphere calmly going about their business of flicking toggles and camera switches and watch as water rises around the globelike exterior until it finally swallows them up. At this moment, it strikes me that dropping four men inside a made-from-scratch submersible into the Cayman Trench might be a scene out of one of Giddings's feature films—sort of like *Sphere*, without the gaggle of dazzling women in clingy wet clothes and suspense-building soundtrack.

For the crew and the American scientists, sub dives like this are almost ordinary; but the newcomers see it through fresh eyes. Fagen will write effusively of the event in his journal: "There is an aesthetic to the whole launch-submerge-retrieve operation that is more than techie. It has all the appeal of a helicopter in motion, plus the mystery of the sea. . . . I am reminded of the wonderful illustrations from 20,000 Leagues Under the Sea. I have just seen the Nautilus disappear into the ocean. It is thrilling!" Like Fagen, I am still fresh enough at this deep-diving oceanography business to be awed by it, as well. And, before the expedition is over, I hope to get at least one chance to ride along inside the JSL—even though I am more likely to be squeezed into the aft compartment than to bask up front in the roomy pilot sphere.

There are other submersibles around that go deeper and stay longer—indeed, the Russian *Mir*, from which Giddings once filmed underwater segments for the film *Titanic*, has a depth range of four miles. The look-alike HBOI subs, JSL I and JSL II (which we have), max out at three thousand feet—when not cracked—but have distinct advantages over the deeper divers: with nine separate battery-powered props each, all aimed in different directions, the subs are also far more agile under the sea. Armed with devices like robotic manipulator arms and vacuum suction tubes, they have a better chance of chasing down and capturing fish and free-swimming invertebrates, including the diverse family of deep-dwelling jellies. And, with cylindrical, water-filled collection vats mounted on a sort of lazy Susan just under the pilot sphere, the subs have the capacity to return critters to the surface, still kicking. In contrast, collecting deep-sea animals from other subs is notoriously unreliable—processes that either mangle the animals or, more likely, fail to catch anything faster than a sponge or sea squirt. Ed Link, the inventor of the Link Trainer, the world's first flight simulator, conceptualized the subs that bear his name. His personal interests were closer to sea-bottom archaeology than biology: Link was one of the first to explore the sunken "pirate city" of Port Royal, Jamaica, and he relished the idea of using a sub to poke at old wrecks and submerged ruins. Whatever his motives, Link clearly transferred his knowledge of soaring through the sky to "flying" through the sea.

There is, of course, another major advantage to these JSL, one the HBOI folks don't much like to talk about: the sub we are using today has been well tested to eliminate flaws over the years. But that development involved its share of trial and error. And the worst of these errors was heart-wrenching. In 1973, during the early experimental phases of the newly invented sub, four crew members—including Link's son—were stranded on the bottom off the Florida Keys. The sub was exploring a sunken ship there and became entangled in the wreckage, unable to ascend. Like today, the tight aft compartment with its two occupants was sealed and separated from the fore pilot sphere for life support—even to the point of having a separate "scrubber" system that recycled exhaled carbon dioxide. But, at the time, the aft was not as well insulated as the sphere, and the delicate components of the scrubber were crippled by the colder temperatures upwelling from the depths. By the time the sub was freed from its entanglement hours later, both Link's son and his fellow crew member were dead of asphyxiation.

Since then, HBOI has worked fervently to develop safer subs, as well as more reliable deployment and recovery techniques. As a result, both *Johnson-Sea-Link*s feature failsafe backup systems, in which a stranded crew has enough food, water, and air to survive five days on the bottom. Moreover, the ship carries along a smaller tethered ROV (remotely operated vehicle) to dive to the rescue if the sub becomes ensnarled or disabled. Indeed, the *Seward* itself functions chiefly as a large sub tender: equipped with bow and stern thrusters, twin propellers and rudders, it has the unique capability of staying in place on the surface over the JSL—to "station keep" with precision and accuracy when the sub is underwater, a giant mama duck hovering over her little duckling. With its delicate 360-degree maneuverability, the *Seward* could be described as a giant surface version of the JSL. Compared with a lumbering freighter of the same size, the sophisticated *Seward* responds more like a virtual image of a ship in a video game than any nautical real-life counterpart.

Once the drama of the sub launch is over, most aboard go about their day in a routine they concoct or have concocted for them. The on-watch ship crew take their posts; the cooks prepare lunch; the off-duty crew sleep or watch blood-and-gore videos on the giant screen in the meeting room. Lipscomb and his assistant, Taima Hervas, huddle together on upcoming photo ops. Claro and Alcolado unload their meager scientific gear in the dry lab, amid the microscopes and pickling jars. I retire to my own work station, a slab of a counter hidden behind banks of computerized videos, a sort of rabbit warren outside the commotion of ship activity. Here, I have enough room for a laptop computer, a digital electronic camera, the map of Cuba I bought in Santiago, a pile of connective computer wires and plugs, and a dictionary. I have Velcroed the laptop down to the counter so listing won't knock it to the floor. From here, I write a short essay about the last forty-eight hours, review a half dozen digital photos I have taken, and, using the satellite phone line, upload the package of copy and photos to the Discovery Channel Online offices back in Bethesda, Maryland. When finished, I then download any E-mail coming in from virtual visitors to the Web site.

The E-inquiries are widely disparate: enterprising teachers with online access have their class follow the progress of the expedition as part of their own learning process. Grad students and scientists pose questions about oceanography; sport divers ask about opportunities to scuba dive in Cuba; curious lay readers wonder about the condition of the coast and the reefs. Occasionally, reactionaries will send hate mail accusing us of consorting with the enemy. A typical one arrived today: "Traveling to Cuba and meeting with the island's slave driver has left your research trip and your vessel stained with the blood of Cuba's victims." Although I try to respond to most of the incoming mail, or in the case of the technical inquiries, ask the scientists to do so, it is clear that the visceral politics of the place are beyond logic.

Certainly, the most gratifying missives for me are the ones from younger readers, such as one that just came in signed "Atlantis":

> This expedition that y'all are doing is a remarkable triumph for science to even attempt to dive down into the depths of the ocean. I myself am going to be a scientist (dolphin biologist) and I am looking forward to going on an expedition just like this one. I was wondering though, exactly how deep can the *Johnson Sea Link* go?? I'm very interested and would appreciate it greatly if you wrote me back. I hope you find what you are looking for.
> —Future Dolphin Biologist
> Atlantis (My real name is Tracy)

As I am also to learn, riding herd on the only E-mail aboard the ship is a bit like being the only bartender on an island of heavy drinkers. A decade ago, the idea of keeping in touch with others by E-mail on an expedition wasn't even an option. But now, E-activity worldwide has habituated us to its maddening presence. Otherwise normal people—some scientists, some crew—will stop whatever they are doing when they hear the *zzzz-oomm-eerrgg* of an Internet connection being made and position themselves just feet away from my laptop, as Pavlovian as any addict has ever been. To protect Discovery's investment in the four-dollars-per-minute satcom transmissions, as well as to keep others from shanghaiing my time, I make a rule: the online access is simply not mine to give away. However, if friends send public E-mail to the site with relevant questions about the voyage, then I'll treat them like Tracy's question and provide a response. With a crew as well educated and sophisticated as this one, my solution is soon trammeled by devious trickery: the "relevant questions," of course, nearly always require technical answers. As a result, the person schooled in the applicable science ended up fielding the question, adding personal notes at the end.

Before this day is over, we will have our first three JSL deployments under our belt. After the Giddings dive is out of the way, the sub makes two science dives, each of which carries along a Cuban scientist. In the second dive, chief scientist Gilmore and Claro descend; in the third, Alcolado rides down in the pilot sphere. It is the first time the invertebrate specialist has been in a submersible since the now defunct oceanographic ship from the Soviet Union visited Cuba with its clunky *Argus* submersible in 1984.

This easterly mountain slope turns out to be almost as barren underwater as it looks from land. But after poking about at fifteen hundred feet, Alcolado saw and collected several inverts—mostly sponges—unknown to science. Of the day's haul, the most visually spectacular is a pink-spined sea urchin, *Araeosoma belli*, a tiny pincushion of spines plucked from its forever dark world by the nimble collection devices of the sub. Along with it came a minuscule deepwater shrimp, which, consigned to living its life in symbiosis with the urchin, clung to its cohost to the very end. Vats of cold seawater (sixty-five degrees Fahrenheit) brought up by the sub from the depths are emptied into the wet-lab aquarium, creating a temporary home for the new specimens. This gives Giddings the opportunity to remove one of his cameras from its housing, position it on a tripod, and shoot macrowork of critters far beyond his diving range, using the glass tank as a sea-bottom stage set.

Neither abyssal critter is scientifically new, but they provide a photo op that otherwise wouldn't exist. Randy Wimberg, a diver with Giddings's team, clamps a thick black cloth over the back of the glass tank to help recreate the dark natural habitat—as well as to block the first aid kit, coffee mugs, and other wet-lab background appurtenances from the shot. Then Giddings fills the frame with the grandeur of the salmon-colored invertebrate and its crustacean buddy. When I watch a small video monitor that shows what the Betacam is capturing, I am amazed at how well the *tableau vivant* has captured reality: I can imagine the specimens existing not here in a glass container on the stern of a ship lab but at depth. If the shot ever makes it to the final cut, the exacting detail of the urchin and shrimp will enlarge so that their tiny world will stretch from one end of the American large screen television to the next.

All the scientists aboard studying deepwater animals are eager to use the sub, and certainly, the seat of choice is the pilot sphere. To the aft, the metallic compartment is cramped and uncomfortable; worse, its only view of the depths is courtesy of two nine-inch-diameter portholes and a tiny black-and-white video monitor, which sends images back from the front of the sphere. Nonetheless, sub time is a valuable commodity, and any opportunity to use it is considered a stroke of good fortune.

Although the Cubans have been guaranteed equal time on the JSL, our strange hybrid of cinematically driven science has already begun to alter that equation. Indeed, Alcolado will get bumped from his second scheduled dive on the JSL in favor of Pomponi, a last-minute addition to the expedition. He will not get a chance to ride in the JSL again until we reach Cayo Matias on December 23—two weeks after his first dive, and after we had left two-thirds of the southern Cuban coast in our wake. By the time Alcolado again climbs into the pilot sphere, Giddings will have ridden in it six times. Although I didn't fully realize it at the time, the shifting equation was a harbinger of the way both Alcolado and Claro would be regarded in the final version of the film.

Ironically, Pomponi had initially been allowed to join the cruise only after Giddings and Lipscomb—who were unfamiliar with her or her science—warned that she should not interfere in the planned mission, would not take sub time away from the other scientists, and would stay out of the filming. Certainly, Pomponi, as chief of HBOI's biomedical division, had also made hundreds of dives throughout the Caribbean in the JSL, while her Cuban counterpart, Alcolado, had been limited to the handful made thirteen years ago in the *Argus*. (Indeed, Pomponi's biomedical division is routinely given the use of the subs for three months out of every year by HBOI; in contrast, Gilmore's biology division must write grants to support its operation whenever research biologists want to take the JSLs to sea.)

Yet Pomponi is articulate, charming, and, with her mane of dark hair and toothpaste-commercial smile, physically attractive. The filmmakers clearly take note of this. As scuba ops begin to emerge regularly, as they do today, Pomponi readily volunteers, and she is quickly paired up with McCosker as his on-camera diving buddy.

Although I am anxious to get into the water, the site for today's late afternoon scuba dive near the volcanic shoreline seems wholly uninviting. Pomponi and McCosker head off toward shore with a camera crew for the first shallow dive of the cruise. Afterward, McCosker tells me the pickings were slim—no grouper, snappers, barracuda, jacks, or eels. Not even any coral, just stony channels lined with sponge and algae. McCosker wonders if this area has been overfished or if the sloping rocky bottom is just all wrong for the tropical ichthyofauna he was hoping to find. Before sunset, a large sailfish fires itself entirely out of the water, about a mile from shore, twisting and flashing magnificently in the golden tropical light. McCosker says it was the first decent fish he's seen since our arrival in Cuba.

Right at the moment the sun sizzles down into the oceanic horizon, I see the fabled green flash, a rare astronomical refraction of light special to southern latitudes. I tell one of the crew about it, and he says he's seen it before too, but he always thought the green tint came from the bottle of Heineken he was holding. Since the *Seward* is a dry ship, he affects a particular look of yearning when he tells me this.

Later at dinner, Lipscomb—a bit less anxious now that we have actually begun to put bodies and high-tech gear into the water—stands to recite some lyrics from Eugene O'Neill:

> It's back to the sea, my brothers
> The sea gull calls and the scents.

It is a nice touch, a bit like having your own poet in residence aboard— what Darwin called the "Philos" in his voyage on the *Beagle*. If the ship's crew seems composed of rugged individualists, they are also better educated than their merchant ship counterparts; many have forsaken better-paying terrestrial jobs for the adventure. They listen attentively; Lipscomb's lyrics are not lost on them.

Wednesday, December 10

El Uvero

El Uvero is a smattering of thatched-roof *bohíos* tucked away in the creases of the green valley that cradles the Río Macambo. When I go on deck early this morning, Uvero is already there, emerging from the foglike mist that shrouds the Sierra Maestra, occupying a special cleft both in geology and in time. As the tropical sun rises higher in the sky, the cumulus burns quickly away. Only the peak of the mile-high Pico Turquino holds tight to the vapor, disappearing convincingly into a ceiling of white. From the stern of our ship, I can see a roadway curling in and out of the boulder-strewn coast barely a quarter mile away, skirting the edge of the turquoise sea. Fast-lane locales in the Caribbean might have a road like this clustered with time-share condos and billboards and tourist shops with varnished blowfish wearing little sombreros. But along the waterfront road to Uvero, there is only wild tropical foliage—interrupted, momentarily, by a cow out for a stroll.

The *Cristóbal Colón*, the largest and most fearsome of Spanish warships, was sunk nearly a century ago just off this beach during the Spanish-American War—which is known among nationals as the "War of Cuban Independence." When it was chased out of the Santiago harbor by American gunships, its Spanish captain—knowing he was defeated—grounded it to keep the *Colón* from being used by the enemy. He need not have bothered: the newer and more proficient American ships were running circles around the Spanish navy, which was at the tail end of its glory in the New World. Oddly, Cubans aboard the *Seward* still seem riled over historical reports attributing at least part of the *Colón*'s failure to escape the American ships to "inferior Cuban coal," which it used when the "high-grade Cardiff coal" ran out. Observer Ricardo reminds us all that the fuel came from Europe, along with the ship. "We have very good coal here in Cuba," he says, agitated over a century-old historical footnote. "That was never the problem."

Regardless of where its fuel originated, we will scuba dive on the *Colón* this morning to see what we can find. I am not certain what our adventure on the shipwreck will turn up for natural science. But it will surely make impressive theater, and I, for one, am looking forward to getting a front-row seat. As I gather my gear out of the Tuffy can, our small jet boat zooms ashore with Ricardo aboard to get a fix on the wreck site. But as it approaches the coast, its engine dies, a large wave washes over it, and it bobs helplessly in the rise and fall of the sea. Up goes a flare to get our attention. I worry that locals—based on the history of the last four decades—might be a bit rattled by gringos shooting off rocketlike devices near their shores. But no one stirs, save a goat, which now occupies the road. The reaction back on the ship is equally underwhelming. "Where is Falco when you need him," cracks one crew member, evoking the omnipresent Coustean TV expedition diver who was always enlisted when a daunting challenge arose. "Yeah," says sub engineer Jim Sullivan, "I always thought 'Falco' was French for 'dumb shit.' Here's a job that could drown you: 'Hey Falco, come here.' "

A crane lifts a larger and more seaworthy vessel off its cradle and sets it down in the water to aid in the rescue. It is a sort of Boston Whaler, but with a large rubber Zodiac-like bumper around it. As it zooms off to shore, another crew member uses a faux French accent to describe the hapless jet boat. "Zee boot, eeet is, how you say, becoming leek a flon-der." All soon return to the ship, the good skiff pulling the bad with a towrope, its passengers soaked but unharmed. As they putter up to the side, Giddings shouts down to a soggy but smiling Ricardo, informing the official Cuban observer that he has just logged his first dive of the expedition.

Back in the conference room, Giddings previews the action with panache: "We'll make an exploratory dive on the wreck, and if it's spectacular, we'll make a film dive later. . . . Okay, now, let's go! It'll be rock-and-roll out there in the water, and don't expect good viz." In fact, the best visibility off this southern coast is normally from February to June, the driest months. By winter, cold fronts move through scouring the waters clean of sediment and plankton. Today, it is surely dry enough, but that alone may not be enough.

I load my own scuba gear aboard the larger rubber-sided launch, and five of us head out to the general vicinity of the coastal wreck site. Giddings tells me that when he was first here fifteen years ago, a portion of the *Colón*'s deck stuck out of the water, providing an easy marker. But today it does not. Seaman Mike Conda drives the Whaler up and down the shore, while all aboard—including McCosker, underwater cameraman Wimberg, and associate producer Karen Straus—peer over the gunwales into the aquamarine sea, searching. The bottom falls quickly here; barely 300 yards from shore, the depth finder shows 400 feet of water under us, well outside scuba range. Conda steers us in 50 yards or so closer, and the slope rises to 100 feet. Giddings decides a better view is needed and volunteers Wimberg, who, wearing only mask, snorkel, and fins, is pulled behind us from a ski rope, his long frame skimming like a log through the water. Still no luck. Nearby, on the brown flat beach, what must be most of Uvero finally arrives—nine men, women, and children and one dog. They wave at us. McCosker says he will swim in to the beach and ask if they know where the *Colón* might be.

"Do you speak Spanish?" asks Giddings, obviously forgetting he spent a month in the Galápagos with McCosker, during which the ichthyologist routinely conversed with Ecuadorian naturalists there in their native language.

"Naaah," says McCosker. "I'll just ask them where 'El Wrecko' is."

With that, McCosker jumps overboard and swims ashore. When he returns, he tells us we are very close to the site. As for the once protruding wreckage, the locals told him it is in their homes and farms—hammered into useful tools and hardware. The people of Uvero are fiercely independent rural campesinos, making a meager living from livestock and farming, augmented by whatever else comes their way—including the maritime fodder of history. Like the Cubans who keep the ancient American Pontiacs and Studebakers running back in Havana, they have learned to do a lot with a little.

With McCosker back in the boat, Conda starts the engine, and we move slowly through the sea until we see the Uveritos waving their arms frenetically when we finally reach the site. Down goes an anchor. Giddings free dives here and returns to tell us that after a surge-churned layer of sediment under the surface, the water clears at around forty feet and the wreck can be seen below that. Then, the Alpha filmmaker puts together the dive plan on the spot: Giddings, Wimberg, and McCosker will descend to one side of the wreck; Straus and I, to the other. Straus is a quiet, handsome woman and, at the moment, also Giddings's girlfriend. Born in

South Africa, she is an accomplished underwater still photographer and a dive instructor, as well as a producer. She seems to know exactly what she is doing and goes about her business of assembling her gear with an unruffled confidence. After he announces the dive plan, Giddings turns to me to explain that Straus is a veteran diver, possibly to reassure me because I was unacquainted with her.

With our tanks on, we fall backward overboard, Giddings and team first, and then Straus and I a couple of minutes later. Just under the surface, Straus and I fin over to the anchor line and pull our way down through the surf-churned sediment, hand over hand. Giddings was right—the first ten meters are murky and stiff with current. But once we are beyond the upper layer of surge, the visibility begins to clear, and one end—the stern or the bow?—of the once mighty three-hundred-foot-long *Colón* gradually emerges. Earlier, in a shipboard briefing, Fagen had given us a condensed version of the *Colón's* demise: on July 3, 1898, this armored steel warship steamed westward on the remote Cuban coast out of Santiago Bay, firing 120-millimeter shells at its American pursuers. Realizing he was outgunned, the captain grounded it on the rocks at Uvero and opened the sea cocks. Americans boarded it later and, inexplicably, towed it back out to sea, where—with the plugs pulled—it sank. Later, the *Colón* settled down on the sandy bottom, one end at forty feet, the other below one hundred. And here it has been ever since.

I reach the uppermost tip of the wreck and duck down in its lee as soon as I can to avoid the heavy surge whiplashing back from shore. I am carrying one of Straus's still cameras, which she will use when she exhausts the film in her Nikonos. Although the camera is nearly buoyant down here, it is bulky and cumbersome and requires some adjustment to my diving style. It gives me far greater appreciation for what Giddings and Wimberg must have to deal with constantly, for the video housings they carry are each the size of a small TV set. Certainly, holding anything underwater will affect what divers call "trim," the dynamic in which even dangling gauges make movement less efficient. As we fan out on the wreck, Giddings, Wimberg, and McCosker disappear over a distant edge of the ship. Straus pauses and touches her forefinger to thumb, giving me the OK sign; I respond in kind, and we both fin away to the opposite side and then sink to ninety feet. The deeper I go, the more the *Colón* reveals itself to me, a slow filmlike dissolve in reverse. Just as Spain once colonized this island, obliterating the indigenous Taino culture with its own, the sea has colonized the *Colón*. Nearly every inch of surface is covered with invertebrates—delicate feathery hydroids and bryozoans; red and yellow sponges molded into fingers and branches; soft corals configured into rods and fans and whips. A newly vacated cowry shell glistens, while tiny blennies the size of a pencil point poke their heads cautiously out of worm holes, ducking back in as I pass over—I must seem like some giant holiday parade balloon to them.

Time and tide have collapsed the hull in upon itself, ripping holes in the deck, as well. I flipper down through a jagged maw of one, shining my light in dark crevices below. Back in one corner, a school of copper-colored glassy sweepers cluster, shy of the light. Thin and discus-shaped, the juveniles in the school are almost transparent. Behind them, a still-round porthole looks out over the seascape, and I position myself just inches from it, imagining long-gone Spanish crewmen once pressing their faces up against this same port, half a world away from home. Nearby, giant gears from the engine room lie askew, as does a metal ladder that must have led to the upper deck. I feel like I am inside a movie set of a wreck.

Straus has been firing off shots with her Nikonos in and around the *Colón*; whenever she does, her camera's strobe immerses everything in a blinding white for a nanosecond, adding to the surreal nature of the experience. She fins over to me, blond hair suspended above her in the water, points to the camera, and gives me a shrug. It is a wordless message: out of film. We dawdle some more on the bottom, until our gauges show that we have only just enough air left in our tanks for a five-minute safety stop—a precaution against the bends—and we both begin our slow ascent.

On another exploration of the *Colón* later in the day, diver Rod Farb will find a pile of thickly encrusted brass 120-millimeter shell cartridges deeper inside the hull—remnants of the *Colón's* hapless sea battle. Later, back on the surface, a crew member takes one of them to the machine shop and, using some combination of mechanical scraping and chemical washing, cleans the base of the shell so well that the original stamped numbers can be clearly seen on it. Ricardo, who seems impressed with the artifact, says he will have it placed in a historic museum back in Santiago.

By early evening, I climb our own metal stairs, up to the captain's bridge. Veteran sub pilot Santos is there, watching the shore through a set of powerful binoculars. Twilight has colored the hills of Uvero bronze. There are now odd geometric incisions on the slopes that I hadn't noticed before. Santos, a personable, good-natured man with a strong Boston brogue, is trying to figure out if the incisions are a trick of light or a hastily constructed message of some kind.

Around us, consoles with half a dozen computerized screens glow with their own unworldly radiance, reporting radar and sonar and other arcane data, pinging and buzzing with static. As I watch, our submersible ascends to just under the surface with its latest cache of deepwater prizes, its strong lights making the black sea around it smolder in an electric blue. Aboard is Claro, and in the collection vat with him will be an apricot bass, a deepwater species first described by Dick Robins off Curaçao years ago. A strikingly colored palm-sized member of the grouper family, the little fish sports a large yellow dorsal, with three red blotches and a bronze tail fin. Until this sub dive, it has never before been found in Cuban waters.

It is fully dark now. Ashore at Uvero, wood and charcoal fires begin to burn. The golden blur of kerosene lamps flickers from the windows of the *bohíos*, thatched-roof homes that are intimations of the original Taino architecture. With the filter of darkness, the reality of Uvero seems especially fluid, easily existing in the now, or a thousand years earlier. However it appears, I am struck by the proximity of two vastly disparate eras—ashore, a simpler, preindustrialized past, and at sea, a complex and elaborate techno-future.

Santos, who has finished studying the terrain, puts down his binoculars. I am curious about what he has seen.

"Trick of light?" I ask.

"Nope," says Santos. "It's a message, for sure."

"What does it say?" A pause.

"Send lawyers, guns, and money."

4

Chivirico and

Cabo Cruz

Thursday, December 11

Chivirico

This morning, we get a good dose of the special Orwellian spin the Cuban government sometimes applies to reality. Thanks to Claro and Alcolado, who alert us to its existence, we plan to dive on a seamount a mile and a half offshore, one that ambitiously rises up three thousand feet from the bottom as a steep volcanic summit, to just forty feet beneath the surface. Alcolado tells me there is a fishing village ashore here called Chivirico, distinctive because it is nestled inside a well-protected cove. But my otherwise detailed map shows no Chivirico.

Brit writer Simon Charles has also tried to figure out this geographic black hole: "There has been a strange reluctance on the part of [Cuban] officials to allow visitors here," says

Charles, author of *The Cruising Guide to Cuba*. "I have even had 'Not allowed to visit Chivirico' scribbled onto my *guía de recalas [map]*." The most reasonable explanation for Chivirico's nonexistence is that the peninsula and cove surrounding the village may have strategic importance for prospective invaders from the sea. While extremely cautious, this is not as paranoid as it sounds: in his lame debut assault on Batista, Castro and his meager, poorly equipped "army" of seventy revolutionaries—including Raúl Castro and Che—came ashore west of here at Playa Las Coloradas on December 2, 1956. Commanding an old leaky cabin cruiser named the *Granma*, Castro and his seasick crew had spent several days being tossed about in the ocean after leaving Tuxpán, Mexico. Finally, the *Granma* grounded in the shallows two miles short of its goal, losing the planned ground support for the "invasion." But the arrival did mark Castro's return from exile. From here, he found his way up into the Sierra Maestra, where he based the grassroots campaign that would eventually overthrow Batista. In inimitable fashion, Che Guevara later said: "This was not a landing, it was a shipwreck."

To the east, another wreck from the "War of Cuban Independence," the *Viscaya*, sits on the bottom of the Aserradero Harbor. A turret and cannon still protrude from the water, marking the *Viscaya*. I wonder if the locals there are prosperous enough not to have to resort to salvaging it, as their neighbors did with the *Colón*. Neither Chivirico nor the *Viscaya* make the roster of possible stops today. But the seamount—with its promise of large roaming pelagic animals like dolphins, rays, and sharks—offers more theater. "Whales are very rare here," says Claro, "but whale *sharks* may be possible." Unlike the whale, which is a mammal, a whale shark (*Rhincodon typus*) is an enormous shark, sometimes reaching fifty-five feet in length. Marked with a particularly striking leopardlike skin, it cruises slowly through the water with its mouth open, sieving plankton, squid, and even small fish. I have seen whale sharks off the Pacific coast of Central America before and was impressed with their elegance and magnificent grace. They are the world's largest fish, and running across one would surely be a coup for the underwater film team.

The film crew loads up for a dive on the seamount. Claro has told me that many locals come here to fish, since the seamount is close to shore and thus highly accessible. This will likely not bode well for the marine life: the easier fish are to catch, the more likely they are to be hammered in need of cheap, high-protein food. Indeed, the annual harvest of pelagic fish that roam out to seamounts like this around Cuba peaked at 120,000 metric tons in the early 1980s and then plummeted to below 10,000 today. This is not a practice special to Cuba; impoverished countries like Jamaica, Haiti, and the Dominican Republic have virtually depleted their traditional fish stocks.

(Certainly, overharvesting is not limited to developing countries. In U.S. waters, nine of eleven grouper species are now designated by the National Marine Fisheries Service as overfished, while most of the other major stocks have peaked and are now in decline. Solutions to safeguard fish populations in "no take" zones are derailed by both sport and commercial fishers: in the United States—and in territories managed by it, such as American Samoa and the Northern Marianas—barely 3 percent of the 10,600 total square miles of coral reef are designated as "no take" zones. Yet conservation biologists stress that a bare minimum of 20 percent should be so protected. A recent study has shown that when such sanctuaries are in place for only one to two years, population density increases by 91 percent and species diversity by 23 percent. When in place, the no-take zones effectively become seed factories to repopulate surrounding waters.)

Despite apprehension over what we may not find, I am still looking forward to getting a close-up look at the bank underwater. The sub has already been launched and is busy surveying the deeper slope of the mount that falls away into the abyss. In the distance, we see a roaming school of tuna move through, scattering the bait fish in great explosions of green water and tiny silver fins. It is the first school of big fish we have seen at the surface.

Shallow volcanic peaks and plateaus like this jutted far above the water after much of the oceans were locked inside the polar caps during the last Ice Age. Indeed, most of the islands that now rim Cuba were then a part of its mainland. But as the ice melted and the seas rose an average of three hundred feet, the peaks were inundated. The taller ones became islands, and the lower ones turned into submerged "seamounts," hidden just below the surface. Seamounts allow floating animal and plant plankton—such as coral and sponges and sea fans yet to be—a sunny place to settle, reveling in the photosynthesis delivered by the strong tropical sunlight not far above. Coral will surely grow in deeper waters—sometimes to two hundred feet and more—but it is penalized by its distance from the light and with the colder water by a loss of species diversity. Shallow seamounts like this offer an oasis of marine life, a virtual buffet for smaller predators that live here, as well as those oceanic species that roam deeper waters in search of a meal. In many ways, they are little "islands" unto themselves wherever they appear, as the natural communities inhabiting them are isolated from the coast and other seamounts by the depths. (Back in my own country, I think of the Flower Garden Banks, the set of peaks in the Gulf of Mexico now protected as a National Marine Sanctuary. Nearly 120 miles off the shore of Texas, those banks support the northernmost coral reefs of the continental United States.) This seamount is unique in that it exists along a volcanic coast otherwise too steep to support the richly textured coral reefs.

It is overcast and choppy, and as we gear up for our dive, our small dive boat rises and falls in the wave troughs. Between the rough water and the loss of sun, the surface appears slate gray today. But as soon as I fall backward off the gunwale, the sea floor materializes, and I slowly sink down to it, at seventy feet, clearing my ears to compensate for ever building pressure as I go. This seamount seems to stretch out in all directions, and I fin just a few feet above it, looking every which way for signs of marine life. Soon I am rewarded by a foot-long red hind—a member of the grouper family with peppermintlike spots over its entire body. It is sitting motionless in a rocky cleft, between two sponges. The grouper's mouth is open, and it seems to be panting. I move down just a little closer, trying not to disturb the fish, and see that this is a "cleaning station" in which small gobies and shrimp peck at parasites carried by the larger host. Other fish seem to be queuing up for their own turn, much like patients in a waiting room of a doctor's office. I have seen this behavior on reefs before, and it is heartening to find it again here, the sophisticated result of a learned symbiosis fueled by thousands of years of reciprocated experience. I wonder, as I often do, at the intricate and sensitive concept of animal intelligence, figuring that there may be more to genetic memory than we could likely ever imagine.

Sunlight loses a primary color every ten feet or so as it penetrates the depths in the Tropics. But today, with the cloud cover, there is scant natural light to illuminate the world down here. Everything around me on the seamount—a coral rubble of fans, rods, whips, and bowling-ball-sized heads—is tinted in shades of gray-blue. Later, Giddings's tape—enabled by powerful lights and computerized digitalization—will tell a different story, making the seamount come alive with false light. For now, my feeble human eyes see only monotone. Within this monotone, fish the size of the red hind are rare, and anything more than a foot in length is missing altogether. Finally, I reach the edge of this underwater peak where the reality of gray-blue falls away into the black of a profound depth. I hang here at its edge and let the nutrient upwelling from the abyss wash around me. It feels electric, as if charged with energy, and I have the otherworldly feeling that I am somehow soaring. The effect is enhanced by the schools of tiny forked-tailed blue chromis clustered here in the gyre, glooming algae sent up from the depths. From above, a shaft of sunlight briefly penetrates the water around me, illuminating the chromis so they seem to glow iridescently, as if someone just plugged them in. It is a moment of supreme wonder and light, one that bores deep into the aesthetics of my own spirit.

No whale sharks or sharks of any kind show up during the dive. But once we return to the *Seward*, we again see a tuna school thrashing off in the distance from its gunwales. "This could be our chance," says McCosker, who suddenly appears holding several spinning rods and reels. We ask Seiler if we can commandeer the dive boat, which is still in the water, and he says sure. McCosker enlists Fagen in the outing, and the three of us climb down to the small boat and head out with the sport fishing gear. We spool out mono with spoonlike lures on the other end, trolling them behind us as we go. If we can get close to the school, we will try casting to it. The sunshine has broken through the late afternoon clouds for good now, and the sea under us shimmers like turquoise. McCosker and Fagen each get a hard strike, then nothing. By the time we reach the feeding frenzy, the tuna have gone deep and moved on.

It is getting late in the day, and the low sun is just now brushing the ocean's surface. We run along close to the rocky coast here, passing a little valley with a deserted beach wedged between the rocks. The valley is filled with a grove of towering royal palms, a magnificent tree that looks as if its trunk is made of marble, bulging near its top. This royal palm has great utility for campesinos; its trunk is used as lumber and its fronds for *bohío* roofing. The fruit-covered nuts are even fed to livestock. There are some thirty different species of palms found in Cuba, but despite its ubiquity, only the royal is protected—in fact, it appears on the national seal.

As we cruise slowly along a steep clay-colored cliff, I see two young boys perched on separate ledges, hand-lining for fish. The ledges are so isolated from the rest of the rock that it is hard to imagine how they were able to find their way out here at all. Each boy waves, a small diffident wave, and then they vanish as if they have see a ghost, using their hands and feet to feel their way over the rock.

The entire scenario—the palms, the valley, the cliffs—is now tinted golden by the late-day tropical sun. As I look off to the easterly horizon, I see the *Seward Johnson*, which by now has been dwarfed into a toy ship by the perspective of the distance. It has become deeply bronze, too. As the sun settles down under the water, twilight turns quickly into night, and the *Seward* becomes a silhouette on the Cuban seas. A placid breeze wafts out from the land, and gentle swells move across the water. Above, a gibbous moon begins its timeless ascent into the black sky. We turn on our running lights and head back to the ship, which is lit now like a magician's parade in the ebony Antillean night.

Before dinner, Giddings rousts up everyone to see the daily "rushes," a replay of the rough digital video he shot underwater today. A video monitor is hooked up to a VCR in a corner of the dry lab, on a space where there are no microscopes or bottles of formaldehyde to preserve fish specimens. There is enough room for twenty or so of us to squeeze back in here. Giddings cheerleads these events, making folks feel it is all a rare treat—and indeed, out here on a ship off the wild southern Cuban coast at night, it surely is.

As Fagen observes in his journal: "Al Giddings is the Fidel Castro of the R/V Seward Johnson. He has the same presence, the same charm, and the same 'Aquí mando yo!' He orchestrates everything not directly in the hands of the skipper: Who'll dive when and where, who'll ride in the sub, which science project gets first crack at scarce resources (sub time, etc.). Most importantly, he displays ego and talent in a way that is not objectionable—at least not to me. When he 'orders' us into the film lab to see [new] footage, it's a command performance. Fortunately, the footage is spectacular. What these big digital cameras can do is amazing. And after the shot, if you don't like the brightness or color balance, you can change it with the twist of a dial. . . . Most immediately, you know while the tape is still in the camera exactly what you have on film!" Impromptu screenings like this are also good for morale, as they give the ship and film crew a raison d'être, a sense of belonging to a mission larger than themselves.

Tonight, a bright red-yellow polychaete worm captured by the sub undulates on the screen. It is a rare animal, seen alive by only a handful of people in the entire world. Lipscomb asks Giddings what the hell it is. Dick Robins says he knows of only two people who really have studied this worm, but both are dead. "Yea," says Lipscomb, "but are they in this room?"

On the monitor, McCosker and Pomponi are scuba diving on the seamount, poking at the organic lumps of all that lives atop it. The colors of the video are so crisp and the water so clear, it is as if they have been diving somewhere else altogether rather than on the same site I just visited. In this incarnation of the dive, there are Technicolor coral caves and immense barrel sponges and scads of small tropicals. But at the edges of the wall, there are also strings of fishing line and an anchor rope snagged from a fishing boat. Despite the health of the benthic marine life, heavy fishing has taken its toll here too; few larger fish are present. "If Fidel comes to visit us in Havana, you should mention to him this place should be protected," says Alcolado. "It could be a 'seed colony' [nurturing breeders] to help populate the coast with fish along here."

On tape, McCosker is squirting rotenone from a small plastic ketchup bottle into a sponge, trying to stun a goby he has found here. The chemical is organic, found in the wood of certain plants native to the Latin America mainland. In heavy doses, it kills fish by inhibiting a biochemical process in their cells, keeping them from using oxygen. Indeed, indigenous fishermen beat the water surface with branches from plants containing rotenone to harvest fish. But in milder doses, it simply stuns the fish, making it easier to catch in a plastic bag. Unlike arsenic, used by aquarium fish collectors in the Philippines, the use of rotenone doesn't destroy surrounding marine life, and if it is used judiciously, the fish collected will even regain consciousness. McCosker opens a plastic bag and with one hand pushes the spotlight goby into it—it will become another new record for Cuba. At 130 feet, he sticks his bare hand into a cluster of fire coral to grab another fish and pulls back reflexively, as if bitten or stung.

"Now," says Pomponi, who still has mask lines from the dive still imprinted on her cheeks, "that fire coral is a good indicator of water quality."

Aptly named, fire coral also stings so acutely that it can feel like a sudden burn. "How did it feel, John?" asks Lipscomb, who although not a diver, is certainly aware of the peril.

McCosker appears stoic. "Ohhh—like sticking your hand into a fucking wasps' nest."

Later, Lipscomb films Pomponi as she watches the footage and comments on some of the captured fish—which are now swimming about in our tank in the wet lab. Although Alcolado or Claro, with far more knowledge of their own waters, would be more appropriate subjects, their thick accents and their diffidence seem to have taken them out of the entertainment game already. Pomponi, a vivacious and self-confident brunette, is another story. I think of Matthiessen's account of the documentary search for the great white shark in 1970 and how a much younger Lipscomb had also preferred the on-screen presence of the attractive diver Valerie Taylor over other, more substantial options. In *Blue Meridian*, Matthiessen critically described the effect as the "Adventures of Valerie approach." As he observed: "It seemed to me that the surface footage depended too heavily on Valerie's lovely face and . . . acting ability in a film where acting has no place, and that these winsome excursions all over the shores . . . would slacken the tension of the film, and rot it with cuteness."

Back in the conference room, Taima Hervas has slipped a cassette of a Lipscomb documentary, "Tall Ships," into the VCR for the night's dose of recreational viewing. Lipscomb's graphic narrative is a welcome respite from the TV room's bloody fare, as well as a working example of a film in which females weren't objectified to carry the story line. Despite the pitch and yaw of the sea, we settle in to watch another sea story. And for the moment, the film seems more real than our own expedition, a validation only the media can so thoroughly provide. It is art imitating life imitating art.

Friday, December 12
Cabo Cruz

The cloud-tipped Sierra Maestra abruptly falls away into the horizon this morning as our ship moves westward, rounding the lip of the supine Cabo Cruz. We are entering the mouth of a broad bay—the Golfo de Guacanayabo—book-ended on its westerly shore by the truncated peninsula that is home to the port of Santa Cruz del Sur. This is mangrove country, a geologically young region of *cayos* and wild sandy beaches, as dramatically different from the worn volcanic relief we have just left as mambo is from Mozart—one new and vital and ever changing, the other symphonic and distant and haunting. There is a diminutive nineteenth-century limestone lighthouse perched at the tip of Cabo and, nearby, a fishing village, its mud-and-stone *bohíos* painted in bright splashes of pastel. Roads in this part of the country are still primitive, and the region remains disconnected from the rest of Cuba. I remember Pedro Alcolado telling me that even Santiago—the second largest city in the country—could be reached only by sea as recently as the 1960s. In his sea assault on Batista, Fidel Castro and his band of revolutionaries ran ashore only six miles from here in the yacht *Granma* in 1956.

All the off-duty crew, the filmmakers, and all the scientists are clustered around the stern railings of the *Seward* this morning. There is yet another feeding frenzy going on, a miasma of fins and tails churning the water over an area about a hundred feet in diameter. This time, McCosker identifies the fish as albacore tuna, which appear to be rampaging on smaller anchovy-sized bait. "Sooner or later, we're going to see a shark in these schools," says McCosker, and just as he says this, up comes a large crescent-shaped black fin, cutting menacingly through the water, as if on cue. "Hammerhead," says the ichthyologist. Cook Grant picks up a heavy spinning rig that was lying against the arm of the A-frame crane and throws a spoon lure at the school and shark, but they are out of his casting range. After fifteen more minutes, the feeding frenzy stops, as suddenly as if someone has thrown a switch, and the crescent-shaped fin sinks low and then disappears. The buzz among the scientists is that we are reaching a more productive region of the coast, and perhaps soon we will see more life underwater as well.

Gilmore, McCosker, Cuban biologist Claro, and I climb down into the skiff with snorkeling and fish-collecting gear. Seaman Mike Conda steers us away from the *Seward* and toward the mangrove coast, past the light-house and the seines held in place by whittled tree branches. The waters beneath us are inviting, clear as glass. The map I bought in Santiago shows good cartographic detail: little red half-moon slashes representing *arrecifes coralinos* begin to appear here just inside the shallow lee of the rocky cape. So do small islands, sand-covered limestone and fossilized coral left behind from thousands of years' worth of work by reef-building polyps. There are two major groups of these islands, each chain splayed out across the outer rim of the coast's gigantic shallow bays.

Here, the island chain is mapped as Archipiélago de los Jardines de la Reina, the Gardens of the Queen, and it serves as a geographic breakwa-ter for the twin gulfs of Guacanayabo and Ana María, a bit farther west. Afterward, the coast will turn deep and become bereft of *cayos* and reefs until we reach the second and final southern island chain. There, count-less islands will spread out in a half-moon crescent encircling the Golfo de Batabanó, the gigantic Isla de la Juventud skulking on its outer edge. There are an estimated two thousand islands encircling the edges of these three giant southern bays—and perhaps as many shadowing the northern coast, between Varadero and Cayo Romano to the east. In fact, a Geographic In-formation System satellite survey shows that, if the intricate shorelines of all the four-thousand-odd satellite islands are accounted for, the amount of land considered "coastline" in Cuba jumps dramatically from 3,563 to 5,580 miles. As naturalist Silva Lee observes in *Natural Cuba*, the rocky basal portion of the major island serves as an "insular platform," widening under the sea up to fifty miles offshore. "At the outer edge of these shallows is generally a chain of keys. The waters between the keys and the island are usually of reduced transparency and the bottom there is sandy or muddy," he writes. "The scenery of the shallow bottom is dominated by seagrass species, the turtle grass, which centuries back was pastureland to innumerable green turtles."

Between the shallow waters inside the keys and the reefs under the clean deeper waters just on the outside, a nearshore marine environment is created that Silva Lee describes as "among the most biologically productive ecosystems on earth." In the wealth of this long and meandering sub-aquatic system, some 38,228 species of crustaceans, 1,501 of mollusks, and 341 of starfishes, sea cucumbers, and sea urchins have been identified. But, as Silva Lee notes, "not a single one is endemic. . . . They are all common to the coastal waters of neighboring territories."

During the peak of the last Ice Age, all the *cayos* were high bluffs, connected to the mainland. Even today, figuring out where an island starts and stops is tricky business. "No one, apparently, has ever defined at what point a mangrove stand is sufficiently large to qualify as a key, or what width a water channel must have to consider two pieces of land as separate keys," says Silva Lee.

Whatever the definition of an island, this place is exhilaratingly wild. I can imagine the conquistadores sailing this same coast five centuries ago and, like the fated expedition in Werner Herzog's film *Aguirre: Wrath of God*, pronouncing every portion of land and water they passed to be the property of Her Majesty the Queen.

Charting and naming places in that era seemed to be akin to staking a claim of ownership, unfurling the flag to warn off competing colonialists. Indeed, six weeks after Columbus landed in Cuba, he forbade "any foreigner to trade or set foot there except for Catholic Christians."

Extracting the native population of indigenous people from the queen's territory would come later. Certainly, it helped that the native Taino, who inhabited most of the island, were—despite their strength and intelligence—a peace-loving, almost timid people. It also helped that, as Columbus noted in his journal, the Indians believed "that the source of all power and goodness [was] in the sky, and they believe[d] very firmly that [Columbus], with these ships and people, came from the sky, and in this belief they everywhere received [him]." In other words, the Spanish lucked out.

As gods, the Europeans would prove to be vengeful deities; ravaging most of the native population in Cuba within half a century of their arrival through enslavement, torture, and disease. Brutally forced to mine gold, the free-spirited Taino and their westerly Guanahatabey neighbors (also called Ciboney) fared poorly. Entire families hanged themselves or took poison rather than endure the inhumane *encomiendas*, the forced labor camps. When the gold and slaves ran out, Cuba became a supply post for other Spanish who sailed off to plunder the treasures of Central and South America.

Some Indian bloodlines survive, with many of them found in the remote northeast around Baracoa. Surviving, too, are some meager but impressive artifacts retrieved from caves, submerged village sites, and inland cenotes (deep sinkholes) throughout the island. But perhaps the most profound hint that the Taino were here is the many descriptive words they left behind—*canoa* (canoe), *hamaca* (hammock), *huracán* (hurricane)— and place-names, like Maisí, which we have passed, and the Gulf of Guacanayabo, where we are headed today. Saying these names out loud pays some homage, however simple, to the voice of a vanquished people.

Today, inside this gulf, the scientists plan to inventory and collect fish at edges of the mangrove *cayos*. By doing so, they can compare this site not just with others we have seen along the volcanic coast of Cuba but with other shallow coastal wetlands back in Florida and in the more heavily developed Caribbean. (Data vary widely, but at least one source reports that 70 percent of this southern shore is given over to mangroves.) I am along for the ride—to fin about in a place few have ever seen and to discover what adventure I can have while doing so. Conda handles our little boat well, slowing and veering off when we approach a white-capped line of breakers, *arrecifes coralinos* lurking just under the surface. He skirts around the treacherous, hull-splitting coral heads, into the illimitable seagrass pastures abutting the stunted mangrove forest. Once in the lee, Conda slows and then idles. "Looks just like the Bahamas," he says, and it does.

We all slip on our masks, snorkels, and fins and tumble over the gunwales, having no idea what lies beneath the surface. As soon as we are clear of the boat, Conda heads back to the *Seward* a few miles away, planning to return to pick us up in a few hours. We are left utterly and totally alone, grateful hostages stuck squarely in the tropical moment—in fact, up to our chests in it.

Of the three small skiffs we have at our disposal aboard the *Seward*, only one is large and seaworthy enough to hold heavy gear and film crew safely, and there is much competition between Giddings and Lipscomb for its use. The jet boat had demonstrated its lack of stable maneuverability when it was nearly swamped near El Uvero; the other boat, dubbed the "Baby Whaler," is only a small twelve-foot skiff, and its gunwales hug the sea with only four passengers aboard. The best I can tell, the Baby Whaler is useful only in the flattest of waters, and then, only for auxiliary work in which expensive camera gear is not at stake.

Here in the shallow Guacanayabo, I stand up to adjust my mask. As soon as I do, I sink a good ten inches through the soft bottom. The substrate here is soft, full of the rich decay of detritus from the mangrove leaves. But it is also carpeted nearly end to end with jellyfish, which collectively have the texture of a large sponge. The jellies are a genus of Cassiopea, normally found undulating through the water upside down. A member of the phylum Cnidaria, the jellies are related both to the reef-building coral polyps, which live in great communities, and to the individual anemones. Among the Cnidaria are the deep-dwelling medusas and siphonophores, all of which sport stinging nematocysts to capture food or ward off predators. Like the constellation, Cassiopea is named for a mythological Greek goddess banished from the right-side-up world for her jealousy. Under me, they are situated thusly, tiny, ribbonlike tentacles tinted purple, green, and ocher, pulsing hungrily in the nutrient-rich shallows. There is so much competition for food among the jellies that there is hardly any space left between them. This bottom is organic, Technicolor, alive, ready and willing to sting whatever comes its way—planktonic fodder or human leg. I'm glad I wore a wet suit today. When I hear shouts coming from the others, I realize not all of us are so protected, and as a result, the Cassiopea will hit all of our group with low-grade stings whenever it gets a chance.

As the sound of the Whaler's engine is finally lost, a silence settles down on this remote place. The scent of sun-warmed mangroves, along with the thousand tiny deaths of tide-exposed organisms hunkering down inside their miniature canopies, transports me quickly from the known world of the *Seward* to one that is timeless, untamed. The effect is commanding, a coming-to for the senses. Conquistador Diego Velázquez, the gold-hungry Spaniard who founded the original European settlements around the coast of Cuba in 1511, could have sailed through here just yesterday. We flipper away in all directions, headed for the jungle of red mangroves, bow-legged at the rim of newly created islands that are neither water nor land. Naturalists sometimes describe the red mangrove as "the tree that walks to sea" because of the way its elegant mahogany-colored roots seem to be stepping away continually from its foliage. In truth, the tree does "walk" to colonize open water, but its stroll is lost to all but a time-lapse camera sequence. Or as naturalist Silva Lee notes: "The coast and keys, alive with a thick mangrove belt, constantly steal space from the ocean: The daily inch of advance translates with the passing centuries into square miles of newborn soil." Indeed, under the best conditions, a red mangrove "walks" at a rate of more than a hundred yards a year.

Gilmore and Claro, with their PVC buckets and seines, hope to catch fish specimens flitting near the bottom of these roots. Gilmore, who has ranged nearly the entire Caribbean studying mangroves, finally gets his chance to inspect them now in Cuban waters. I can only guess how exhilarating this must be for him.

McCosker and I fin beyond them, past a portal of mangroves and into a small isolated cove, a shallow pool indented with natural tidal canals cutting back into the shore. I float over the jellies and the seagrass and the bright green clusters of algae shaped into miniaturized shrubs with fanciful common names—bristle ball brush and mermaid's fans, pinecone and teacup. Much of them belong to *Halimeda*, a genus that crumbles into white sand upon demise, providing a key piece of the bottom-making ecological puzzle—from here all the way down to the depths traveled by our submersible.

As I move along, the value of these mangrove flats as a colossal sea nursery also becomes clear. Scattering before me under shafts of golden sunlight are Lilliputian schools of shortband herring and silversides, cubera and dog snapper, four-eyed butterfly fish and cocoa damsels. The snapper and parrot fish are juveniles and, as such, bear little resemblance to their eventual adult coloration. Of these, the redband parrot fish effects the most sweeping change.

When it is young, two bright white lateral lines stretch across each side of its black body, with traces of scarlet under each eye and a patch of yellow around the mouth. But when it becomes an adult, the stripes fade, except near the head, where what is left of the stripe turns red. The rest of the body is a muted blue-green. All that seems to remain constant is that wonderful parrotesque mouth, a fish beak that will serve it well in scraping algae from coral and rock throughout its life. Other juveniles, like the foot-long barracuda, are simply scaled-down replicas of adults, slender and toothy now, with much more of the same yet to come.

I remember an earlier conversation I had with Gilmore in which he compared fish to birds: both change coloration through life, many school (or flock), and some even migrate, "flying" through the water for countless miles to mate, spawn, or search for food. There are recognizable habitats where certain fish can be expected to be seen almost all the time—garden eels in sand, hamlets near coral, and mackerel in open water. Octopuses hide in little caves, leaving empty shells strewn outside; parrot fish endlessly chomp at coral; squirrel fish avoid the light. Like birds, most fish lay eggs, and many make mating calls, although those songs are often lost to all but another fish. Gilmore has studied fish songs back in the Indian River for years using a hydrophone, and now, like a good birder, he can even identify a fish from the surface by the grunts, chirps, and groans it makes underwater. Such sound makers, says Gilmore, even have regional accents, tiny audio modifications influenced by the geoenvironmental differences of their special place on earth.

There is, of course, one major disparity between fish and birds, and it makes fish watching far more complicated: some fish, such as those in the sea bass family, change sex. And if a harem of females is bereft of a dominant male to carry on the serious business of propagation, a female will rise to the occasion and transform into a male. Unlike birds, some fish—notably the yellowfin grouper and longlure frogfish—will also change color with mood or for camouflage. There may be only one species of scamp grouper, but it can dress its way through four distinct colorations in a matter of minutes.

I turn and fin up one of the natural canals, and the bottom under me turns to barren sand and mud, becoming deeper almost immediately. Fish disappear, and the visibility drops by half, both from an increase in sediment and because I am now under a sun-blocking canopy of foliage. The rare and endemic Cuban crocodile lives along this coast; aquatic cuts like these must be good avenues for them to move back and forth between the interior mud flats and the food larder of this fish nursery. McCosker has a disconcerting habit of disappearing during dives, and as I look over my shoulder, I realize he is no longer with me.

The notion of heading upstream inside one of these mangrove tunnels seems not as wise as it did a few minutes ago. I slowly turn, not wanting to cause any unnecessary splashing that might imitate some morsel in distress, and fin a few hundred yards back out to the open cove.

Here, I am again in the midst of a virtual aquarium of tropicals, a food chain that begins with tiny fish, worms, and crustaceans, all grazing on the organic buffet of the dropped and decomposing mangrove leaves. The clarity of the water on the outer edges of these *cayos* allows turtle grass the light it needs to thrive on the bottom, helping to anchor this food chain in slender, undulating blades of green. As I float next to the mangrove roots, I catch the reflection of something large and metallic from the corner of my eye. Turning my head ever so slightly, I see a three-foot-long tarpon hanging back inside the labyrinth of bow roots. A ray of sunlight bounces off his silver scales, reflecting like a swirling disco ball from the 1970s. I turn my entire body to get a better view; as I do, he vanishes in a swirl of silver and mud and light, disappearing so completely that I have to wonder if he was ever really there at all.

I am beginning to feel comfortable by myself now. I stop finning and simply hang in the water, not unlike the juvenile tarpon had done, to let the uniqueness of the place wash over me. I take long, relaxed breaths of air, as if I am scuba diving, letting each exhale audibly mark one more used portion of my time here. There is a be-here-now element to controlled breathing, and the more relaxed I become, the more I slip into the essence of the moment. Alone on this untamed Cuban shore, I think not of Castro or of crocodiles but only of the rarity of this place, and as I do, I allow myself to become informed by its sanctity. I realize I am in a cathedral, one as sacred as any on earth. An intellectual fragment surfaces, and it is not a warning or a nag but a lyrical reminder of the ephemerality once described so well by Latin American poet Pablo Neruda—of a place "between shadow and space, between trimmings and damsels, endowed with a singular heart."

Then, I hear the distant, buzzlike sound of the Whaler's motor as it returns from the *Seward*, a metallic whirling amplified many times by the conductivity of the water. Manatees have been observed flinching when they hear such sounds, and now I know why. Regretfully, I release the hold on my solitude and flipper out of the cove for the pickup.

By the time I fin back to the Whaler, everyone else is on board, Gilmore and Claro with their five-gallon bucket of live tropicals and McCosker with his list of fish he has identified. In the bucket are a single beaugregory, a squirrel fish, a reef silverside, and a blue hamlet. The two-inch-long hamlet (*Hypoplectrus gemma*) is over-the-top blue, a bright shimmering cerulean. It's widely reported, even by sport divers, throughout the Caribbean basin, including the Florida Keys. But this is the first confirmed sighting of it in Cuban waters. "We expected to find fish like this," says Gilmore, "but no one's been out to look before, so they're not recorded as 'officially' living here."

Indeed, this site at Cabo Cruz turns out to be the healthiest of the mangrove areas Gilmore has surveyed in all the Caribbean, with more than thirty-six different fish identified in just a couple of hours. In a report he will put together back on the ship, Gilmore will list smaller fish like shortband herring and reef silversides as the most predominant—as they are found here by the thousands, while juveniles of the redtail, stoplight, and striped and princess parrot fish are counted in the hundreds. I wonder what else we would find in this bay if we had more time to search. But the *Seward* is ready to pull anchor and continue its westward journey, on its quest for an image-driven story, and our time here is up.

We return to the ship, beyond the stunted little lighthouse and the weirs and the coral heads. Frigate birds soar and glide, elegant and aloof, in the incalculable blue vault of the tropical sky. Back aboard, we strip off our wet gear and put it back in our blue garbage storage cans. I head for a hot shower down on the lower deck. In the middle of the shower I hear the ship's engines power to life and feel the *Seward* move off again into the sea, bouncing me against the walls of the narrow stall as it does.

5

Laberinto
de las Doce
Leguas and
Tortuga Hotel

Saturday, December 13

Laberinto de las Doce Leguas

By night, the *Seward* has traveled across the open mouth of
the Gulf of Guacanayabo, beyond the *cayos* of Manzanillo and
Balandras and the mainland fishing harbors of Santa Cruz del
Sur and Manzanillo. In a strategy meeting up on the bridge last
night, the captain told us a winter front is preparing to move
through. Winter cold fronts in Cuba usually scour the waters
clean, leaving better visibility in their wake, but they can be
troublesome, even dangerous, when it comes to driving small
boats about for scuba ops. "We'll get a blast out of the south,

maybe twenty-five knots," says Seiler. "It isn't a big deal, we'll just point our nose into it. Then, after it passes, the wind will then come out of the north and, down here in the lee, we'll be protected."

Claro said that the prettiest and the clearest shallow water scuba would likely be found in the last leg of our cruise, from Isla de la Juventud west. After the meeting, I had strolled out by myself to the stern and stood there, gripping the railing as the props churned the black sea into furrows of white just below. I knew that somewhere due south are the Cayman Islands, although all I could see was the endless gloom of the night. A full moon in a clear winter sky was overhead, surrounded by streaks of high cirrus clouds with their icy crystals, interrupted only where they haloed around the moon. It was haunting, a striking distinction from the familiar moisture-rich banks of cumulus that have been puffing up over the landscape during our run along this coast.

We are now anchored fifty miles west of Cabo Cruz, off the shore of a subchain of mangrove *cayos* mapped as Laberinto de las Doce Leguas, Labyrinth of the Twelve Leagues. Some 130 square miles of the Laberinto is designated as a marine "Protected Area" by the government— one of several "Areas de Manejo Integral" in the country. There are some forty-odd protected areas around the entire Cuban coast, according to the International Union for the Conservation of Nature (IUCN). Some are "managed" for wildlife, some for rare and endemic plants, and some for nature tourism. But the truth is that enforcement is scant: managers here face the same dilemma as marine sanctuaries do throughout the entire hemisphere—lack of funding. The good news is that this southern coast is generally low and isolated and difficult to reach by road from the mainland. Its protection, even within its own country, is more a result of sheer inaccessibility than anything else. If the best places are found at the end of the worst roads, then this southern Cuban coast surely claims some of the best places in the entire world.

Using the results of yesterday's rich survey of the Cabo Cruz shore, Gilmore lobbied to include mangrove forests in the filming. Mangroves provide storm protection, anchor the marine food web, and serve as a genetic storehouse of plants and animals. In fact, the mangrove is the tropical version of the more temperate tidal saltmarsh found rimming estuaries back in the coastal United States. But, limited by its subtropical range, the mangrove is concentrated in the poorest countries in the Southern Hemisphere, places where its health is anything but guaranteed. Certainly, the lack of prosperity has kept most of the coastal zone in Cuba from being developed. As a result, an estimated 3,030 square miles of such wetland plant communities remain in the country, according to the World Resource Institute. Yet only 208 square miles of them are protected by law in preserves and parks.

Ironically, stands of red mangrove—low, impenetrable green forests of prop roots, often surrounded by soft mud—are the antithesis of the tourist-postcard image of a beach. And when coastal development is proposed, the fiscal prosperity of hotels and resorts more often than not prevails over the biological prosperity of native plants there.

The filmmakers and a few of the deepwater biologists remain unconvinced of the import of the mangrove story to the larger expeditionary mission. And the sub is beginning to turn up more exciting finds from the depths—including a spectacular ghostly white nudibranch that McCosker recently captured at 1,802 feet as it undulated through the darkness. The nudibranch, a mollusk without a shell, usually hunkers down along the bottom in search of fresh meat, including other marine invertebrates, and even plants. But this one seems lifted out of a tale by José Lezama Lima, perhaps one of his seductive dancing spirits forever writhing in slow motion, bulging with tentacles and tiny false heads, struggling to awake from a dream. In comparison with the sizzling sci-fi splash of the sub dives and the visual thrill of sunken wrecks and coral reefs, mangroves and seagrasses seem tame, even aesthetically redundant. Too, there is scant menace in these habitats, little of what Giddings calls the "sphincter factor."

Realizing he is bucking the tide, Gilmore continues to argue for aquatic plant systems as a reliable way to distinguish the health of "forbidden" Cuba from conditions in the rest of the developed and known Caribbean. In doing so, he hastily composes a memo to the filmmakers that sounds a bit like an outline for an undergrad course on ecology. Entitled "Cuban Mangroves—Seagrass Meadows," Gilmore's paper lists major points of their utility:

1. Sunlight: Source of All Energy on Earth (Reveal sunlight in association with the tree and seagrass meadows)
2. Mangrove: A Tree of the Sea, giving . . .
   A. Shelter from Predation
   B. Food to begin the food chain of the sea (the leaves can be carried out to sea, floating on the tide carrying their trapped energy from the sun to the open ocean and deep sea).
3. Seagrasses: Fertile Meadows of the Ocean Margin

Indeed, not only do seagrass pastures nurture small fish and crustaceans, but they are also a major food source for green sea turtles and manatees—two endangered species found here. Like mangroves, the grasses stabilize the bottom, keeping the vital nearshore coastal zone from churning itself into a mud-driven froth every time a good blow surges in. Where tourism prevails in the Caribbean, shallow seagrass beds are often crossed with the prop scars of powerboats and smothered with sediment runoff from land. Mangroves are cut down to provide affluent visitors with an open vista of the sea. But here in the Laberinto de las Doce Leguas, both seagrasses and mangroves are largely unscathed, and the desolate nature of the place helps make them so.

Lipscomb quickly grasps the role of these plants in defining the larger picture of the marine landscape. Giddings remains unconvinced but is game to give it a shot. Now, the vital story of the Fertile Meadows of the Ocean Margin just needs to be captured on film with some theatrical verve if it is to be useful to the eventual documentary. I take care of my online chores by answering another half dozen questions from Web site readers and dashing off a quick essay, which I upload with some digital photos. Incoming questions arrive from school kids and scientists alike—including a patronizing missive from the Discovery producer, who signs it as "The Envious One." There is a startling dose of magic surrealism to this entire online reportage in which words and photos created on the geographic far side of the moon can be made available to the world on the Web within hours. Lipscomb has asked if I would post the essays on the corkboard in the hall outside my workspace, in the belief that—like video rushes—they will provide some sense of immediate realization about the expedition for all aboard.

Generally, my shipmates are good sports about this peculiar and self-conscious process of turning yesterday's actions into today's Web news. Since there are nine Ph.D.'s and many college grads on board, more often than not, I find editing changes scribbled on the hard copy of the dispatches. Only chief engineer John Terry seems baffled by it all. After reading several dispatches, he asks me if "we are on the same trip." Since Terry shows little interest in the local culture or environment, it occurs to me that his version of the expedition would quite naturally end on this side of the ship's gunwales.

By late afternoon, the mangrove contingent is ready to cast off. The weather front seems to be on its way: waves are already pounding the stern, and although the sun is still bright and warm, the ocean is becoming rougher than it's been since we arrived in Cuba. I climb the metal ladder down into one of the skiffs, holding tight as the *Seward*'s hull sways in the building seas. Since both topside and underwater film crews are along today, we will be taking both boats. Claro told me that there is a ramshackle bargelike houseboat back here somewhere, a floating lodge used mainly by Italian sport divers who—like other Europeans—don't mind rustic accommodations in order to be near pristine diving conditions. Several of the *Seward* crew are giddy with the idea of encountering female Italian sport divers, who they have already imagined will be sunning themselves naked between dives. Before casting off, we try to raise the houseboat on the radio, but no luck. Finally, just when it seems we will be on our own in the mangroves, a Whaler-like center-console skiff comes zooming out from shore. It moves alongside, and two men aboard shout to us in Spanish, identifying themselves as Noel López, the boat pilot, and Vicente Hernández, the fishing guide with the floating "hotel." They assure us they will lead us back to their lodge. It sounds like a plan, so off they go with their fifty-five-horsepower Yamaha blazing a white zigzag wake through the thick tangle of green, and off we go, in hot pursuit.

It is low tide, and Seaman Corbin Massey has our motor wide open to keep the boat up on a plane, swerving at drastic angles, deeper into the foliage jungle. Although the Cuban boat quickly disappears into the mangroves—where rounding each corner reveals four or five new potential channels—Massey expertly traces its path by following the bubble-froth trail it has left behind. This backcountry looks for all the world like the Ten Thousand Islands of the western Everglades—or the Florida Keys, without its concrete and Golden Arches. It seems as feral today as when the Spanish first named it.

The houseboat soon appears. It is a rickety two-story barge with a funky *African Queen* charm. Fagen later writes in his journal about our trip: "It was like a high-speed chase from Miami Vice; and the old steel barge looked like it would not be out-of-place on the Amazon!" As we draw near, the scent of fiberglass and marine paint makes it clear that the barge is currently under repair. No Italian divers are anywhere, naked or otherwise. The rusty hulls of two metal and wooden Cuban fishing boats are tied up next to the barge. Fagen says they are old Cayo Largos, boats custom-designed to be effective in both catching and transporting seafood. One is a working lobster boat, wire traps stacked on its bow. The other, I soon learn, is a floating classroom for young Cubans training to be captains for fishing boats. Their school, Escuela Superior de Pesca, is back on the mainland at the edge of the Golfo de Guacanayabo in Manzanillo.

The barge has a sign in English identifying this, a bit grandiosely, as the "Tortuga Hotel." Although run by Cubans, it is owned by an Italian tour company that offers package deals for up to two weeks for divers and sport anglers. To do so, the company somehow bought exclusive fishing rights to a six-square-mile area around the Tortuga. This sounds more like the sort of bucks-for-resources deal often found in developing countries—but there is a covenant: the sport fishing here is all "catch and release" rather than consumptive.

I walk inside the main structure on the lower deck of the barge with Fagen and our official Cuban navy observer, Ricardo. Tacked to the walls are sets of shark jaws and varnished blowfish (sans sombrero) and photos of anglers with large jewfish and barracuda. In one picture, a man holds a bonefish that is at least ten pounds. A certificate in English declares a "Grand Slam" was accomplished here on May 5, 1997, when a Mr. Silvano Capro caught a 3.5-pound bonefish, an 18-pound tarpon, and a 22-pound permit, all on the same day. An aerial photo illustrates the spur-and-grove reef system that occupies much of the space between the mainland and the *cayos*. A rectangular hole in one wall opens to the kitchen, revealing the tops of a few liquor bottles, indicating that the hole in the wall is also the bar. Above the hole is a hand-made sign, La Cucaracha Borracha, the drunken cockroach.

Hernández assures Ricardo that everything is indeed released after capture—except Spanish mackerel and jacks and large grouper, which they keep to eat. On one wall is a large display of anglers' lures—Super Shad Rapala, Sinking Shad Rapala, and a lure the exact color of the flying fish Ricardo netted our first night at sea. Under the display of lures is the banner logo of the American company Rapala. "Uhhh-oooh," says our official Cuban observer, affecting a singsong Ricky Ricardo I-caught-you-Lucee tone. "Some-body's been vio-lat-ing the em-bar-go."

Although all dive shops in Cuba are government owned, they are run as joint ventures with foreign investors, with Germans, Canadians, or, in this case, Italians. Of the three major dive outfitting companies—Cubanacan, Puerto Sol, and Faviota—Cubanacan is by far the largest. But visiting sport divers used to on-demand service in dive destinations like the Caymans and Cozumel are warned up front about the lack of infrastructure. As one sport-diving guide advises: "You should be prepared with all [backup equipment] spares needed for diving as these are either not available or excessively expensive. A well-stocked medical kit is recommended, for although Cuban medical professionals are well trained, supplies are limited. Dives can sometimes be delayed for a number of reasons, including limited available fuel, Coast Guard clearance to depart port, etc., so patience is needed." This same guide also identifies seven separate dive sites just west at Cayo Anclitas, on the outer rim of the coral and sand islands sheltering the inland gulfs. It includes coral pinnacles, plunging coral-covered walls, and a deep garden of rare black coral—Cabezo de Coral Negro. Blacktip, bull, and silky sharks routinely cruise these sites, but the guide reports that they do so because dive masters from the Tortuga release bloody chum in the waters to draw them in. Of all the underwater stops along this southern coast, this is the only one so far in which a shark encounter—an opportunity for the sphincter factor!—might be guaranteed. But the weather choreographs opportunity here, and if good viz and large marine animals don't appear during our brief stop, then we'll simply do without.

By now, Lipscomb, Giddings, and their crews have disappeared, back somewhere in the red and black mangroves. I savor the opportunity to spend a little time with real Cubans. Under the tattered awning of the fishing boat, older men, their faces lined from long days under the Cuban sun, play dominoes. Any of them could be drafted by Central Casting to play the role of Hemingway's fated Santiago. On the other boat, a gaggle of teenage Cuban boys take turns diving off a railing, sometimes sharing a ragged dive mask or kicking about on a broken fiberglass surfboard, which likely came to them as flotsam. In the water, they look like sleek brown otters. A cook is preparing their dinner, and the scent of grease and *jutia*—a local giant rodent—fills the air. Once I get a look at the in-progress main course, I realize the *jutia* is similar to muskrat, a regional food I ate in stew while growing up back on the Eastern Shore of Maryland. But there are two major differences: this Cuban rodent is endemic; and, unlike the commonplace muskrat, its popularity as regional cuisine threatens it survival. "Jutias are an Antillean invention," naturalist Silva Lee has observed, having evolved from a South American ancestor that invaded the islands about 20 million years ago. While they can be found in the Bahamas, Hispaniola, and Jamaica, there are ten different species of the rodent here in Cuba. Of them, the *jutia congo* bottoms out at ten pounds—the largest of its kind.

On the battered stern of the school boat, I meet Angel Herrero Pacheco, one of the teachers, a sturdily built, thoughtful man who used to be a fisherman and who now passes his knowledge along to the youngsters. Angel refers to the kids as "my seventeen *tiburónes* [sharks]." The school, says Angel, doesn't just teach navigation and other skills to future fishing boat captains—it also tries to nurture an appreciation for the sea. "And, also," says Herrero, smiling broadly "to have some fun." They are in the first year of a two-and-a-half-year course; their classroom training is augmented with field trips like this, during which they stay out as long as a month at a time. "Most of these boys come from fishermen families, and we try to show them that life on the sea can be rough—the sailor's and fisher's work is very hard. . . . It is work, work, work." Clearly, Herrero is trying to balance for his charges the utility of the work with the romance. But the reward of commercial fishing can also be far beyond both. In fact, those who fish for lobster, as I will later find, fare better than almost any other Cuban because they catch a valuable commodity that can be exported for cold cash—and as a result, they receive a bonus for it.

During their anchorage here, the kids will go to the beach at night to watch and count the loggerhead turtles, as this is the season in which they crawl in from the sea to dig their nests and lay their eggs in the sand. Although the endangered turtles are protected by Cuban law, locals still hunt them for both eggs and meat. When possible, eggs are collected or new hatchlings are captured by the boys and taken to a "turtle farm" on Isla de la Juventud, where protection from predators—including humans— will give the tiny and vulnerable turtles a head start for a couple of years before being released to the sea. We had planned to stop near that farm on Isla de la Juventud, and I now have an additional reason to look forward to it. "We maybe find six or seven nests on this small island nearby, when the turtles finally come in from the sea," says Herrero. I wonder when that event will take place, and Herrero flashes me a smile. "Only God knows these things."

As part of their training, each student is given the helm of the fifty-foot-long boat at the end of the trip into the field. "We tell them: now, you have to take the boat straight home." Most live on islands or the coast, a hundred miles or more away—somewhere between Manzanillo and Santa Cruz. After several weeks at sea, they are homesick and eager to steer their floating classroom to their *casas* as soon as humanly possible. "They learn a lot, and when the time comes, they are very happy to show they can drive the boat—and very happy again to see their families."

Herrero shows me the claustrophobic engine room, dark, sooty, and smelling of burned oil. An ancient Russian 150-horsepower marine engine looks dangerously unpredictable. Berths are bunks stacked up against one another in a single, narrow room with a few inches of water under planks slotted over the V-bottom. Back on deck, the "bridge" has four pitiful little gauges, a wind-up clock and a single, battered two-cell flashlight. "Our ship is very old—it barely goes six or seven knots. We have some leaking here, some leaking there. We must always stop to repair it. We are always asking for a new boat," says Herrero, a bit despondently. "But it never comes." He waves his hand in the air, as if to signify something that has just flown away and may never return. "Our country is not in good condition, you know. Economically. It seems to be a curse."

Still, it is not all despair. The boys seem to be having a great time. Sea turtles still come to nest on the beaches, and whale sharks can sometimes be seen just offshore. And there are, says Herrero, tales of pirate treasure buried somewhere in the *cayos* of the Gardens of the Queen. "Everybody wants to discover it," he says, visibly brightening at the idea. "You never know what you might find . . . if you only try to look."

The film crew returns to the houseboat. Taima Hervas makes a point to ask me what the story is with the kids. I tell her about the aquatic schoolhouse, hoping the unique aspect of Angel and his *tiburónes* might fit into the story line. Lipscomb has joined us; he listens and nods his head. He is intrigued, but not enough to include them into the film. "Maybe if we had them up on the beach, hunting for turtle nests or something," says Lipscomb. "Not much action, otherwise."

Over a cup of espresso, I ask Gilmore how the shooting went. Underwater, he says, the site was rich with colorful tropicals flitting around the mangrove roots, not unlike the collecting stop we made earlier at Cabo Cruz. Topside, though, foliage on the mangroves was dead or dying—likely because of some natural environmental condition, such as hyper-salinity stress related to low rainfall or low mainland river outflows. Later, better topside shots of other mangroves will be found to match up to the submarine images put in the can today.

Then, Gilmore tells me a bizarre story of another disagreement between Giddings and Lipscomb—this time over the *jutia*. "We're way back in the mangroves, and after Jim found out the *jutia* was endemic and rare, he wanted to film it. Somehow, one of the guides captured one and is holding it, petting it. And Al goes, 'no fucking way am I filming a rat!' Jim and Al go back and forth, and finally the guide tosses the *jutia* back in the water. Instead of disappearing, it swims in circles around the boat, sometimes trying to crawl back inside. Al just stands there in his wet suit, with his arms crossed, glaring at it. It's like a Mexican standoff. Finally, the *jutia* gives up and pulls itself out of the water and onto the prop roots of a mangrove."

Monday, December 15
Tortuga Hotel

The wind is howling this morning and predicted to get worse—both the temperature and the barometer have dropped, signaling the full arrival of the winter cold front. Last night as I tried to sleep, it felt as if I were on a waterbed mounted on a slow-motion Tilt-a-Whirl. This morning at breakfast, green water was slashing up over the portholes, making it look like the wash cycle of a Maytag was taking place just outside.

As our ship lists heavily from side to side, life aboard becomes just a little trickier. Cook Grant deeply cut two of his fingers this morning while slicing food, and the wound was serious enough to need stitches—had there been a doctor to provide them. Despite the high seas, Giddings's film crew made a dive late yesterday with guides from the Tortuga Hotel, trying to find some black coral or sharks in 110 feet of water. McCosker reported that the bottom stair-stepped away on the outer edge of the keys, first down to 30 feet, and then—after crossing a 900-foot plateau—down again to 100. Guides López and Hernández fed some groupers at the top of the reef and encouraged the Americans to do the same. Giddings moved in with his cameras on, and as McCosker started to feed a grouper, the fish promptly bit him on the finger, taking a piece of flesh with it. Despite the depth, everyone on the dive ended up being soundly thrashed by a vicious current, and little good footage came from it.

A series of midlevel descents planned for the JSL submersible later today have been scrubbed. With heavy listing, the water in the aquarium in the wet lab has sloshed out, so it is now barely half full. The aquarium's lone occupant, a redeye gaper (*Chaunax stigmaeus*) taken by the sub at fifteen hundred feet the other day, looks even more baffled than normal, affecting that grimace of eternal bewilderment that its cousin the batfish permanently wears. McCosker had been hoping to find a bioluminescing flashlight fish somewhere at scuba depths along the coast after dark, and this is the first good coral bottom where it might live. But clearly, the weather is not cooperating.

In the brief lull in our work last night, Alcolado strung Twinkle Lites around the galley and assembled a three-foot-high artificial Christmas tree—propping a lead dive weight on its base to steady it after a particularly nasty list knocked it over. The tree is trimmed with tinsel and candy canes and compressed, hand-painted Styrofoam coffee cups that just returned from a recent sub dive to two thousand feet. Inexplicably, a rubber arm from a doll baby plucked from a sandy *cayo* also adorns the tree. Unlike the inside of the sub, which is pressurized at the atmosphere of the surface, the cups rode along in a mesh bag on the outside. As a result, they were squeezed down to about one-fourth of their original size—squashed by the pressure of sixty-one atmospheres. On the cups were names of our loved ones and friends, tiny links back to a world getting ready to celebrate a holiday without us, emotional icons compressed by the Cuban seas.

Even though winds and waves canceled the sub launch, filmmakers and biologists load gear and prepare to head ashore anyway today, hoping to find enough of a lee in the thick mangrove wilderness of the *cayos* of Jardines de la Reina to continue shooting more mangrove footage. With no science to perform, the women aboard—Frank, Widder, Pomponi—ask to be put ashore so they can at least stretch their legs on a beach. The boatman promises to return to pick them up after dropping us off in the mangroves.

The riskiest moments in this entire expedition usually aren't in deep water or the midst of circling sharks but in the precarious windows of time when we climb from our large ship down into our smaller boat—especially when we must carry cumbersome gear. As I prepare to do this today, a massive wave hits the hull of the *Seward Johnson*, washing across the stern and, briefly, floating heavy metal boxes and a lighting rig from the sub about us before it drains through the scuppers. I dodge the flotsam, climbing down a ladder over the edge of the ship to the smaller boat, which is now bucking wildly. As it rises nearly six feet on a heavy swell, I quickly climb aboard and ride it back down like a very fast elevator.

Soon we are off, headed the mile or so ashore to the tight Pasa Piedra Grande, a shallow natural cut that will take us behind the low berm of *cayos* that stretch across the mouths of the two inland gulfs, Guacanayabo and Ana María. We ran this same pass two days ago on our way to the Tortuga Hotel, and I welcome the chance to run it again, for there are hundreds of wild islets back here—some higher ones with snow-white sand, low tropical shrubs, and stunted silver palms; others a miasma of the elegantly bowed red mangrove roots and soft ivory-colored mud. In we go, across shallow green water and past flocks of cormorants with their snakelike necks, soaring frigate birds, and roosting roseate spoonbills, their plumage spectacularly pink. It seems primal back here, a place freshly tossed up from the sea, in the lee not just of the wind but of the shift of time itself.

Columbus had a "fairylike fascination" with this natural Cuba, describing it in his journal as "the prettiest that human eyes have ever seen." And other observers have followed his lead—including the two modern writers whom Cubans hold in such high regard today, expatriate Hemingway and countryman José Lezama Lima. "Ernesto," as the former is fondly remembered in Cuba, pitted man against the sea in macho resolve, while Lima explored its more mythic nuances—writing of "the sacred silver of scales and tails that seemed to have been polished by Glaucus."

This afternoon, it is the rough Hemingway sea that strands us. When we reach the edge of the cut at Pasa Piedra Grande, we face a stout line of eight- to twelve-foot-high waves rolling in from the sea. Although it is barely a mile offshore, the *Seward* seems impossible to reach, and trying to run through the waves with the expensive camera gear is not an option.

We head back inside, the houseboat barge our only possible refuge. As we approach, I find that Herrero and the boys and the fishermen are still here, socked in like us by the weather. In our two days away, almost nothing seems to have changed: the dominoes still click, the boys still swim, the old fishermen still laugh and joke with one another.

The only disconcerting blip on the screen is our Norteamericano sense of urgency. But even that will be muted by the capriciousness of the weather. Clearly, we won't be going anywhere soon. Giddings, who is in contact with the *Seward* by hand-held VHF radio, tells Captain Seiler we'll overnight on the barge rather than risk returning through the dangerous seas. Seiler tells him that's a good idea, especially in that the wind on the outside is expected to hit eighty knots per hour. The Tortuga, under repair, has no other guests, and all its spartan rooms are made available to us for the night. We have only the clothes on our back, or in some cases, just the wet suits and neoprene booties we are wearing. But the spontaneity of the moment is a heady antidote for such worries—and, after all, we are in the business of discovery.

We have a few hours of daylight left and decide to make the best of it. McCosker, Gilmore, and I arrange to have Hernández take us out bonefishing in the local mangrove flats. We have left our fly rods back on the ship, but the guide produces several light spincasting rigs, complete with lures, and fires up a small skiff. After a twenty-minute zigzag through the mangroves, we enter a small cove where Hernández has promised that bonefish are always found. A slender, dark-skinned man, he cuts the engine and stands up on the bow and poles us toward the edge of the mangroves.

Bonefishing is a business of sighting and casting to the fish, which give themselves away with their distinctive "tailing" as they root for small inverts in the sandy bottom. Although rippled with waves, the water is still clear enough to let us see several giant bones—at least ten-pounders— just under the water's surface. But they are skittish fish, made even more so by wind and sudden barometer drops, and they hang motionless near the mangrove roots, trying to be invisible. We cast to them anyway. But instead of gobbling our offerings, they spook, bolting away in a flash of fins and tails as soon as our spoons hit the water.

After we return, Hernández takes us up on the top deck to show us our rooms for the night. Each is austere but clean, identified with the name of a different marine animal on the door. Along with McCosker and Fagen, I'm in Palometa (permit); others are in Macabi (bonefish) or Sabalo (tarpon). Back downstairs, from inside the Drunken Cockroach, Hernández serves us cups of high-octane Cuban espresso. A freshly caught skipjack tuna is cleaned and readied for dinner, along with three spiny lobster.

As we are relaxing, we are handed a bill for the bonefishing. It is about three times the price we had agreed upon, the additional padding added by the rental of individual spinning rods for seventy-five dollars each. It is clearly a rip-off, and I want to complain, but Fagen is officious about the cultural differences: "You're in Cuba, man," he says. "They do things differently here." I figure fairness is universal regardless of where you are in the world, and to justify it as a cultural disparity is specious. But Fagen remains adamant, insisting it would be politically incorrect to argue the point, and I let it go.

The tropical sun dips below the mangroves, taking the thick golden light of the late afternoon with it. I quickly forget about the bonefishing transaction, determined to immerse myself in the flavor of the moment. It occurs to me that, when money is not at stake, the Cubans are pleasant and affable and sweetly charming. But when their lives are driven by profit making, they can become just as excessive as us North Americans.

Thanks to the unbridled power of nature, the official portion of the expedition is on hold, and there is nothing any of us can do about it. And so, with no personal duties calling to us here, in the most distant heart of these southern *cayos* of Cuba, we gather around a rough-hewn wooden table on the back deck and do what Ernesto likely would have done: we drink round after round of cold Cuban "Cristal" beer, washed down with local rum, Havana Club, dark and sweet.

Herrero generously brings us a couple of guava-colored slabs of mullet eggs that had been drying atop the awning over his bow; they taste salty and piquant, a sea-driven memory. From the kitchen a plate of albacore sushi appears, marinated in fresh lime juice. We talk some more, and Herrero asks me if I would contact his adult daughter Jehane, who now lives in Boston, when I return to the United States. "I have not heard from her for four months now. Her birthday is soon and I wonder if you would let her know I am okay and also want to wish her a happy birthday." Then, in a dash of Cuban stoicism, Herrero adds: "You know, telephone communications between our countries isn't restricted. It is just . . . impossible." I ask Herrero to join us for drinks, but he says, no, it is not so good for the boys to see him drinking.

Fully exorcised of civilization, we tell jokes and laugh until the cool Antillean night consumes us all, scientists and filmmakers, gringos and Cubans. The rising tide swashes gently against the hulls of the barge and the Cayo Largos, and in the mangroves nearby, a *jutia* scuttles through the shallows, setting off blue-green sparks of bioluminescence. "The world," says Ricardo, "is becoming a much better place." Overhead, the stars are again stretching across the sky, the oblong splatter of the Milky Way glowing as if it had been airbrushed onto the night. Lipscomb, in his bathing suit and T-shirt with a towel around his waist, stands, clears his throat, and recites lyrics from "Trade Winds," a poem by John Masefield:

> In the harbour, in the island, in the Spanish Seas,
> Are the tiny white houses and the orange-trees,
> And day-long, night long, the cool and pleasant breeze
> Of the steady Trade Winds blowing.
>
> There is the red wine, the nutty Spanish ale,
> The shuffle of the dancers, the old salt's tale,
> The squeaking fiddle, and the soughing in the sail
> Of the steady Trade Winds blowing.

I am astounded that he remembers the lines so well and am touched by the relevant nature of the lyric. The film and ship crew, accustomed to his public declarations by now, have begun to call Lipscomb "the Ancient Mariner."

McCosker has launched into a long convoluted joke in which sex and fish both play a role, although by the time he reaches the punch line, most everyone has forgotten how the story began. Lipscomb's associate producer, Taima Hervas, the only gringa with us, scurries about, at least pretending to organization, although clearly there is little need for it at this juncture. Fagen has now put on a cheap clear plastic poncho to keep himself warm. McCosker informs the esteemed Latin American scholar he looks like a giant condom. "Noooo," says Fagen. Then, thinking it over: "Really? Do I look like a condom? Really?" Soon, there is dinner, broiled tuna, white rice, fried plantains, and chunks of spiny lobster, swimming in a spicy cream sauce. Dinner could have been beef jerky and this crew would have been very happy. But now—away from a dry ship and with no work to do—they are in bliss.

Sometime before midnight, I climb the stairs and open the door to Palometa. Aboard the Tortuga, I have found a copy of José Lezama Lima's *Paradiso*, and I struggle through the Spanish to try to identify a passage that describes the fuzzy magic surrealism of tonight. Finally, I stumble across: "For him, every awakening was a discovery of the infinite expansion of each of the starfish's radiations. . . . On each of the plates, a fish appeared, its face enlarged and corroded by the beginning of sleep."

The last sound I hear before I fall into my own vibrant, dream-filled sleep is the bulletlike crack of dominoes being slammed down on the table under the stern canopy below. There is no talking, no laughing, no other sound at all but the smack of the dominoes on the hard tropical wood.

6

Cayos de las Doce Leguas and Banco Jagua

Tuesday, December 16

Cayos de las Doce Leguas

After a quick breakfast of plantains and rice, Cuban bread, and espresso, we load into the boats and make a run for it before the wind picks up again. Skies are overcast, and the seas are still rough, but the waves are half the size they were yesterday afternoon. By the time we reach the stern of the *Seward*, several of the crew—most notably the women biologists, who were hoping to be retrieved for some shore leave yesterday— are leaning over the railing, hooting at us. "Yea, some science you guys did," says Frank. And from Widder: "Hope you had fun out on the town while we had to stay here on this ship and rock ourselves to sleep." It is an odd shipboard equation that has developed just in our few weeks at sea; now I am feeling like a wayward husband who went out for a loaf of bread and didn't come home until the morning.

Back aboard, we stow our gear and gather in the conference room for a briefing. The seas have calmed enough for a sub dive, and Liberatore and Gilmore are slated to take the JSL down to twelve hundred feet, along the slope of the outer wall. "The plan is to hang around at depth for a while, then start back up, doing transects along the way," explains Liberatore. A transect is simply a lateral hover at which time the sub electronically records data—like temperature and current velocity—while the scientist and pilot try to capture whatever is nearby via the suction tubes and claw arms.

After the meeting, I retreat to my rabbit warren and discover that last night's rough seas have knocked my chair and books onto the floor—everything, in fact, except for the laptop, which is still safely Velcroed to the counter surface. I straighten up the desk and review the images I took last night at the Tortuga Hotel on the digital camera. Although amusing, few will be useful for the family-rated Web site: most, shot long after we were stranded, show various renditions of our crew around the table, on their way to becoming thoroughly hammered. I print out some of the incoming E-missives and tape them up on the bulletin board in the hallway outside my workspace. They are the usual mix of curiosity about Cuba, mean-spirited criticism and even threats (from anti-Castro zealots), and veiled greetings from friends and family back home. Also in this batch is another from the in-house Discovery producer ("JIM OR AL OR TAIMA OR KAREN OR BILL, PLEASE SEND ME AN EMAIL!"). After I attach the E-mail to the board, I later notice that someone has scribbled on the hard copy a reply to the producer's E-mail:

Dear Sr. Producer:
    We all miss you so much. Meanwhile, we are asking the doctor to correct your medication.
    —Your Friends in Cuba

I struggle through lunch, still a bit fuzzy from last night. I stroll back to the dry lab and watch as Claro carefully pins a small goby-looking fish down in a shallow pan with formaldehyde on the bottom. It is an apricot bass, captured on a deep sub dive by Claro and Dick Robins.

There may be some twelve hundred different species of fish known to live in Cuban waters—well over twice the number in Florida waters—and while a scientist as expert as Claro will know most shallow reef fish from simply having seen them more frequently, the deepwater fish must be studied with care. Historically, specimens that represent the "first" of their kind to be described scientifically are sketched, preserved, and cataloged. New specimens recovered by the subs benefit from being photographed as soon as they are brought to the surface, providing color integrity that collections a century ago didn't allow. And, the JSL, with its high-resolution digital video camera mounted outside the pilot sphere, also captures valuable movement and clues to behavior in situ.

In the past, ichthyologists often sketched or painted newly harvested fish. In the early twentieth century, Henry Fowler, William Beebe, and Margaret Smith were known for such work. Later, biologists Joe Tomelleri and Guy Harvey—who most often illustrated fish described by others—became so adroit that they actually became commercial artists. Gilmore, who carefully renders images of captured fish using colored pencils, may be one of the last practicing ichthyologists to still hand-draw and color specimens he describes. Gilmore tells me that his eyes can see tints and hues that even the camera misses. "Cameras can fool you with the color, so I keep pencils handy and try as quickly as possible to make a rendition," Gilmore says. But clearly, there is another dynamic going on here, one that links the scientist more viscerally with the animal he studies: "It also gives me an intimate association with the fish and its characteristic morphology."

There are two major problems with the original specimens—the "holotypes"—first used to describe species around Cuba. Snatched by hook and line or trawled up from the depths, the fish started out in poor condition and got worse with age. Or, more often than not, they simply disappeared from Cuba altogether, traveling away with visiting scientists into the natural history collection of whatever country happened to be cruising their waters at the time. The most notable such exodus of specimens from Latin America in modern time was courtesy of the "Atlantis Harvard-Havana Expedition to the West Indies of 1938–39." Earlier collecting trips in the nineteenth century include the "Thayer Expedition to Brazil" in

1865–66 and the "Hassler Expedition of 1871–72." Louis Agassiz, a Swiss-born naturalist who studied fish as well as developed the theory of ice ages by analyzing the movement of glaciers, organized both. On the Hassler expedition alone, some thirty thousand specimens were collected, which required thirty-five hundred gallons of alcohol to pack and preserve. Most of the fish gathered from Latin American waters during this period were placed in the fish collection at the Museum of Comparative Zoology (MCZ) at Harvard.

In fact, almost all the fish captured or described by Cuban naturalist Filipe Poey are in the MCZ Collection. Besides the imperialistic implications, having those specimens in the States creates its own conundrum. As biologist Mike Smith of the Washington, D.C.–based Center for Marine Conservation had told me before I left on the trip: "Cuban scientists need to be able to study information on their own country's biodiversity—which is critical because of the high rate of endemic species and high rate of extinction. . . . To do this, though, they need to access their country's specimen base. But that base is in the country that has had a blockade against them, including travel restrictions, for the past thirty-four years."

Gilmore hopes that one of the postexpeditionary rewards will be to help Cuba rebuild its collection by stocking it with ecotypes—the surviving animals descendant from the originally described species. To this end, Gilmore seems to have a personal quest for a certain Cuban deepwater spiny ray fish, *Verilus*. It is one that Poey first described as *Verilus sordidus* in 1868 from a dead specimen brought to him by a Chinese fisherman. (Later, in Havana, we hope to see Poey's original sketch at the home of one of Cuba's most distinguished ichthyologists.) Gilmore has been chasing the live *Verilus* all over the Caribbean since 1982 in one or the other of the Harbor Branch subs. But the little perchlike fish has been as elusive as government funding for field science. "It lays on its side on a slope underwater on seamounts, like it's saying: 'Come get me, if you can.' It's like a cat-and-mouse game. And so far, he's winning." If Gilmore catches *Verilus* during our trip, he will leave this fresh specimen behind, bringing the taxonomy full circle. This seems particularly important to him as a symbol: not a single specimen of *Verilus* has been recovered anywhere—including Cuba—since Poey's first description.

The gesture of capturing such a fish and placing it in the collection at the Instituto de Oceanología is a generous one, reflective of Gilmore's own strong respect for Poey's work as well as his regard for his Cuban colleagues. To help make this happen, he has promised a bottle of the finest Cuban rum to the sub pilot who helps him capture the little fish.

Thomas Barbour (1884–1946), who published *A Naturalist in Cuba* in 1945, never met the pioneering Cuban scientist. But he spent years in the earlier twentieth century tracing the work of Poey and his fellow Cuban scientists, such as Carlos de la Torre y la Herta (1858–1950). More of a Renaissance man back in the days when scientists weren't as confined to specialties as they now are, Poey collected and identified butterflies, insects, and land snails, as well as fish; his knowledge of fish included both marine and freshwater, including a genus of blind cave fish found in western Cuba. A professor at the University of Havana, Poey wrote his country's definitive book on its environment in 1851: *Memorias sobre la historia natural de la isla de Cuba*. He was, Barbour explains, "one of those old-fashioned naturalists with a curiosity about every living thing." Ironically, he was "better known to the great naturalists of Europe than he was to his colleagues in the U.S." Barbour also provides a different light on the issue of "curation exploitation" by noting that Poey was extremely generous in donating original specimens to museums outside Cuba: "He knew perfectly well that the day had not yet dawned in Cuba when such things as specimens of natural history would be appreciated." After all, Poey lived at a time when Cuba was still a colony of Spain. The wealthy sugar dons who ran the country were a harbinger of the oppressive twentieth-century dictatorships, first of Machado, and then Batista—rulers more attuned to agricultural commodities (and later, casinos) than the mysteries of natural history, marine or otherwise.

By evening, the downrigger on the stern of the *Seward* is baited with a fish head and dropped to its two-thousand-foot depth range. I ask Gilmore what he expects to catch, and he says anything from ten pounds to four thousand. A few of the crew putter a bit around the stern, killing time. I return to my work space and check incoming mails. In the last day, I have posted a digital photo of the nudibranch McCosker thought was a *Melobe* on the Web. Using the E-mail, McCosker contacted a colleague at the California Academy of Sciences who specializes in such mollusks and asked him to take a close look at the photo on the Web. A return E-mail now informs us that the nudi may instead be a species called *Fimbria occidentalis*. As I am becoming gradually more suspicious about how the entertainment component drives such online access, I am heartened to see that the Web can be a tool for real science, if the right people are involved in the process.

As I am reviewing this new long-distance stab at taxonomy, I hear shouting coming from the stern. I push away from the counter, rush out into the hallway, and step reflexively over the six-inch-high bulkhead that separates the enclosed working quarters from the open deck. As soon as I do, I spot Gilmore and McCosker moving frenetically around the downrigger. One of them is trying to crank it, but the thick metal arm of the device is bowing heroically with the down pull of what must be an extraordinary weight. Something big and deep is on the other end, and the others gathering out on the stern begin to speculate on what it can be—six-gilled shark? Manta ray? Sub tech Jim Sullivan suggests it may be Verne's giant squid, returning to haunt us for ever doubting its existence. By the time the line is reeled in, the giant hook on the end has been straightened by the force of whatever had its mouth around it, a steel question mark turned into an exclamation point.

Wednesday, December 17

Banco Jagua

Banco Jagua is a massive underwater mountain rising up from a mile's worth of sea bottom, some thirty miles due south of the bustling sugar port of Cienfuegos. This port and its natural harbor are nestled in a valley between the Sierra de Escambray to the east and the Zapata Swamp to the west. Although first sighted by Europeans during Columbus's second voyage, Cienfuegos wasn't settled until 1819—and then by a small group of French adventurers from Louisiana, who founded the colony of Fernandina de Jagua here. Today, the port handles about one-third of all of Cuba's sugar exports, relying on some twelve mills that process *cana* from local fields. But for most of the world, Cienfuegos is known more for its Juraguá Nuclear Power Plant, a set of twin 440-megawatt nuclear reactors based on the Soviet design of Chernobyl. Construction began in 1983 but was only partially finished by the time the Russian aid ended in 1990. An operating plant like this one would be a nuclear catastrophe waiting to happen, according to experts who have studied it—with a scatter potential powerful enough to dust Florida and beyond. A dead zone with an eighteen-mile radius would emanate from any accident, pushing a fallout that could extend for three hundred miles, all the way to Tampa. Like fish larvae, nuclear radiation doesn't recognize the boundaries of an embargo, either. Even staunch anti-Castro critics say that Juraguá is reason enough by itself to engage the country in diplomatic dialogue. More irony: the flirtation with nuclear power dates from the Batista era, in which that government was offered U.S. funding under the "Atoms for Peace" program. The first plan to build a nuclear power plant was canceled with the break in U.S.-Cuban diplomatic relations in 1960 and the subsequent loss of U.S. funding.

Our nautical map shows that Banco Jagua is clearly distinguished from other seamounts by its enormous size and shape. It is configured more like a mesa in the southwestern United States, with a vast flat top supported on all sides by plunging walls—not dissimilar to the limestone mogotes that dot the westerly Cuban landscape of Pinar del Río. Peaked near its middle, the plateau rises up to within fifteen feet of the surface, which is nearly shallow enough to scrape the bottom of the *Seward*. But most of the mesa is in fifty to sixty feet of water. Surely, it is shallow enough to allow for the sunlight-to-energy conversion corals require to flourish. Like the smaller, nearshore seamount off Chivirico, its tapestry of marine life may also draw in roaming oceanic pelagics from deeper waters. We are hoping that the remote location of Banco Jagua—and the fact that few local fishermen likely have enough fuel to bring them out here on a regular basis—will have kept it less accessible and more intact.

Lipscomb has been anxious to get four good minutes of topside tape in the can a day, and the stress of that is beginning to show. Just yesterday, as he was setting up to film Claro and Alcolado, he shouted to Hervas to "cue the Mexicans!" Hervas informed him that they were Cuban, and

Lipscomb said he knew that. We have already been here two weeks, and our remaining time is limited. Once we round the horn at the tip of western Cuba and arrive in Havana, the science of the exploration will be over for good. Peculiar-looking fish and inverts—jellies and shrimps and other lumpy organisms lacking a backbone—are being harvested by the JSL, but they are almost all known species. Our voyage has been slight on the "marine marvels," and the gee-whiz epiphanies of new discoveries have been more sublime than dramatic.

In the treatment that pitched this project to Discovery, comparisons were made with the Galápagos expedition and its film ("Galápagos: Beyond Darwin"), in which this same ship and most of the crew participated two years earlier. But the Galápagos Islands were six hundred miles out in the Pacific and were renowned for being a "cradle of evolution." Nearly every time the sub went down, it emerged with an undescribed deepwater fish or invert, and another dozen or so critters were found by divers using scuba. That expedition played big to the "newness" of those uncharted depths.

We *are* certainly navigating a coastline few ever see and diving in waters never before filmed. Fish found elsewhere in the Caribbean but unknown in Cuba are being encountered and identified. There may even be a couple of new species aboard, sucked up from the depths by the JSL. And Gilmore is still hot on the track of *Verilus*.

Yet Cuba is not the Galápagos, and our own discoveries are more circumspect: ecological theories are being developed or reinforced. From scuba dives, we are learning that the rocky volcanic shores are nearly devoid of life, whereas the more shallow mangrove coasts are swarming with it—as a result, the farther west we go, the richer the shallow waters become. (Claro, who has written a book on the marine environment of his country, and Alcolado, who is an expert ecologist in the wider Caribbean, already knew much of this.)

And Gilmore is finding that a complex theory of his about deepwater fish—based on hundreds of sub dives throughout the wider Caribbean—is also being supported by our work. He had speculated that we would see deepwater fish known from igneous rock bottoms in the West Indies on volcanic "substrates." But over sedimentary bottoms—like limestone and fossilized coral—we would observe deepwater fish associated with the Central American coast. Since no plants are typically found below six hundred feet, fish life at those depths is influenced mostly by temperature and the composition of the bottom rock, Gilmore reasons.

Nonetheless, this sort of byzantine ecology seldom provides the revelation that makes documentary expeditions "sexy." Since our contact with Cuban locals along the coast has so far been limited, I worry about how the real Cuba will be eventually portrayed. Herrero and his fishing school, the villagers of Uvero, even Santiago and its caffeinated bustle didn't make it to film. So far, the emphasis has been on oceanography, without a geographic context and the related cultural connection. The particular "sense of place," while gradually being revealed to all of us aboard, is still unformed on film. I wonder if the Discovery producer's shipboard tirade to disembody Cuba from its waters has had a tacit impact, one that is more subtle than any of us realize.

If these waters are truly forbidden, a good dose of melodrama is plainly needed: everyone is hoping that a visit from Castro—El Jefe, the old spearfisherman himself—might provide that when we reach Havana. Certainly, Castro is a hot potato politically. But, with his extensive first-person knowledge of his island's waters, he might provide the sort of provocative component journalists always seek to punch up a story—especially one immersed in natural history. We are also awaiting permission to stop at Castro's vacation villa at Cayo Piedras, as well as the nearby Bahía de Cochinos, the Bay of Pigs, which has been off limits even to Claro and Alcolado in the past. We will approach both locales in the next day or so as we continue to steam west; stops there could add sorely needed local flavor to the story. Certainly, a few more new discoveries—or a dangerous shark or two—wouldn't hurt either.

Today, our sub will run a transect along the sloping edges of the bank to its two-thousand-foot limit. Along with scientists and film crew, I will scuba dive on the immense platform at its top. We have arrived at an opportune time, at the peak of the lunar cycle in the early winter when the Nassau grouper (*Epinephelus striatus*)—the sea bass with the gregarious personality—gather in mass congregations to spawn on shallow banks like Jagua. Here in Cuba, it is the time of the Grouper Moon. To reach this place, we steamed southwestward, from the enormous shallows of Golfos de Guacanayabo and Ana María—with their splendidly wild *cayos*—into the deep blue of the open Caribbean.

As I scan the horizon from the deck of our ship this morning, I see no trace of land, only the endless scrolling of the stout seagoing waves. It seems a tabula rasa, ripe for our own palette of experience to define it. With no geographic reference point, this ocean surface beneath our ship strikes me as the cusp between the conscious and the unconscious mind of the earth itself. And with our educated technology, we are again preparing to breach it, like some psychologist probing the internal shadowlands of the most primitive biological urges. Perhaps this analogy is not a stretch: Jungians say that 90 percent of our brain rests in the gyre of the unconscious; deepwater scientists say that 99 percent of the ocean is hidden beyond the range of surface-skimming vessels and shallow scuba gear. And the deeper one probes, the more primordial the marine life becomes.

Down goes the JSL submersible, lowered off the stern by the **A**-frame crane, spitting bubbles and churning water into eddies as it settles into innerspace. Aboard today are Gilmore and McCosker.

Giddings has also asked several of us to make an exploratory dive on Banco Jagua to hunt for the grouper. So, while the JSL is flying along the deeper edges of the seamount, I load up my scuba gear for a visit to its top. If the visibility is good and if critters are plentiful, a film dive might be scheduled for later. Since we are far at sea, the southwest fetch—which I imagine begins to gather energy somewhere off the coast of the Yucatán— makes the surf look wild and unpredictable. Still, I have just had an enlightening chat with Gilmore about the Grouper Moon, and I am thrilled about the possibility of seeing some of the pre-spawn grouper roaming the bank. Gilmore, who has studied mating rituals of grouper for years from inside the JSL, has told me that the Nassau grouper congregates in great numbers and spawns over a couple days before and after the December full moon throughout the Caribbean. At this time, its olive-brown bars turn nearly white—especially the pronounced lateral hash mark across its head. Gilmore asks me to keep an eye out for fish like this on my dive.

Gilmore's study of the grouper is typical of the unsung work practiced by dedicated ichthyologists everywhere—in that it often takes place far beyond the attention of the air-breathing surface world. It is a quest that trails in the wake of the Sirens' call itself, inextricably pulling the scientist underwater to a certain place, as if he too is drawn back by the waxing and waning of each full December moon. Using the Harbor Branch sub, Gilmore has descended on the deep Oculina reef system off the Atlantic coast of Florida; he has perched on the bottom with lights off, sitting stealthily in wait for the seasonal ritual to begin.

Certainly, sitting still anywhere in nature—as opposed to crashing about—usually brings rewards to the good observer, and the sea is no exception. In one study, Gilmore watched from the pilot sphere as the scamp (*Mycteroperca phenax*) went through a total of four color phases in minutes as part of a way to demonstrate dominance as it prepared to mate. On other dives, Gilmore watched in awe as the fish preparing to spawn returned to the same site that they had gone to the year before, jockeying for position like hotshots in a singles bar.

"It's like they're taking stock," Gilmore explains. " 'Where's Charlie? I don't see him this year.' They are making note of who is there and who is not. . . . When a big male disappears—say, he is speared or caught by a fisherman—and he doesn't return, then a female can change into a male to take his place. But there is still much we don't even know about its life cycle. For instance, how long does the gender change take?" Unfortunately, the biggest, fattest grouper are also the oldest, living to thirty years and more. Functioning as either a mother fish or a stud, the big slow-growing grouper are key to the survival of their species. Yet, because they present fat targets—and are relatively slow moving—they are the easiest to spear underwater. Each ready-to-spawn female grouper holds some million eggs, and the loss of each mature fish whittles away at the grist of the sea mill just a bit more—not just for Cuba but for the southeastern United States, where many of the drifting young larval fish may float. "If you want to wipe out a population of any fish," Gilmore said, "all you have to do is to catch as many as you can during its spawning stage."

I also learned from Alcolado that, despite Banco Jagua's thirty-mile distance from land, the bank is not as protected by isolation as we have been led to believe. The Cuban ecologist told me that the lack of fuel doesn't stop those determined to fish. In fact, fishing boats have been *sailing* out to these submerged banks for years during the Grouper Moon, taking the large fish before they even have a chance to spawn. (Others on the ship suspect that sport fishing and scuba guides with access to fast boats from tourist lodges have been padding their income by zooming out here to capture the big, valuable fish and selling them on the black market.) When he was a young man, says Alcolado, the waters here would be white with milt and eggs for many square miles, and other fish would move in by the thousands, drawn by the chumlike slick. But now, he wondered how many such fish still come to Banco Jagua for their annual rite at all. After all, Cuba's yearly harvest of grouper—a prize food fish—is barely 15 percent of what it was twenty years ago, he said. Nonetheless, we simply don't have the luxury of spending days in one place along the route to finesse the science. If legions of spawning grouper don't materialize during our overnight stop, then the Grouper Moon and its congregations of serranids—if they still exist—will go into the ether of our wake.

Banco Jagua is directly under the *Seward* this morning, and when I climb the ladder down into the smaller dive boat, I can see the beams of sunlight bouncing back up from its white patches of sand fifty feet below, the brown-red slabs of coral barely visible in the clear green shallows. There are other banks isolated out here this far from shore—the nearest are Banco Bucanero and Banco Paz to the east. But at thirty-six square miles in size, Jagua is surely one of the most prominent. As we putter away from the *Seward*, Jagua takes on the persona of a looming giant—sleeping, perhaps, but very much alive—and our little skiff seems to be the tiny *Pequod* to Banco Jagua's inexorable Moby Dick.

Certainly, we could have simply dived on the bank from the *Seward*. But Giddings is more interested in capturing the ways in which Banco Jagua makes its sensational plunge into the deep at the edge of the mesa. The dive boat takes us to the camber, where the depth finder shows that the shallow plateau sharply drops off the screen. We are nearly a mile from the ship now, and the water under us has changed from green to deep blue. This is too deep, and we return a hundred yards or so to the shallower green water and anchor here atop the underwater canyon rim. Then we stagger in the bucking seas to strap on our gear and splash over the gunwales, sinking down—we hope—to the ridge where the bank gives way to the mile-deep ocean.

My dive buddy, associate producer Straus, has entered the water first and is ten feet under me, sinking slowly toward the bottom, her blond ponytail wreathing out into the light current. As we descend, the silvery domes of her exhalations brush against me on their way to the surface, each carrying a miniature of my own reflection inside it. Although the depth finder showed the edge of Jagua as fifty feet here, we are falling beyond that, to sixty, seventy, eighty, and more. I look around and see we are sinking into a black chasmlike gash that forms a **V** shape as it pulls away from the higher platform. Realizing we have overshot our mark, Straus and I stop, look at each other quizzically, and then simultaneously point back up to the edge of the precipice, silently agreeing that is where we want to be. We then fin back up to that lip, weightlessly mountain climbing with no ropes or pitons. We skim up and over the ledge, to where the mesa top is covered with a truncated garden of soft corals and white calcareous sand. The sea has done a magnificent job of upholstering this seamount with a thick fabric of coral and worms, sponges, and tiny invertebrates, all united here in their isolation from the mainland.

Visibility is barely fifty feet, and in the distance I can make out the lanky frame of underwater cinematographer Randy Wimberg and another diver I don't recognize. I slowly poke along, with my head down, allowing the tiny details of this coral city to reveal themselves. Smallish tropicals like fairy basslets flit through sponges and sea fans, bicolor little serranids glowing with bright violet and gold. Just under a patch of white sand, a yard-wide ray wiggles and then, realizing his cover is blown, scuttles away. A pair of four-eyed butterfly fish, drawn together as a couple for life, swim through in tandem, their disklike bodies actually seeming to flit like butterflies in the light current. Earlier, Alcolado—proud of his country's heritage—had shown me a ten-peso Cuban coin, which sports the image of a four-eyed butterfly fish.

I sense something watching me and look up. It is a great barracuda (*Sphyraena barracuda*), a silvery torpedo-shaped fish, and it is hanging in the water about ten yards away. This one is huge, maxed out at nearly six feet in length and as big around as a log. It is opening and closing its underslung jaw, as if it is barely able to accommodate all the long, sharp teeth in its mouth at once. On first blush, it seems to be a predator with an attitude, ready to Cuisinart anything in its path. Since barracudas also appear to stalk you as you move through the water and fix you with an ichthyological version of the thousand-yard stare, larger ones can be disconcerting—especially in that they almost always see you before you see them. Sometimes they circle, as if preparing to feed, as this one is doing now. But its metronomic jaw work is a means of respiration for the fish, a way to help it suck more oxygen into its oversized body. And when it escorts you about, it is merely being territorial—at least that is the theory, and right now, I am eager to buy into it. As for the rest, the barracuda does far more damage to humans who spear it or catch it on hook and then cook it for a meal. Barracuda flesh—particularly that of larger fish—often carries ciguatera, a neurotoxin so disabling that people who eat it après dive sometimes think they are suffering from decompression sickness.

I turn my attention away from the barracuda and back to the organic mosaic of the bottom, trying to make some sense of it. Using a yellow plastic slate and pencil, I jot down notes of what I see, teasing each part away from the other to reveal identifiable creatures—a nearly transparent Pederson's cleaner shrimp, a lettuce sea slug curled like a piece of romaine, a small black feather star. The star, which is also found at great depths by the sub, fascinates me. Unlike its fat-bodied sea star cousins in the Echinoderm phylum, the little feather star—also known as a crinoid—is the most ancient of the starfish, a living fossil. Its arms appear as feathers, delicate and fragile limbs that may number as many as twenty. With only its long, thin arms exposed and waving in the current, the feather star can easily be mistaken for a soft coral—perhaps a sea rod, fan, or whip. It dates from that time in oceanic history when sea creatures were genetically busy trying to figure out what worked best for them, an ancestral forerunner that was delicate and brittle, with far too many arms for its own good. Yet, if the sea can be treacherous, it can also be forgiving in regard to evolution: today, this Neanderthal star survives in the same environment as its more efficient modern descendants. Like other invertebrates that creep slowly or not at all—including valuable protein sources like the giant queen conch—the feather star colonizes the sea not by its movement but by the release of its spawn, which may drift hundreds of miles away from it with the current.

Just as I am looking down at my slate to make a note about the basket star, I feel a hard thump on my thigh. Reflexively, I gulp a large mouthful of air, and my heart races. My primal reaction is that the barracuda has decided after all to make full use of its impressive array of teeth. But as I turn, I see Wimberg next to me, gesturing and making repeated sweeping motions with his arm. His eyes are wide behind his mask, and he seems particularly animated. I have dived with Wimberg before, both here and in the Galápagos, and since his usual demeanor is calm and steady, his excitement does not particularly bode well. But I have no idea what he is trying to tell me. I hand him the slate, and he writes the word *shark* in large letters. Then, he hits his shoulder hard to show me that the animal was inches away from running into him. (Later, back at the surface, he tells me that his encounter was with an eight-foot nurse shark. Normally docile, nurse sharks [*Ginglymostoma cirratum*] share the same "carpet shark" family with whale sharks. They have been known to attack and bite if provoked, but I have never heard of one actually swimming into a diver on its own before. Maybe the Grouper Moon has excited more than just the serranids.)

With the shark business out of the way, I hang in the water and slowly rotate 360 degrees, which gives me a more panoramic look at the mesa top. As I do, I notice what seems to be a large fish duck behind a clump of coral about twenty yards away. I hover, motionless, hoping it will emerge. And soon it does, poking its head out just enough to see if I am still here. It is a ten-pound Nassau grouper, in full spawning regalia, and I realize he is so curious that he has been following me across the bank. I pull up from my position and continue to fin on with my head down, stopping every couple of minutes to look over my shoulder and see if my new friend is still there. Every time I pause and turn, the grouper darts behind the field of sea whips, plumes, and rods, like a little kid playing hide and seek. Oceanographer Sylvia Earle once compared groupers to cocker spaniels for their friendly, tail-wagging inquisitiveness, and clearly the metaphor was a worthy one.

I stop one last time and fix my attention on what I can see of the grouper, which by now is only partially hidden by a slender sea whip, a soft-bodied coral that looks like a terrestrial bush that has lost all its leaves. The distinctive olive-brown slashes of this stout-bodied fish are fired with white, reconfigured by its ancient urge to survive, an animal reflecting the pale colors of the Grouper Moon itself. The Nassau is gregarious, curious to a fault, and perhaps too tasty for its own good. I hope its spawn has been safely exuded, that it has consummated—for this year at least—its timeless dance with the sea. The fish continues to follow me, until my air wanes and I surface.

Back on the *Seward*, I tell Gilmore about the lone pre-spawn grouper I have seen, and he says it is the only one anyone has spotted on Banco Jagua during the dive.

By late afternoon, the sub emerges from its dive, its one-knot propulsion moving it against a light current until it is where the crane can reach it for retrieval near the stern. At the surface, it seems more to wallow than to move with purpose, a giant leviathan struggling to keep itself from toppling. I realize the current—as scant as it is—is close to overwhelming the vehicle. Unlike better streamlined submersibles, it strikes me how poorly built the JSL is for aerodynamics. Instead of reconfiguring Ed Link's original vehicles, HBOI engineers seem to have been instructed to continue to add to the original prototype over the past three decades. Although it is capable of harvesting living organisms from the water much better than its counterparts, the accessorized nature of its ad hoc technology makes it look outrageously clunky—a glockenspiel of a sub if there ever was one. The disadvantages of this are becoming increasingly clear: its poor speed puts it at the mercy of underwater and surface currents, which often rage far beyond one knot an hour. And its jagged array of appendages makes it more likely to become snagged on sharp rocky ledges or sea-bottom wreckage. (A final dive to explore artifacts at the mouth of the Havana harbor at the end of our journey will turn treacherous for this very reason.)

A crew member in a wet suit—this time, sub engineer Dan Boggess—jumps from the deck of the ship and swims over to the top of the sub, which rises and falls for several feet at the surface. There, he crawls up onto it and, grabbing the heavy titanium "plug" swinging at the end of a thick rope from the crane, jams it down into its pneumatic slot right behind the pilot sphere. The thick line holds the sub in place while the crane can be lowered to pluck it from the sea. It is astounding that millions of dollars of high-tech oceanography rely on a few seconds during which a human must perform a low-tech—and dangerous—chore like this one. The potential for error on the part of the "swimmer" is immense, from getting caught in a surface eddy and washing away to getting knocked unconscious by the swinging metal plug. And though sharks in this part of the world are normally uninterested in divers, they often mistake swimmers of any kind for a thrashing, wounded prey, thus adding one more risk to the exercise. (Nonetheless, the recovery of the JSL is said to be the safest in the business; other subs—like the *Alvin* and the *Pisces*—must be secured with multiple lines by swimmers, sometimes from *underneath* the sub itself.)

Boggess, with whom I have closely worked to frame-grab digital stills from Giddings's underwater footage for the Web site, seems an unlikely candidate for the job of swimmer. A bright man, he is also thin and intense, with thick glasses and a preoccupied air. He is also a heavy smoker—hardly the sort you expect to be performing a physically challenging Falcoesque chore in the uncertain seas. Although Boggess seems more at home tinkering with the never-ending electrical system maintenance of the JSL, he is as game as any of the other crew when swimming duties come his way. Today, he performs well, and the sub is soon cranked aboard, dripping on the stern like a giant wet dog.

Giddings, who was riding next to the pilot, emerges from the hatch to tell everyone that he has brought them "a Christmas stocking—something for everybody." Lipscomb, balancing his heavy camera on his shoulder, moves toward the sub as the crew begins to unload specimens from the rotary plankton-collection vats mounted under the sphere. Out come two very curious-looking deepwater fish captured at the edge of this seamount: a foot-long leopard-striped cat shark (*Scyliorhinus boa*) and a big-eyed tinselfish (*Grammicolepis brachiusculus*), which looks like a permit on steroids. Despite the mystery that deepwater fish hold for all of us who live at the surface of the earth, both specimens are familiar to our scientists. The tinselfish, which lives up to its name, has been videotaped by the JSLs on other missions, its narrow rows of comblike fins undulating to move it through the everlasting darkness of deep water. In fact, several specimens from the Bahamas now reside in the HBOI museum back in Fort Pierce. The colorful little shark, known commonly as *gatica* in Spanish and the Boa catshark in English, was first described in 1896 from specimens captured off Barbados. The pupils of its eyes are strikingly vertical, almost felinelike in composition. Also collected were a bone-white deepwater sponge and a delicate silvery anemone.

Cinematically, this haul might make a nice Christmas stocking for chair-bound, TV-surfing naturalists, but it hardly sends our ichthyologists into rapture. At least all the specimens are alive and, once ensconced in the wet-lab tank, make great film. Giddings said that during the capture the tinsel fish was so "stupid" that it actually backed into the clawlike "manipulator" arm of the JSL.

Later, Gilmore tells me that the tinsel fish isn't really "stupid" at all. "The fish never enters sunlit waters and lives in eternal darkness. We brought the sun down with us and stunned the fish." Gilmore, whose sympathies clearly lie with the animals, says the tinsel fish is not unlike the nocturnal possum blinded by car headlights at night. "The possum has been around since the Cretaceous, when it was running about between the legs of *Tyrannosaurus rex* some sixty-five million years ago." It's not a matter of stupidity, says Gilmore, just perspective. The tinsel fish, the possum, and all the other animals with long, extended evolutionary track records will likely still be here long after we humans—who repeatedly back into one cosmic manipulator arm or another—have vanished.

Despite the visual productivity of this site, there is a sense of urgency to continue moving westward. McCosker thinks it is a bad decision to leave Banco Jagua because scuba dives along the top might reveal most anything this far out in the ocean. Although the next two tentative stops on the itinerary have five-star entertainment value—Castro's vacation villa and the nearby Bay of Pigs—we have not yet been given permission to visit them. As a result, we will steam past them to the edge of the next and last set of islands, Archipiélago de los Canarreos, which encircle the edge of the Golfo de Batabanó and are punctuated with Cuba's largest island, Isla de la Juventud.

By the time we reach this Isle of Youth in a few days, we will finally receive official permission to visit the Bay of Pigs, but by then there will be no turning back. Gilmore will tell me that if this had been a pure science expedition, the Bahía de Cochinos was so important that he would have backtracked to survey it. In fact, by now, he has seen enough of this southern coast to have created a scientific wish list in his head: "From an ecological standpoint, I'd pick three very different sites along this course—one somewhere off the volcanic shore of Santiago, then Playa Girón, and finally the western tip at María la Gorda, where it's flat and extends out into the sea. I'd compare each site with the next, to see who's eating whom."

The Bahía de Cochinos—named for local wild pigs that once formed the staple of the Taino diet here—would have been impressive as a stop, environmentally as well as historically. Columbus was the first European to see it; in 1494, he reported seeing naked Taino carrying "in their hand a burning coal, and certain weeds for inhaling their smoke." The weeds were a form of tobacco, and the coals were charcoal. Today, self-sufficient Cubans still make charcoal from wood using a method similar to that of the early Indians: they cut wood, stack it in an oven made of earth and straw, light it, and let it smolder for several days.

Still, most of the world knows the Bay of Pigs for its more modern celebrity: in April 1961, some thirteen hundred well-armed Cuban exiles trained by the CIA came ashore, both here at Playa Girón and at the nearby Cayo Largo, the large island at the easterly tip of the Canarreos chain. Organized by the CIA, the mission behind the invasion was threefold: it formed a Cuban government in exile back in Florida, trained a paramilitary force for future guerrilla action, and began its four-decade-long campaign of covert action inside Cuba. The Florida government-by-proxy was created from within the Frente, a loosely organized group of zealous anti-Castro exiles, many of whom were also widely known as corrupt Batista-era politicians.

The plot seemed doomed from the start: although warned by several Cuban experts that the dark splotches seen in aerial photos of the waters near the landing sites were coral reefs, the CIA insisted that they were seaweed. As a result, the first wave of invading landing craft grounded on the reefs, and the soldiers had to slog ashore. Boats carrying other battalions capsized. Local defenders, including student cadets bused in by Castro, took up M-52 Czech-made rifles and fought the invaders for seventy-two hours, until finally they prevailed and the exiles retreated.

The invasion became institutionalized in the minds of Cubans on both sides of the fence, living on far beyond the three-day event itself: it galvanized nationals inside Cuba who saw the United States–funded invasion as an imperialistic strike—one that would reclaim American-owned property seized by Castro with the help of a friendly reinstalled Batista-themed government. And back in the United States, it gave wide credibility to the anti-Castro exiles enraged over executions, imprisonment, and totalitarian rule that followed the revolution. Despite all that has happened over the past forty years, both paradigms remain largely intact.

"Live" is scheduled tonight, a "call-in"-style program with a guest and a host—but that appears only on the Discovery site on the Internet. Those who wish to ask questions don't call in but simply type in their question on their computer. An audio software will then "broadcast" the program to those who are tuned in. Last week, the "Live" producer had called on the sat phone to get recommendations for the "guest"; I had facetiously suggested Castro but, after receiving dead air in return, recommended McCosker.

The host will be Neil Conan, the NPR personality, who apparently is moonlighting for this new medium. Using the sub engineering lab, I make contact with Conan by the sat phone near one of the workbenches. Conan comes on, sounding very officious. To make small talk, I ask how the weather is back in the D.C. area. "Well, you're the one down there in the Caribbean, aren't you," says Conan. Then abruptly: "Put John Mc-Cosker on."

Conan then toggles his on-air voice, resonating with the practiced cadence peculiar to TV anchors and radio hosts. When he speaks, I picture a Slinky methodically walking its way down a semantical stairway: "On the TV commercials, all those Caribbean Islands look pristine and unspoiled. But there's only one that really has long undeveloped coastlines. The good news is it's the biggest island in the Caribbean. The bad news is that it's Cuba. . . . Estranged relations between Washington and Havana make it impossible for most Americans to visit those as yet uncrowded waters. . . . Journalists and scientists, though, are allowed to work in Cuba." Then he introduces McCosker, as "an evolutionary biologist with the California Academy of Sciences."

"Where are you exactly," asks Conan, and McCosker tells him, describing the country of Cuba as looking like a giant potato chip, with us between its curls, on the underside. "We're approaching the Isle of Pines right now, on the high seas. We've just finished a long day of diving, and we'll be up in the morning, sub diving and scuba diving."

Questions come in from California, Puerto Rico, Arkansas, and Istanbul, Turkey. They reflect the sorts of inquiries I have been receiving by E-mail—from very erudite to wildly inquisitive. Albert from Key West wants to know about underwater archaeology. "There's no limit to the wrecks here," says McCosker, reflecting the sum total of what most of us aboard know about marine archaeology. "And hopefully, we won't be the newest."

Ricardo from Honduras wants to know if there are coral reefs here. "Yes there are, Ricardo, and it's a Garden of Eden. It's untouched," McCosker says. "I would suggest the reefs you experience in Honduras are less well developed than here . . . because we're right in the heart of the Caribbean. It's extraordinary!"

During a lull in questions, Conan asks about the sub. McCosker gives him the shorthand history, spouts data on its size and weight—"I believe twelve tons"—and compares it with the deeper-diving *Alvin*: "*Alvin* hits the bottom like a bag of rocks and just creeps slowly along. The JSL lets you 'fly.'" There is a slight problem, admits McCosker, when the sub's modest speed is overwhelmed by a three- or four-knot current, which might carry it smack into the side of a wall or deep reef. "If it was gas powered, it would go faster," he explains, "but you can't use gas-powered engines underwater, and all the devices on the sub must compete for the battery-stored electricity—lights, collection tubes, thrusters."

There is some discussion about bioluminescing marine life, about biomedical work, about ecology. Claro and Alcolado are cited as "leading experts" in their respective fields. McCosker is animated and showy, going theatrically blow for blow with Conan.

A final question is how long the waters here will remain pristine—an inquiry that begs the contradiction of Conan's original introduction, in which a surge of American visitors may likely not be compatible with marine health. McCosker drops all traces of exaggeration from his voice. "They won't stay this way," says McCosker flatly. I notice Boggess nervously pacing about, clearly not happy about the way the sub tech lab is being expropriated. Here, in the middle of a real expedition, the interview is starting to feel calculating and manufactured. I'm glad it's coming to an end.

"When decisions are made that the governments of America and Cuba can tolerate each other, there will be a massive investment in this beautiful environment—hotels, marinas, tourism—that certainly will be harmful," says McCosker. "You can't ask Cuba not to develop its coastline, but we hope it has the wisdom to not make the same mistakes we have." And then: "We're just fortunate to have seen it the way it is now."

7

Archipiélago
de los Canarreos

Friday, December 19

Archipiélago de los Canarreos

In the last day, John McCosker has performed brain surgery on a jaw fish, Richard Fagen has ridden the sub back into time, and our cook has made an emergency medical trip ashore. As for me, I have explored a lonely, undefiled island that glistened with pink sand—and in doing so, inadvertently helped divine the mystery that made it so.

We have skirted the open sea from the submerged mesa of Banco Jagua, moving onto the edge of the sprawling underwater platform that stretches out from the southwestern coast of Cuba, the Golfo de Batabanó. This gulf is shallow, the remnant of a coastal plain that once rose above the water during the height of the last glaciation. Claro gives me the rough draft of a comprehensive book he has written, "Ecología de los Peces

Marinos de Cuba." Batabanó contains all the major marine fish habitats in Cuba—coral reefs, beds of Thalassia seagrasses and patches of sand, mangroves, coastal lagoons, and oceanic waters. Fish migrate back and forth between these systems, using various habitats at different times in their life. Batabanó is so rich and diverse that some animals never leave. The heart of the country's spiny lobster fishery is here. And manatees and sea turtles roam through its waters. Everyone on board is excited by what lies in store.

Due north from us on the main island is the flat peninsular swamp that looks like a shoe on the map, Península de Zapata. It is a refuge shared by both crocodiles and flamingos. Indeed, most of the endemics that live on the island of Cuba are found here: the bee hummingbird, the Cuban parakeet, Gundlach's hawk, the Cuban trogan, the Zapata wren and rail. The snail kite—known in the United States as the Everglades snail kite—feeds on aquatic snails that live in the clean, shallow swamp waters. Also here is a small, gaudy land snail, like those living in hardwood hammocks back in the Glades and the Keys—*Liguus*—with its colorful bands spiraling around a triangular porcelainlike cone. *Liguus* is microevolution in action, as it is often speciated from its brethren by the particular hammock where it lives. Much of Zapata's natural wealth is preserved in a national park, Ciénaga de Zapata. The park in turn is divided into 182 protected areas with various sustainable uses, an attempt to accommodate the seven thousand souls who live here (mostly around its edges), protect the rich biodiversity of the region, and even encourage "ecotourism."

By its purest definition, ecotourism requires that the destination be closely monitored for visitor impact and that locals be trained in grassroots guiding programs. Neither will likely happen until money is available to staff the park with rangers and to train guides.

Zapata curls to the west, as if it is one leg of Guillén's giant lizard of stone and water that is Cuba. Inside that leg is the Ensenada de la Broa, a massive lagoon. Clearly, we could spend weeks just poking at the edges of the Zapata: at 1,633 square miles, it is the largest peninsula of Cuba, as well as its most important wetland region, a sweeping moist prairie of sawgrass, reed, and thorny *marabú* bush, edged with red mangrove and punctuated with tree hammock islands. Claro, who has visited the Florida

Keys and the mainland Florida cape, says that the Zapata is a mirror of our own Everglades. But the sparsely populated Zapata is far healthier. Like the Glades, sugarcane fields, citrus groves, and processing plants do push right up to the edge of the swamp, concentrating at the crossroads town of Jagüey Grande to the north. Unlike the Glades, though, millions of wetland acres elsewhere have not been expropriated for residential development, and the natural sheet flow of water feeding the plants and animals of the swamp remains largely intact.

This giant shoe of land sits atop a limestone plateau, overlaid with peat and pocketed with caverns and even cenotes. The peat reserves, said to be the eleventh largest in the world, were eyed as an energy source after the Soviets left and the "Special Period" began. If peat was mined here, the terrain supporting the rich fauna would be destroyed, as would the buffer that protects interior farmland from the seep of coastal salinization.

Although we are seeing a Cuba we regard as unspoiled, the truth is that the impact of humans here is far more pervasive. By 1945, American naturalist Thomas Barbour reported that many critters found in the Zapata once roamed throughout Cuba, but farming claimed that natural landscape, forcing animals into the more remote areas, like the Sierra Maestra, which we have passed, and the swamp, which is now due ashore. "Agriculture has robbed most of the central part of the island of its glory of forest and glade, and replaced the woods with wide reaches of green cane, rippling rhythmically in the brisk trades," Barbour wrote in *A Naturalist in Cuba*. Schemes to exploit this wilderness date from 1912, when the American-owned Zapata Land Company was formed to drain it for development—in imitation of such "reclamation" taking place back in Florida. But the sheer inaccessibility kept the Zapata safe: a dated survey from the company declared this to be "a place of fogs and death where alligators are absolute masters." Thanks to the intact nature of this place of fogs and death, Zapata remains an overwintering stop for scores of North American migratory birds, including sandhill cranes, tricolored herons, wood ibis, and roseate spoonbills. If a sensitive strategy for nature tourism is ever developed, Zapata could become the premier wildlife viewing region in all of Cuba—indeed, one of the finest in the hemisphere.

The easterly tip of Cayo Largo is just off our starboard bow. It is the beginning of a chain of islands fanning out from the Zapata, girdling Isla de la Juventud, and then curling inward toward the limestone-rich hillocks of Pinar del Río Province. This is the Archipiélago de los Canarreos, and it is the westerly version of Los Jardines. Here hundreds of *cayos* are scattered along and inside the reef line of the shallow sea rostrum occupied by the Golfo de Batabanó. In his book, Claro counted "672 isles, keys and islets" in Batabanó alone. As a chain, they separate this shallow basin— which averages from nine to eighteen feet—from the Caribbean Sea. To the east, the lip of the basin is outlined by coral reefs; to the west, by a series of *cayos*, banks, and shoals, stretching from Isla de la Juventud to the mainland. Because it is easier to reach from land than our other sites (as it is due south of Havana) and doesn't require diving gear to survey, Batabanó has been studied perhaps more than any other single coastal region in Cuba. Earlier research here includes low-tech snorkeling and collecting trips organized by the Center for Marine Conservation (CMC). During some of those outings, a number of marine invertebrates were discovered, small squirmy critters like segmented worms. Other trips here to study biodiversity or collect species have been organized by the Smithsonian, the American Association for the Advancement of Science, and the New York Botanical Gardens in the Bronx. (In 1997, a team of U.S. and Cuban scientists led by the CMC's Mike Smith found fifteen new species of Amphipoda, a group of shrimplike crustaceans, on a single trip. "The fact it's still possible to make such a large increase in the knowledge about a marine fauna, especially in shallow water, is an indication we are still at the very beginning of the exploration of Caribbean biodiversity," said Smith at the time. But he warned: "It is chilling to realize that as fast as we are discovering new marine species [in Cuba], they could be disappearing.")

Cayo Largo, out here some twenty-five miles due south of Zapata, is the largest island in this archipelago at forty-five square miles. Long and slender, it has its own set of smaller satellite islets fringing its leeward edges: Cayería las Majaes, Cayo Iguana, and Cayo de los Pájaros, among them. To the west, a tiny cape is mapped as "Punta Sirena," and I wonder if it was charted for the taxonomic order (Sirenia) of the West Indian manatee or for the mythological Siren, the universal bewitchment that drags seafarers to their demise. Somewhere here is a small sea turtle farm, Granja de las Tortugas, which we will bypass in favor of a larger one on Isla de la Juventud.

As I look shoreward, I see a few buildings and a long deserted dirt road that deadends in a small airstrip. Not much seems to be happening. But in fact, there are several villages mapped here, and the longer I look, the busier the road to the airstrip becomes. I ask about Cayo Largo, and Alcolado tells me this is a "famous resort" and lets it go at that. Fagen explains that it is heavily commercialized, along the lines of the upscale tourism ghetto of Varadero on the north coast. Simon Charles, the yachting guide writer, has described Cayo Largo as "Cuba's premier foreign Cuban resort along the Southern cays," with an airport, six hotels, and a marina that rents both sailboats and Jet Skis. Live-aboard dive boats with Germans, Canadians, and Italians frequently visit the area to scuba dive the reefs around Cayo Largo and other nearby islands.

Not surprisingly, it was a U.S. firm that launched the trend by building a resort here on the island in 1957. Although that project was abandoned during the revolution, a new building boom took hold in 1985 with Soviet support. Desperate to court foreign capital, Cuba—via its internal PuertoSol tourism enterprise—has remade this onetime fishing village over into something else entirely, excising its original sense of place in favor of the traditional "sun, sea, and sand" umbrella-drink appeal. The Moon Travel *Cuba Handbook* by Christopher P. Baker writes it off as "imminently appealing to those with no interest in interacting with or understanding local culture." Cayo Largo—like its northern cousin Varadero—could be the worse-case scenario of what all the Cuban keys could become if traditional Caribbean beach tourism prevails.

As we steamed along the coast, the steady and predictable pitch and yaw of shipboard life was abruptly interrupted. Before dawn, our affable cook, Jay Grant, was rushed ashore for medical treatment. The pain of his two deep finger cuts was compounded by disabling flulike symptoms. Infection was suspected. Over breakfast, second mate Sharky Martin told me he drove the boat with Grant to Cayo Largo, just before dawn, and found a clinic there. Ricardo was along as an interpreter and facilitator. Despite the early hour, a doctor soon appeared, and a dozen townspeople spontaneously assembled for the event, graciously serving up espresso to the crew members who accompanied the wounded cook. "It was as relaxed and friendly as a family reunion," Martin tells me. "It was like we were old friends and they were glad to see us. And no one charged us for anything—not even for the espresso. They wouldn't take our money." Grant's cuts were stitched. and he was given antibiotics and ordered back to bed.

For the rest of the crew, the most obvious consequence of the cook's bed rest is that assistant steward Robert Haverty will commandeer the kitchen over the next few days. Haverty, a big man who seems a bit tightly strung, was a last-minute replacement on the expedition. (Once, as I was putting together a list of all crew in order to give them credit on the Discovery Web site, Haverty came to me and asked that I not use his name. He was afraid this sanctioned visit to Cuba would be a "black mark" on his "official record" if he ever applied for a government job.) He seems unfamiliar about how the kitchen works, even confused at first about where utensils and food are stored. As soon as he learns the whereabouts of food stocks and spices, he becomes relentless about making sure everyone attends all meals, at the appointed time. To do so, he polices the stern and even the captain's bridge, where, standing only a few feet away from hapless crew members late for a meal, he shouts out, "lunch!" or "dinner!" For his effort, other crew members begin to call Haverty the "Soup Nazi."

Beyond Cayo Largo, other keys appear—mapped as Rico and Perases and Campo. Many of these unsettled *cayos* are also maternity wards of brown pelicans, double-crested cormorants, and magnificent frigate birds. As naturalist Silva Lee points out, the more prosperous colonies turn the mangrove leaves white with guano and spark a vigorous growth by fertilizing the roots. But there is a separate category of mangrove keys apart from those underlaid by mud or sand. Using a term employed by Cuban fishermen, Silva Lee describes these as "scraped keys"—*los raspados*—as they are distinguished by scarce and stumpy vegetation, seldom rising above knee-high height. Geology is the hand shaping *los raspados*: usually long, narrow, and very rocky, the scraped keys are fossilized reefs, exposed a few millennia ago by a falling sea level, with ragged colonies of stunted mangroves hanging on for dear life. They include the *cayos* of Ballenatos,

Inglés, Oro, Sal, and Trinchera. Although they are biologically impoverished, the lack of predators make them great seasonal roosts, and by each
May, the scraped keys turn into aviaries for roseate terns, sandwich terns,
royal terns, bridled terns, sooty terns, brown noddies, laughing gulls, and
brown boobies. A single tiny key may host up to six species of nesting
birds, says Silva Lee. Despite their distant wanderings, the seabirds return
to the same scrubby little islands when they are ready to give birth, year
after year.

We slow to a stop just off Cayo Rosario, an uninhabited, thirty-square-
mile crest of sand and dwarfed maritime shrubs, shells and driftwood. It is
what a wild beach looks like, when beachcombers aren't around to scour it
clean of little treasures. Rosario's beaches are also inexplicably tinted pink,
a phenomenon I have seen once before in the Bahamas on the island of
Eleuthera. There is nothing scraped about Rosario.

Our sub will penetrate the deeper waters here several times over the
next couple of days. Political scholar Fagen is offered the chance to ride
along in the rear observer compartment of the JSL on one dive and is
ecstatic about it. In his journal, he writes of preparing for the dive: "I have
already put on my wedding ring and the shark's tooth I always wear for
flying. Why not? Good karma is needed up there, and *down* there. Up
there, if the hull cracks, you're blown outside. Down there, if the hull
cracks, you're squashed like a grape."

Before Fagen's dive, the recuperating cook offers the novice sub rider
the loan of his folding hunting knife, calling it an "oxygen doubler." "If
the air supply goes, you kill off the other guy and there is twice as much
air for you." Fagen calls it "submarine humor."

Once underwater with Fagen safely stashed in the aft, the JSL sinks to
a fifteen-hundred-foot-deep shelf. "The bottom itself," writes Fagen, "is a
barren snowfield with decaying bits of shallow water sea grass motionless
in the current. . . . The overall impression is of a lunar desert landscape
of whitish silt and sand, sterile, silent, not ugly, not pretty, just plain and
unrelieved except where a bit of rock pokes from the silt."

The detritus of the seagrass and other shallow-water foliage signals the
presence of energy, a food source for bryozoans and other tiny animals
that in turn attract larger predators. Indeed, the severed blades of grass

represent encapsulated slivers of sunlight, Gilmore's "Source of All Energy on Earth." As such, they can be regarded as tiny batteries bringing energy to a world bereft of sun.

But there is a twist: to go deeper into this ocean is to go back into time, settling into a forever-dark netherworld where the ancestors of surface-dwelling fish still live in the protective womb of the depths. The deep is where the primitive lobed, finned fish known as the coelacanth—thought to be extinct for 50 million years—was living when it was discovered off the coast of Madagascar in 1938. "The animals down there don't know the dinosaurs have died," Gilmore told me a few days ago, and I thought that nailed it perfectly.

Once the sub carrying Fagen settles down, critters initially frightened by its presence begin to show themselves, astounding the novice sub rider. Hundreds of lancet fish, from six to eighteen inches in length, encircle the sub, flitting in and out of its bright exterior lights. "They are pencil thin, flashing silver like Mylar, and endowed with a very mean set of barbed, backward raked teeth," Fagen writes in his journal. "They hang vertically in the water column and evidently dart *upwards* to nab their prey. My favorite visitor is a small squid who comes to my five-inch porthole and starts to do loops, mouth open, catching small creatures as he goes. He has those big squid eyes, quick and intelligent looking, and his movements were more fascinating than anything else around. He looks almost transparent in our hot lights, as he darts about in this planktonic soup."

Fagen's sub ride gradually takes him up the slope leading to the light and the coral reef, where, after some three and a half hours, the JSL bursts through the sea and, after recovery, is returned to the stern.

On the surface, we are also poking about the edges of time by retracing a surface route early Spanish galleons traveled between the early 1500s and the mid-1700s for the purpose of hauling plundered gold, emeralds, silver, and pearls back to Spain. Historians who have studied archives of ship manifests and logs in Seville now understand how the early treasure fleets crisscrossed the Caribbean: those bound for Cuba left the stronghold of Cartagena, New Grenada (now Colombia), and sailed north, skimming the edges of Los Canarreos at Isla de la Juventud. From here, they followed the prevailing current, swerving up and around the horn at Cape

San Antonio and docking in La Habana. At this busy port, they took on provisions and loaded up with more treasure shipped from Veracruz and Portobelo, riches either mined or stolen from the Aztecs and Incas. Then, riding the Gulf Stream, they sailed north to the Florida Keys and out across the Atlantic. During all this sailing about, many went to the bottom, either by blundering into the shallow reefs, becoming swamped in storms and hurricanes, or getting blown out of the water by pirates. Although we have no immediate plans to play archaeologists—at least until we reach the historic, deep harbor mouth of Havana—we are more likely to stumble across a sunken colonial wreck here than anywhere we have traveled so far.

Despite the submerged cultural wealth left behind from this busy maritime era, the Cuban government is too busy just trying to keep its country afloat to establish a policy to direct the careful archaeological survey and excavation of such wrecks. Instead, it works with CaribSub, a quasi-private Cuban treasure-hunting agency that splits its take fifty-fifty with the government. I remember Roger Dooley telling me back in Fort Pierce that CaribSub—which operates nearly independent of government control—actually charters sport-diving tours for the purpose of recovering artifacts. Although Dooley was among the first in Cuba to organize recreational diving tours, he doesn't feel that using untrained pleasure divers to excavate wrecks has much archaeological integrity. "It is not highly regarded by Cuban scientists," Dooley said of CaribSub.

This issue of who "owns" such wrecks represents a bitter controversy taking place throughout the wider Caribbean and in Florida. For their part, treasure salvors argue that currents and storms are in the process of gradually washing away remnants of sea-bottom wrecks. Without their intervention, artifacts would be scattered or destroyed, they say. In contrast, archaeologists reason that ships buried in sand are virtual "time capsules" representing pages of unwritten history. Careful excavation requires gridding the wrecks in meter-square test digs and carefully examining each tier of submerged materials to understand better how people of that era lived. The heavy-handed salvors—who often use powerful prop blasters to blow industrial-sized quantities of sand and debris away from the wreck—may find treasure, but to the exclusion of all else. Just before the *Seward* cast off, I had learned of an exclusive private agreement the Cuban government extended to Vancouver salvor Glenn Costello, who had reportedly found twenty-three wrecks, most along the northwest coast. In response, a marine archaeologist at Texas A&M was outraged: "Treasure hunting is like doing brain surgery with a chainsaw."

For now, we have our own natural treasures to explore. McCosker makes a scuba dive here over what he describes as a "crummy reef of coral and channels." But at forty feet, he sees something small dart behind a boulder. Driven by a combination of good reflexes and intuition, Mc-Cosker has collected dozens of undescribed fish from scuba depths over the years. Feeling this one might also be off the charts, he takes out his plastic bottle of rotenone from a pocket in his buoyancy control vest and squirts behind the rock. Out drifts a little goby, this one almost translucent. Using his hand, McCosker sweeps it into a large clear plastic Baggie. When ichthyologist Dick Robins first gets a look at the Lilliputian specimen back on the *Seward*, he thinks this one might also be undescribed. In his journal, McCosker even draws a detailed sketch of the diminutive fish, which, with its bright lateral line, splotches of yellow, and oddly splayed dorsals, seems just as colorful as the deepwater specimen captured by the sub. Certainly, this new arrival causes a stir at first, as it could present an opportunity to film a brand new species in the process of being discovered.

But on closer inspection, Gilmore recognizes the goby as an old, if mysterious, friend. He first captured a fish just like this one in the Bahamas a decade ago. Since then, Gilmore—notorious for his painstaking attention to minutiae—has been in the process of fully describing the species for science. So far, he knows the fish is not in the genus *Gobiosoma* and must fall either in *Chriolepis* or *Varicus*. It is, for now, a fish with no name. For the rest of the world, this specimen is novel, in that it does not yet appear in any fish identification books; certainly, it is a new record for Cuba.

Gilmore tells me there's more species of goby in our oceans than any other fish. Although they are one of the smallest vertebrates in the world, they have virtually the same anatomy as one of the largest, the whale shark. Backbone, gills, heart, nerve cord, fins. "We take them for granted," says Gilmore, "but they're really intelligent. They produce sound and have territories."

The process of discovery on the *Seward* begins with a thorough visual identification of an animal's anatomy. Spines in the fins are counted, and careful attention is given to how the body is configured and colored. Are there bars, stripes, bands, blotches, and lines? Does it have scutes, a forked tail, barbels, or a single flat dorsal? How many spines are inside the fins? Such careful observations date from Aristotle's own methodical descriptions of wildlife. Meticulous details like this provide a bond linking contemporary scientists to their historic counterparts centuries ago— reminding us moderns that there is no substitute for paying close attention to the world around us, whether it is on the deck of a forever listing oceanographic ship or in tidal pools at the edge of the Mediterranean Sea.

Perhaps the most wondrous new technique delivered by our space-age technology is the capacity to examine new fish further, back in the lab, for molecular similarities and differences. The importance of finding contemporary neotypes that represent long-described species—like the still-elusive *Verilus*—becomes much more urgent in this age of molecular sampling, as it provides a more detailed look at the animal in question. Differences in the same species that are not yet visually apparent—a modification that reflects an ongoing adaptation to the marine environment— can be signaled by a change in the molecular composition. Evolution may take millions of years. Or it can happen over just a few generations, as with the finches of the Galápagos Islands. (Not only did thirteen species develop from one pair of finches, but, as Jonathan Weiner, author of *Beak of the Finch*, illustrates, that speciation is ongoing even today as the birds more thoroughly flesh out their ecological niche.) Fish, by virtue of their inaccessibility, simply haven't been as well studied as birds or other fauna in the air-breathing realm. And with the fuel shortage and general lack of reliable ships and gear, they've been scrutinized even less in Cuba.

Our shipboard aquarium is now becoming a very busy place. As soon as a newly collected form of marine life is deposited there, Wimberg sets up one of Giddings's cameras on a tripod next to the glass tank, and the taping begins. If a stray scientist is around, he or she is corralled into commenting on the newest inhabitants on camera. Sound recordist Ray Day hovers nearby with the boom mike to catch the commentary. Those of us curious about the newcomer either watch silently from the dark edges of the room or gather in the dry lab, where the image being momentarily celebrated is on display via a remote video monitor hookup. As all the specimens will later be pickled in formaldehyde for preservation, the emphemerality of their few minutes on the little screen is jarringly surreal.

When I walk over to the aquarium after lunch today, I see a spindly white arrow crab dancing about next to a deepwater sea urchin, which is balanced atop a chunk of rock, over a bottom of black volcanic sand. The arrow crab is a deepwater version of a crustacean found on the shallow reefs; with its slender pinlike arms, it looks a bit like an albino daddy longlegs. A new wrasse has just been added to the community, a tiny colorful fish commonly known as a "candy stripe wrasse." Gilmore says that the little fish is comfortable at a wide range of depths and is, in fact, the deepest occurring wrasse in the Atlantic. On the shallow reefs, wrasses are one of the most plentiful species. Closely related to the parrot fish, wrasses are generally cigar-shaped and "bucktoothed," courtesy of their strong front teeth, which allow them to crush the shells of invertebrates, like sea urchins. They belong to the same family—Labridae—as the much larger hogfish, notable for its hoglike snout used to root for food, and the smaller razorfish, characterized by its blunt razorlike head.

As Giddings cranks down on the focus and tightly frames the crab and urchin and wrasse, there is no hint that this shot is taking place inside an aquarium instead of out in the ocean. Giddings's cinematic technology is so practiced, it can greatly enlarge the arrow crab's head—which in reality is smaller than the nail on my little finger—so that it fills the screen, with no loss of resolution. The result is an image that is half menacing, half caricature, with a down-turned slit of a mouth and set of beady eyes, not unlike Peter Falk's Columbo on a bad hunch. With the filming over, all but Gilmore and I disperse. He seems concerned that the rare crab might eat the undescribed wrasse, thereby consuming a specimen that took thousands of dollars' worth of time and gear to capture, before it can be properly identified and preserved. "It's happened before," he says, shaking his head. "Crustaceans can never be trusted around fish."

Out on the stern, I look longingly at the deserted Cayo Rosario, hoping to visit it before we move on. A dive team is being assembled, with McCosker, Pomponi, Straus, and the rest of the film crew, and I am invited to come along. Competition to get on a scuba dive is fierce, especially with just the one good dive boat and the limited time we have at each site. The rebreather tech, who shouldn't be diving at all, tries desperately to assert himself onto each dive, with varying degrees of success. Fagen, a veteran sport diver, is eager to get in the water but can do so only after other science and film priorities are met. He writes in his journal: "I'm the low man on the totem pole, when it comes to scuba diving." Other crew members and scientists who dive but who are not directly part of the immediate plan come along only as a distant option. Despite the online reportage, I seem to be afloat in the middle, my cache oscillating between necessity and expendability, depending on the moment. Although my style is normally low key and unobtrusive, if I am to get on a dive at all, I find I have to be forceful about it.

Today, the dive boat takes us to a reef on the outer edge of the underwater slope, where the platform of Cayo Rosario begins its gradual plummet into the deep. We cruise over blue water and then head inshore as the depth recorder reads 400, 300, 200 feet. At 50 feet, driver Mike Conda drops anchor. It is ebb tide, and just a hundred yards away, several inches of the reef crest are exposed at the water's surface. The surf churns between these bare coral heads in a fierce vortex, frothing green and white. Ashore on Cayo Rosario, a long white beach is pinched into a rocky limestone cape.

Pomponi and McCosker, both armed with rotenone and specimen bags, drop over the gunwales, with Giddings and his camera right behind. Kelly Myrstol, an underwater camera assistant, and I enter the water a few minutes later so as not to interfere with the filming. From the surface, the bottom can barely be seen. But as I sink deeper, it appears as a white sand pasture, punctuated with sea fans and small clumps of coral. Off in the distance, the reef looms like an ancient bastion, worn walls and arches and truncated towers.

On the bottom nearby, a bright blotch of color moves, out of place in the monotone of gray and white. It is a coney, a foot-long member of the grouper family. At this moment, it is displaying a reddish-brown color phase, one of several that can transform it from a brilliant yellow-gold to dull brown. As we fin away, the coney follows in typical grouper puppy-dog fashion, about ten yards behind us. As we approach the reef, I see McCosker and Pomponi, on their knees in a sandy alley between the ridges of coral, attentive to something small on the bottom. Giddings is splayed out prone a few feet away, with his back toward us, filming them. This seems to be a classic spur-and-groove reef system, with avenues of sand furrowing the coral, allowing the flush of the tides an easy route to push to and from the island. Although seemingly barren, sand grooves like this shelter all manner of marine life, which live in association with the "spurs" of the coral—from garden eels to shellfish.

Whatever they have found here can't be seen from this distance. Rather than visually eavesdropping by looking over Giddings's shoulder, I leave Myrstol and head for a nearby coral head. Here, I poke my head inside a portal of coral and shine in a small light I carry in a pocket of my buoyancy compensator. Anything may lurk inside, from small sharks to moray eels. In the first cave, I see a spotted drum, which is a very prosaic name for a remarkable three-inch-long fish—particularly one that resembles a punctuation mark, say a parenthesis. With a tiny head on the outside of its angular body, the drum is prominently marked with stripes of black and dots of white. It moves like something choreographed in a dream, a delicate female hand swirling a silk scarf in the darkness, over and over. I think of all the suspect human actions marketed under the limelight of performance art, reminding myself once again that nature has the real thing down all along, with no illumination at all, except what I hold in my hand.

From the bottom of another ledge, I spot the wiggle of a slender tentaclelike spine. Thinking it might be the antenna of a very large spiny lobster, I fin over to it and shine my light inside, pressing my mask up against the lip of the ledge. The spine is the tail of a stingray, attached to a body that is nearly a yard wide, a round organic tabletop nearly covered with sand. I gingerly push back from the ledge and then swim out across one of the sand alleys. As I do, I am surprised to see that what I thought were tiny clumps of rock and coral from the surface are actually adult queen conchs. I let all the air out of my BC and settle onto the sand bottom, watching one helmet-sized conch (*Strombus gigas*) move over the sand in a series of slow-motion hops. A master of unintentional disguise, the elegant, pink-lipped shell has been colonized by an assortment of algae and sponges. Up close, the only giveaway that it is not an inert lump is an astounding set of eyeballs that peer out at the end of stalks from inside a groove at the front of the shell. Later, I tell invertebrate specialist Alcolado about this, and he seems very pleased to know that the animal—largely overfished throughout the Antilles for its edible high-protein foot muscle—is doing so well here. Like the sea star and other invertebrates, the conch spreads its progeny far beyond its ambulatory range by its spawn, which drift with the current far beyond the twelve-mile limit of Cuba.

The dive over, we ascend one by one and swim back to the dive boat. I mistakenly surface next to the exposed reef crest and am nearly sucked into its eddy for my efforts. Finally, back on the boat, I learn that McCosker and Pomponi had been chasing tiny jawfish in the sand. As a result, we now have a pair of live yellowhead jawfish (*Opistognathus aurifrons*) on the *Seward*, each two inches long, slender, and bluish, with elongated brush-like fins. I have seen the jawfish on sand bottoms before, skittish little creatures that seldom stray too far from the burrows they have excavated by mouth from the sediment. Their common name suits them well, for not only do they use their jaws to dig, but the males also incubate the females' eggs inside them. When not busy in this way, the jawfish hover vertically over their burrows, and when threatened with any quick movement, they retreat tail-first to safety—closing the burrow by using a small shell as a door. Except, of course, when scientists with spray bottles of rotenone are nearby to intercept them.

The jawfish join our menagerie in the aquarium, where they both quickly burrow individual holes in the bottom of the volcanic sand. For their trouble, they earn a few seconds of cinematic fame, bobbing and weaving over their new homes like an aquatic carnival game, Whack-A-Mole goes to sea. When the show is over, one jawfish is immediately preserved, while the other falls under the knife. This afternoon, McCosker is the surgeon, and he wields the scalpel carefully, entering through the gill cover and extracting a speck-sized ear bone, the otolith. Fabricated by the fish from calcium carbonate—just as the shell of the queen conch is exuded from the chemicals of the sea—this ear bone helps biologists distinguish one species from another; it also has minuscule growth bands similar to the tree rings on logs. The otoliths come in pairs, one on each side of the head, where they rest atop little nerve patches—sensory hairs that help the fish feel and hear vibrations. When the fish travels up or down in the water column, the otoliths allow it to sense the depth change. "Fish that make noise, like drum, have larger otoliths. The ones that don't usually have smaller ones," McCosker explains. A shark may have twenty or thirty tiny bits of calcium that together function as its ear bone. In addition to identifying the species and aging the fish, the hard otolith often survives in nature long after the rest of the fish has decomposed, especially if it is trapped under the protective sand or mud of the bottom.

"You can look at the deep bottom sediment dredged up and see who was there, through the centuries," says McCosker. If seasonal growth during the life cycle of a fish is slow, the ordinary dark rings become more translucent. When the fish matures, it puts more energy into making itself larger, and that too is revealed by the rings.

"It was the otolith that gave us the bad news about the slime head, the fish restaurants renamed as 'orange roughy,'" says McCosker. "We found we were eating a fish that was extremely slow growing—one that would live to 160 years and more. It didn't mature until it was 60. Commercial fishermen were wiping it out before it even had a chance to mature and spawn." That fishermen were sweeping the depths at 1,000 to 3,000 feet for such species at all was a reflection of the overfishing and the related collapse of fishery stocks far beyond Cuba.

Since humans began to catch fish to eat, their harvest was generally limited to seafood inhabiting the sunlit shallows. Now it goes far beneath that. Other such abyss dwellers on the menu include hoki, ling, skate, sablefish, oreo dory, spiny dogfish, and black scabbard. The dilemma is twofold: little is known about the ecology of the depths, and little management exists to regulate it. Dwelling as deep as a mile beneath the sea, the slime head has a large mouth and very good eyes to help it see and capture luminescent krill, small squid, and lantern fish. But its place on the table is purely a product of spin: to make it marketable, its mutantlike body was cut away, and its meat was filleted. The alienlike "slime head" became the more palatable orange roughy.

McCosker asks if I want a look under the microscope—what he calls a "crash course in graduate ichthyology." As I press my eyes to the scope, this wee tablet of life history metaphorically opens for me to read it. The rings of this jawfish otolith—magnified by a power of twelve—show that it was into its third year of life when it was captured. Far more powerful electronic scopes, McCosker tells me, will even let scientists count the age of the fish down to the exact day of birth. Analyzing the chemical composition of the otolith will also divulge a "home water signature," revealing the location where the fish has lived most of its life. As we are examining the ear bone, sub engineer Boggess walks by on his way out to the stern for a cigarette break. On seeing the other jawfish pinned down in a small tray of formaldehyde, he comments, idly: "Wasn't he just swimming around back in the aquarium?" Then: "That fish needs a new agent."

Meanwhile, expedition logistics are changing. A low-level helicopter flight that both Lipscomb and Giddings had tried to arrange for some aerial footage was sacked because the charter cost was an exorbitant five thousand dollars, and the unexpected overnight at the Tortuga Hotel had eaten up most of the budget for onshore expenses. And a run into the red mangroves of Los Canarreos for some topside filming—intended to match up to the underwater mangrove sequences captured back in Los Jardines—has been postponed until tomorrow. Some unexpected time opens up.

With a couple hours left before sunset, McCosker schemes up a shore trip, contingent on the captain's approval. Captain Seiler is a steady, easygoing fellow, and when McCosker asks if we can use the smallest skiff for a shore visit, he says sure, just be back by dark. The Baby Whaler is lowered by crane off its cradle on the *Seward* down into the water. McCosker, Gilmore, Robins, and I climb down into it, carrying only fly-fishing gear and, in case of emergency, a portable VHF radio. With all four of us aboard, the gunwales of the tiny boat ride low in the water. McCosker cranks up the kicker, and we move away from the side of the *Seward*. As we do, Mike Conda leans over the railing and shouts down to us, asking where we are going. McCosker tells him "to practice ichthyology." Conda, spotting the fly rods aboard, waves his hand dismissively. "I got your ichthyology."

Earlier, Alcolado told me that Cayo Rosario is home to a new "sanctuary" for monkeys and crocodiles, although surely not in the exact same place at once. The crocs likely roam out here from Zapata. But the primates are more troublesome to figure: the precepts of island biogeography eliminate most large mammals. Bats are usually the predominant island species because they can fly here, followed by rats, which may ride on mats of seaweed or flotsam. Other mammals, which must walk or crawl, not only are less likely to reach the island but also find it harder to endure within the boundaries of the limited biogeography. If they are already on board when a continental island is separated from the mainland, their larger size often dooms them, as the bigger they are, the more habitat they need to survive. And when humans with a hunger for meat historically arrive, mammals are among the first animals to disappear as a result of overhunting and habitat destruction. Sometimes, non-native critters that are introduced—like hogs, goats, and dogs—will inadvertently munch up the landscape and its natives as thoroughly as humans ever could. As the Pulitzer-winning biologist Edward O. Wilson pointed out, islands are continents in a microcosm, where ecological and evolutionary trends that take place on a larger scale elsewhere are compressed and made more obvious here.

The only known primate to live in the wild here was the Cuban monkey, *Paralouatta varonai*, a relative of the "titi"—the tamarind—of South America. Naturalist Silva Lee reports that fossils of the now extinct Cuban monkey were found among the mogote mesas of western Cuba in a single cave—Cueva del Mono Fossil. The monkeys of Cayo Rosario are said to live somewhere on the other side of the dune line. But the island is too big to explore in our truncated time here. If we did see monkeys, they would be exotic non-native primates, recently arrived from the mainland and most likely transported here by humans. Oddly, until 1989, a Cuban agency dedicated to the country's flora and fauna had imported a number of exotic species—revealing what Silva Lee describes as an essential "lack of affection towards indigenous animals." The imports included five species of goats, six of antelope, three deer, and five species of monkeys—at least five hundred of the primates in all. After the experiment was over, the monkeys "later disembarked on large keys of fragile and valuable nature." The confusion simply adds to the average Cuban's already imprecise view of nature, admits Silva Lee.

But it is a confusion that comes honestly: "The inhabitants of the Antillean islands . . . are descendents of a European cultural confetti that destroyed with lances, mistreatments, dogs and bacteria, the aboriginal cultures . . . [creating] groups of humans most profoundly alienated from nature."

Robins, officially along on the expedition as a "consultant," was an inspiration to Gilmore during our chief scientist's formative years as an ichthyologist. Gilmore, in fact, has named a little fish, the yellowbar basslet (*Lipogramma robinsi*) in his honor. Robins was the premier ichthyologist at the University of Miami in 1956, helping lay the groundwork for the formation of the prestigious Rosenstiel School of Marine Sciences during his tenure there. Highly eclectic in his own studies, he has produced research papers on billfish, eels, and freshwater fish from limestone sinks, as well as his extensive work on marine gobies. Known primarily for his taxonomy of new fish, Robins—who is the expedition's de facto professor emeritus—has always had a strong interest in ecology and conservation. Cuba, however, remained an enigma for him during his career; he expected waters here to have the richest marine fauna in the Caribbean— possibly the Western Hemisphere. Robins retired in 1994 to Lawrence, Kansas, and from there continues part-time work with the university's Natural History Museum. Gilmore genially invited him along on the cruise in order to allow the venerated ichthyologist a glimpse into the mysterious waters that had eluded him for so long.

Despite Robins's vast knowledge of the marine world, he—like some older ichthyologists—is not a scuba diver. He honed his taxonomic skills by identifying and comparing specimens either trawled, caught by hook and line, or collected by others—from technicians to his grad students to diving scientists, like Gilmore. The bespectacled Robins—with his tattered V-necked sweater and worn binoculars swinging from his neck and his last few unruly strands of gray hair pointing every which way—seems to actualize what most folks imagine a professor to be.

Our Baby Whaler slices through the building waves, whipped up by a less than gentle southeasterly trade-wind blow. By the time we approach Cayo Rosario, the ship is nearly two miles away, dwarfed by the vast expanse of the sea. Field science, when piped back to the safety of the family television, seems fairly manageable business—like a very exotic vacation, perhaps. But it is grueling and even dangerous work at times, particularly when the sea is part of the equation. Scuba gear will misfunction, and boats will capsize. Our little nonexpeditionary run to shore this afternoon is not even a particularly safe or known event—and this is merely a pleasure trip. That all my three companions are nonchalant about the building sea and its relationship to our pocket-sized boat is a measure of the sangfroid their lifelong work requires. "I feel like I've spent half my life on boats," says Gilmore, to no one in particular.

We putter over a deeper sand shoal, which serves as an outer breakwater to the reef rimming the island, and it alerts us to other hazards associated with the shore. The tide seems to be rising, something we should take note of for the return trip—when it may begin to fall. McCosker cranks down the motor and sneaks us over the top of the bank reef, mustard-colored coral heads clearly visible under the clear water a few feet below, a pastiche of fish flitting in and out of its cover. The bar we just crossed has taken the chop off the water, laying the nearshore surf down like a giant pool. Berms of sand under us are tinted pink, made especially more so by the late afternoon sun.

The hull of the Baby Whaler scrapes ashore on the beach, and I jump out and tie the bow line to a small scrubby bush. Gilmore and Robins prepare to go off in one direction to do some birding. McCosker and I will head the other way to fly-fish for snapper and jacks in the green surf. Weathered flotsam—nets and buoys, water-sculpted driftwood and coconuts—is scattered everywhere. Cayo Rosario is a Buffettesque revelation come to life, the archetypal deserted Caribbean beach that tourist bureaus everywhere promise but never deliver. Indeed, this uninhabited slice of sand and limestone is about the size of Grand Cayman Island, a British Crown Colony that is a bustling sport-diving and fishing resort 140 miles south of here. Grand Cayman, now an upscale "travel destination," only began to develop after Cuba and its *cayos* turned illicit forty years ago. Back on the *Seward*, I had compared maps of the two islands and saw, to my amazement, that they were both shaped alike—like giant backward Ls—with protected natural harbors on the inside leeward edges of each letter configuration, sandy windward capes facing the sea.

Gilmore says he and Robins hope to see one of the spectacular little birds known as the Cuban tody, with its hummingbirdlike body sporting a green head, a bright red throat, and a buffish underbody, tinted pink. Locally called the *cartacua*, the tody ranges over the entire country, where it hides in forests, including those on the larger keys, and burrows into the sand to lay its eggs. Todies, notes Silva Lee, could be the "ornithological flag of the Antillean Islands. Each Greater Antillean island is home to at least one [species] of these small birds," and each is speciated by the island where it lives. Gilmore imagines the maritime foliage here, with its stunted brush and miniature silver and thatch palms, to be tody-friendly. Both Claro and Alcolado have also told us that this key is big enough to have its own freshwater river. If so, the flowing fresh water could nourish larger trees and even a forest, somewhere back in the interior.

Throughout Cuba, there are some 355 species of birds, with as many as 124 arriving here each fall after hatching or nesting somewhere in North America. Some of the migrants, like the kestrel and king rail, have remained here to breed over enough generations to create what Silva Lee calls "distinct local races or subspecies." Others were separated from their continental genera by huge storms, blowing them off the mainland of Latin America. Still others "lived in an ancestral Cuba at a time when the island was but the tip of a long strip of land connected to South America, or when it was much closer to Central America." However the local nonmigratory birds got here, some twenty-five of them—like the tody—are now found nowhere else on earth.

Armed with our fly rods, McCosker and I spread out along the shore, gingerly picking our way over the slabs of limestone wedged together like a giant stairway—what Alcolado will later describe as *terracos*. The terraces appear and disappear along the beach. After a while it becomes clear that the rock is the crust of the island, exposed where the sea has washed the sand away from this ancient reef. When the vertical walls of the terraces face seaward, they are sometimes pockmarked with people-sized caves scooped out by the steady action of the wind and tide.

The water is as clear as glass, and where it covers the slabs of limestone, it revitalizes the rock as living patch reef. Young snapper, grouper, and grunts dart about just under the surface, a giant marine kaleidoscope with an untiring dynamic. We wade out to our waists, casting repeatedly like we first did a few weeks ago, back in the estuaries of Florida. In the evenings, McCosker has been tying up a series of flies in a popular saltwa-ter "deceiver" pattern—a small number one hook with an avocado body, a snatch of lime-green feathers, and a sprinkle of Flashabou with the re-flective qualities of a strand of fiber optic. To this he has added a pinch of bright red feathers just under the "throat." The latter touch imitates the flaring red gills of a desperate fish, perhaps one injured or in dire flight.

I toss my deceiver into the flat surf, trying to retrieve it just fast enough so it doesn't catch on a chunk of coral but not so fast that it doesn't elude any possible takers. As I settle down into the rhythm required by false casting, I have enough time to look around and let the lonely peacefulness of Cayo Rosario fully sink in.

Where the sand rises into a dune line, there is a series of dark symmet-rical tunnels, large enough to plunge my arm into, if I were so inclined. These are the homes of iguanas, a reptile tasty enough to have been literally eaten to extinction on many other Antillean islands by sustenance-hungry locals. Here, the lizard is said to reach up to four feet in length, and by the size of the burrows, that is easy to believe. Despite their size, they are shy herbivores, and I have to look carefully before I finally spot even one resting with its enormous head out of its burrow. When it sees me, it vanishes in a splatter of fine sand into its home.

The Taino knew this iguana well—after all, they named it, as they named the island of Cuba itself. They ate the lizard as part of a natural diet that included tubers, which they ground into cassava; queen conch, which they pounded into steak; and sea turtle and fish, which they both boiled and grilled. Other plants and animals they depended on have dis-appeared, thanks largely to Columbus's second voyage in 1493, when sev-enteen ships full of conquistadores wove their way through the islands of the Caribbean. With them this time were living European provisions—pigs, sheep, goats, dogs, and cattle. The domestic livestock, set loose to range, quickly became feral, eating the eggs of native birds, owls, iguanas, and any animal not quick enough to flee. To anthropologists studying the Antilles, the animals from that voyage have come to be known as the "destruction troop." Later, the animals were joined by invasive non-native plants, including forage grasses and sugarcane, imported to feed livestock or humans.

As elsewhere in the Caribbean, the arrival of Europeans spelled an end to an era. "We will never know how much appreciation and respect the Tainos had for their surrounding animals," Silva Lee observes today. "We can [only] be sure . . . Cuba's fauna has been underrated and ignored."

Certainly, I am trying to pay attention to what is left. A few yards away, a small ground dove, like those I have seen back in the Florida Keys, does its mechanical strut down the beach. A sandpiper flutters at the water's edge. A tern soars low, looking for scraps. My false casting and retrieval continues, little bumps by curious fish not strong enough to cause a hookup. Finally, a foot-long snapper soars toward the fly as it wiggles by the fish, and it clamps down with authority, bending my rod impressively with its strength. Its run is strong, and after I pull it in, I reach down and undo the hook from its lip and let it go.

I admit fishing is more of a prop for me, an excuse to immerse myself in the transcendence of the sea rather than actually record catches or tally numbers. With this in mind, I lay my rig down on a large trunk of driftwood and stick the barb into the cork handle of the rod. McCosker is out of sight, somewhere beyond a limestone bluff that juts out in the surf, giving me the illusion that I am the only human on the shores of Cayo Rosario.

I walk alone along the water line of the beach, looking more closely at the seashells scattered here. Among them are small chunks of coraline algae, a branched filiform of calcium frozen like feathering crystals. I bend to pick up a bleeding heart periwinkle, a shelled gastropod the size of an acorn. It is an intertidal snail, one that lives in the cusp between land and sea, grazing for algae on exposed rock or mangrove roots, submerging completely only to lay its eggs. This particular species sports the uncanny look of a minute, bloody tooth—three, actually—right at the crevice where the snail head emerges from the shell to graze. Around me, the beach is glowing in a light pink, but for the life of me, I can't find any single shell large enough to trace the origin of such a color.

The sun has settled under the horizon in a magnificent burst of orange, leaving behind the smolder of twilight. I grab my rod and head back toward the beached skiff, where I find McCosker already there. Gilmore and Robins soon trudge down from their end of the beach, todyless but happy with the opportunity to poke about in such an extraordinary place. We are all in great spirits as we push the skiff away from the shore and climb in. McCosker pulls the starter cord until the kicker finally turns over, and we head out toward the *Seward*, which has just turned on its lights. The tide, which was still flooding on the way in, has pushed several feet of water over the more shallow corals—a good thing, as we can no longer see beneath the surface.

Now that the sun has disappeared entirely, the heat rises off the land mass of Cayo Rosario and mixes with the cooler air of the sea, whipping a once modest chop into rolling two- and three-foot-high waves. We head directly into them, sea water splashing over the gunwales in buckets. Gilmore and I bail, using empty cans floating in the bottom. A few waves are large enough to soak everyone when they hit, even knocking the bow of the skiff sideways. Low in the water to begin with, we are in danger of being swamped by the ever growing sea at any moment, but no one seems concerned by this possibility.

By the time we reach the edge of the *Steward*, it is fully dark, and we tie up and scamper aboard the ladder. Dinner is almost over, but we manage to scrounge up a few plates full of pasta and salad. Between my earlier dive, the fishing, and the constant movement of the sea, I am bone tired. When finished, I pour myself a cup of coffee and go back to the dry lab to see Alcolado, who is studying something of infinitesimal size under the scope. He seems glad to see me and asks about our shore trip. I tell him of the beauty of this island we have seen on the shore of his country, and he nods knowingly. I ask what could have made the sand so pink on Cayo Rosario. He says he is not sure, but if I have a sample of a grain, he would try to find out.

Digging through my dive gear, I find a pinch or so of the sand accidentally captured in one of my neoprene booties. After gingerly dumping it onto a scrap of paper, I bring it to Alcolado for study. He puts the grains under the scope, twists the knobs of the focus, and within seconds looks up. "*Tellina*," says Alcolado, naming the genus. I look puzzled. "You might call it 'tellin.' It is the juvenile of the species. That is why it is so small, so hard for you to see." I recognize the name tellin as a small bivalved clam, a cousin of the technicolored coquina. I ask why there are so many of them, all at once, and why they are all pink. "No one knows," says Alcolado, adding, "Maybe there is a gyre in the ocean that keeps them from dispersing. Maybe . . . it is something more." When Alcolado says this, it is comes out stoically, in what I imagine to be a shared commonality among those whose lives are bound by the fathomless authority of the Caribbean Sea. I think of what Herrero had told me earlier back in the Laberinto when I asked him if he knew when the sea turtles would be coming in to lay their eggs. "Only God knows."

There is something comforting in all this for me, and back in my bunk, just before I fall asleep, I take great pleasure in its profound uncertainty. Something happened to me today—perhaps a critical emotional mass was finally breached, and I stopped thinking of Cuba as a forbidden exotic place and began to feel comfortable enough to let its natural beauty reach down inside and touch something vital in me. It is as if a growth ring has been scored, deep and immutable, into my own emotional otolith, and it will be here for as long as I want to remember.

8

Cayos Aguardientes

and Sambo Head

Sunday, December 21

Cayos Aguardientes

We are over deep water, somewhere south of the Canarreos chain. What are mapped as the desolate islands of Cayos Aguardientes are due north, shimmering like a mirage under the warm tropical sun. I've been given the opportunity to ride in the JSL this morning, and I take it as an early Christmas present, the only one I'm likely to get. Except for the miniature tree in the corner of the conference room and a feeble string of lights strung along the wall, the holiday that consumes everyone's lives back in the United States is seldom mentioned out here on this remote southern shore of Cuba. Most expect December 25 to be just another working day, and a humbuggery atmosphere of denial seems to be growing in proportion to the approach of the nonevent. Oddly, throughout Cuba, the

147

holiday of Christmas—once outlawed for its crass materialism and its con-nection to the Catholic Church—has again become legal.

Before the dive, I walk out on the stern, where the submersible is berthed, and look it over more closely this time. It looms like a large metal insect, with its one single bulging bug eye in front and a clunky thorax just behind. Stuck onto the thorax are an assortment of cylindrical tanks, which could be regarded as giant metallic eggs. Pipes and wires wo-ven over the body might be legs, arms, antennae—who knows? It is the modern incarnation of the *Nautilus*, first entered into the genetic mem-ory of human consciousness as fiction and then spit back out as reality some 130 years later. This may also be the only submersible with a deep-water algae named after it: former NOAA chief scientist Sylvia Earle, in collaboration with HBOI biologist Nat Eiseman, once discovered a tiny green parasol-shaped plant found only in deep water and named it for the JSL as *Johnson-sea-linkia profundia*. ("Discovery of a site where the plants grow has always been from one of the JSL subs," Earle noted, after first describing the species she found in the Bahamas.)

Despite the sub's seaworthy track record, to crawl inside and ride it to the bottom of the sea—even though I've done it once before during an expedition in the Galápagos—requires an emotional leap of faith. My caution, I am admitting, is mostly atavistic, a gut-level response any mam-mal might have when faced with squeezing inside a metal can and being dropped in the ocean.

Once I deal with this issue, however, I am free to consider how fortu-nate I am to participate in such a rare event at all. As I do, the prospect of riding a sub down into deep Cuban waters becomes an exhilarating notion. After all, such an experience is one the entire world could only have dreamed of a century ago. Last night in my bunk, I read of naturalist Thomas Barbour's longing to penetrate these depths decades ago. Near the end of his life, the American expatriate wrote: "I have always wished that I had had more chance to engage in deep-sea exploration. This is the most thrilling and romantic of all the activities in which a naturalist may engage!"

Although William Beebe was experimenting with his diving bell in the 1920s and 1930s and Swiss physicist Auguste Piccard developed the first untethered bathyscaph in the 1940s and 1950s, the reality was that most scientists in the world—until relatively recent times—still used trawls and metal scoops to sample the deep. That was surely the case in Cuba during Barbour's lifetime. In 1938 and 1939, the *Atlantis*, a ship on loan from Woods Hole Oceanographic Institute, made two separate cruises jointly underwritten by Harvard and the University of Havana. Barbour described the prevailing techniques: "Some methods of scouring the deep have been used since time immemorial. . . . What are called 'tangle bars' are a most useful method. This is simply a heavy bar of iron attached by a bridle to a cable. From the bar, long unraveled hanks of rope are made fast and these being dragged across the surface bring up samples of coral as well as sponges and many other objects broken loose."

The *Atlantis*, reported Barbour, also employed the relatively new otter trawl—not unlike those that modern shrimp boats use to bag their catch in midwater. But while the maritime piñatas always revealed surprises, they frequently mangled their treasures. Specimens were "usually terribly injured in the bag; even those caught in the most delicate bolting silk nets are often skinned . . . before they reach the surface." In the rare instance when a deepwater fish was delivered whole, its air bladder would usually explode—in imitation of how a rapid ascent can also cripple a scuba diver with an air embolism.

Nonetheless, animals occasionally survived intact, Barbour reported. In fact, one of the best catches from the *Atlantis* effort was a new "deep-sea fish of the genus *Chaunax*" recovered from 1,070 fathoms (6,420 feet). In a stroke of great irony, perhaps recognized only by Gilmore and the Cuban scientists, we also have a live, sub-wrangled *Chaunax* aboard, and it is, at the moment, in the aquarium.

Edie Widder, a bioluminescence specialist, joins me on the stern. During the dives she makes in the JSL she has arranged for a custom-made, screenlike device to be installed that will help record the presence of certain glow-in-the-dark invertebrates as they collide with it. McCosker dubs it the "widderizing" of the sub. Widder, bright, low key, and diminutive in stature with short-cropped hair, seems much friendlier now than when I first met her, just after the *Seward* begin its voyage. At that time, I was leaning out on the port rail watching the ship slice through the furrows of the South Atlantic. Widder sidled up and, with little prelude, asked what I would be doing on the expedition. I explained the online reportage, and her immediate response was: "How do you rate?" In this context, "rate" was not used as a measurement of skill but as a means to ask the broader question: Why you? She then proceeded to vent her frustration over trying to get a children's book about bioluminescence published. Later, as I was working in my rabbit warren, she brought me proofs of the book and asked for suggestions. Since then, I've written off her initial truculence to media distrust and some eccentric defensiveness. Beneath the surface beats the heart of a teacher with an abiding mission: to alert the world to the glowing animals that inhabit the deep.

Today, Widder seems to welcome me as a passenger on the sub's voyage. She hands me a clipboard with sheets on which the results of the JSL's collections can be made as they happen, including the species, time, and depth and whether they are collected, filmed, or squashed into the "splat screen" atop the sub. Since I am riding in the "observer's chamber" in the rear, I will function as the second scientist—or in this case, scientific technician—on the dive. "We'll be looking for bioluminescent roadkill," says Widder, smiling. If this were a feature movie, Widder would be played with word-clipping panache by Holly Hunter. The loud buzzer rings to signal the upcoming dive, and we gather back in the conference room for the briefing. Don Liberatore will be piloting, with Widder riding next to him in the bubble sphere. In the back, I will be joined by sub tech Hugo Marrero. The sub mission is to "identify, film, and collect midwater invertebrates," and we plan to max out at two thousand feet in order to do so.

All involved in the launch, except for the sub occupants, put on their life vests and move quickly to their posts on the stern. The rear compartment of the JSL is not insulated, and since the three- to four-hour dive in deep water will cool it markedly, I carry along a light jacket in addition to my notebook and clipboard. I walk to the rear of the JSL, duck under it, and raise myself up inside the round port at the bottom, using my arms to hoist myself into the chamber. It is a tight fit, and once I am inside, the narrow compartment is slightly claustrophobic. There is enough room for me and Marrero to lie down, he on one side and I on the other. When first developed, the JSL was used for "lockout" scuba diving, in which a diver could actually open the entry port to emerge at depth and survey the bottom more closely without having to worry about decompression. (As a testament to the early commitment Ed Link had to using diving biologists, all scientists hired at HBOI between 1971 and 1973 were actually trained to lock out of the JSL at five hundred feet.) Once we are both inside, Marrero reaches down and pulls the port latch up and twists a wheel-like lock until it clicks shut.

Marrero, like most crew, has an eclectic background: Puerto Rican by birth, he once piloted a tourist submersible that poked around at the edges of the walls of the Cayman Islands and in the Bahamas. Like other techs, he is in training to become a JSL pilot, and he says he hopes that happens before funding for deep-sea research completely dissolves.

Along with us on the dive today is a life-sized Styrofoam head, attached to the outside of the sub. The head, normally used to display wigs back in the real world, has been colored with Magic Markers by Ben Chiong, another of the sub techs. Chiong has applied great Tammy Faye Bakker lashes to the eyes, generous bursts of rouge across both cheeks, and a big fat red pucker of a smile on the lips. Lashing such an object to the outside of an oceanographic submersible creates one of those special moments of life in which the comically absurd is fused with a lesson in physics: with the pressures of the ocean increasing at each atmosphere of 33 feet by another 14.7 pounds per square inch (psi), the porous head will take a mighty squeeze at depth—as would we, if the sub ever ruptured. From the stern, Giddings films the head before its dive; he will film it again after we return, when it is squashed down to about half its size by depth.

Marrero gives me a safety briefing, explaining how the scrubber mechanism works to recycle our exhaled carbon dioxide and alerting me to fail-safe methods of communication if the sub should become disabled. "We're sealed separately from the pilot sphere, so if they flood, we'll still be dry," says Marrero happily. He then reminds me to not lie back atop the fan that helps recirculate our air supply because we'll slowly lose consciousness and die; I assure him I will not do this. If Marrero passes out and the electronic communications go down, I can use a primitive voice-activated phone to call for help. He then shows me the valve for the oxygen, which, in case of an electrical fire—the worse-case scenario—I am to shut off immediately, before we become toast. For air, I can then breathe from a scuba tank regulator, which, along with survival suits, is stuffed into a storage space behind me. I am assured there is enough food and fresh water for five days, should we become snagged on the bottom. Marrero then hands me a headset and mike I can use to communicate with Widder up front, and he switches on a tiny black-and-white monitor that shows me what the front-mounted camera sees.

The JSL shakes, jarring us, as it is lifted up and off its cradle by the pneumatic **A**-frame crane. I watch through the starboard porthole as we rise into the air and then, ever so gently, settle down onto the sea. The thick cable that tethers us to the ship is popped and then retracted by a shipboard winch. We are on our own in the sea now. I hear Liberatore's voice over the intercom informing the bridge of our readiness to dive: "We have a seal." And from the bridge: "Roger that." Water sloshes outside the port window, lime green from the sunlight. We pitch and roll at the surface as Liberatore moves us away from the *Seward* using the JSL's prop thrusters. The rough sea, barely noticeable back on the deck of the larger ship, tosses us like a giant plastic beach ball, and I feel a wave of seasickness begin to rise inside me. When we finally begin our descent, the sub rides smoothly, the lime-green water turns light blue, and my body calms. With only one knot's worth of propulsion stored inside, the sub sinks by filling its ballast tanks; not only is the descent an energy-saving exercise, but it is also wonderfully silent and sure, with no whirling from the engines.

As we drop, a needle inside a large clocklike depth gauge moves from one number to another, tracing our slow-motion free fall. At 60 feet, we have lost reds and yellows. At 130 feet, there is a beautiful zap blue outside the port. From my headset, Widder's voice comes through clearly. She is telling me that she has designed a "photo multiplier tube" that measures the light at depth and that surface light decreases exponentially as we go deeper. "The spectrum gets more and more narrow." We continue to drop. At 250 feet, Widder tells me we have only 10 percent of surface light left. "Light is so important down here," explains Widder. "We take it for granted. It's the driving force of life."

When the needle hits three hundred feet, it seems almost fully dark outside my window. "There's barely enough light left to measure, says Widder. Under normal conditions, five hundred feet marks the "cutoff point for photosynthesis." It also signals the beginning of the midwater "mesopelagic" zone, which stretches between here and three thousand feet. "This is where most of the action is in the ocean," says Widder. I press my face against the Plexiglass window, scrunching my body around to get a better look. Something the size of a basketball pulses outside in the darkness. It heaves, surges, and billows in waves of protoplasm and cold, blue, unworldly light, seeming to skirt the margin between real and make-believe. I ask Widder what it is, and she says "medusa," an inverte-brate that falls into that large class of animals most lay observers describe as "jellies." My immediate response is that this is something Jules Verne might have dreamed up if he really wanted to get beyond the giant squid thing.

Named for its resemblance to the mythological Medusa, the animal is considered to be among the most primitive multicellular life forms on earth, dating from the Precambrian epoch. Fossilized medusae believed to be 700 million years old have been found in Australia. They were pre-dominant then, representing the first signs of complex life—the ancestors of all that was to come later. I remember Gilmore telling me earlier that animals down here "once owned the world." Certainly, Darwin posited one of the first insights into the time-frozen nature of deep-sea incubation when he theorized that some species can nearly remain intact if they live in "some distant and isolated station." Although some of the contemporaries of the medusae continued to evolve, the depths have protected many of its kin, allowing it to survive within its ecological niche with little change. Would this animal care if it were pulsing through Cuban waters or not?

Marrero dims our small overhead light so I can see the bioluminescence better, and then he lies back, crosses his arms, and shuts his eyes. "Look around you," says Widder, sounding more like a benign mentor than ever. "It's alive down here." And she is right; glowing animals are moving every-where in the darkness: other medusae, siphonophores, and ctenophores, even the occasional deep-sea fish. Although all translucent soft-bodied inverts share a resemblance, they are different enough to be grouped into separate phyla: the medusa—which is a swimming version of a stationary coral polyp—is in the phylum Cnidaria, shared by anemones, hydroids, corals, and true jellies. The siphonophore, also a Cnidarian, is a complex form of unattached colonial hydroids that pulse a gas-filled float to move them through the water. (The best known of the siphonophores is the Portuguese man-of-war, which floats on the surface, dangling its tentacles below to catch unwary fodder.) Yet ctenophores—characterized by eight rows of cilia and the lack of tentacles, or the presence of just a single pair— are in the phylum Ctenophora. Also described as "comb jellies," they beat their cilia in waves to move; when they bioluminesce, the rows of cilia seem to light up nearly sequentially, as if electronically wired to do so.

For most humans, the deep ocean translates into *abyss*—a word with root origins that literally mean "without bottom." Long ago in the history of humankind, deep-sea monsters lived here—from the ogres of Greek mythology to the Leviathan of the Old Testament. Sea serpents rose up from the depths, appearing at the edges of known territory on the maps drawn by cartographers: *Here Be Dragons*. It was not a friendly place to be.

And here I am today, somewhere in the forbidden depths off the shores of a forbidden country, some odd symmetry in all that. Behind me, the "scrubber" hums reassuringly, cleaning our exhalations of carbon and re- cycling them back to us to inhale, again and again. I ask Widder about the devices she had attached to the JSL for this dive. "The point is to get really accurate measurements of how much light the animals are putting out." Light is no small matter. In an earlier experiment, Widder and colleague Tammy Frank studied ultraviolet light and vertical migrations in deep-sea crustaceans. Just after sunset, crustaceans and other animals that inhabit the midwater zone migrate up to the surface, taking advantage of the cover of darkness to feed there. Widder and Frank's test showed that spectrum changes at the surface after twilight were not detectable at the depths, indicating that the shellfish they followed must be responding to other signals. Could it be temperature change in surface waters, or some other unknown genetic clue as time-scrambled and mythologically imprecise as sea monsters?

Widder, at home here in her mesopelagic zone, appears far more confi- dent and actualized than I have seen her. She also seems impassioned not just about how and why deep-sea creatures bloom with light but about what it means to the rest of the earth. "Our planet is driven by the sea," says Widder, "yet we know so little about it." There is an urgency, says Widder, to learn as much as we can before things fall into disarray. This is especially true in the abyss, where the biodiversity rate is high but the size of populations is low. A newly discovered animal could easily be driven to extinction before it is understood. There are not only biomedical salves to be discovered down here but also secrets to the mystery of life—vital links that sustain us all on this water planet. After all, our oceans do more than cover three-fifths of earth's surface, says Widder: together, they create a liquid column of life that accounts for 97 percent of available living space on our world. Once regarded as infinite—reserved as the seldom seen territory of oceanographic adventurers and poets—this vast salty column is now under siege. Ship traffic nearly everywhere crosses over it, commercial fishermen scour it with increasingly sophisticated high-tech harvesting gear, and humans cluster around its islands and mainland edges with their time-released waves of pollution. Worldwide, one-third of the population lives in coastal areas. Shallow coral reefs are becoming diseased with nutrients, and fisheries worldwide are declining. The ocean depths are the last to be affected by our surface malaise, surely. But when will our terrestrial impacts finally reach a critical mass and rain their way down to the solitude of rare ancient places, creating real sea dragons and beasts from the solitude here?

Now we are totally surrounded by darkness, the tiny lights of our sub nearly lost in the abyss. It is noticeably cooler inside, in contrast to the warm tropical surface I left behind just a couple of hours ago. Shivering a bit, I put my jacket on. Marrero shines his flashlight on the gauge behind his head. Its needle points to 1,950 feet.

Outside the port, the sea is indeed alive, creating a fantastic light show that would have played very well in the 1960s, perhaps as a backdrop to a song by the Jefferson Airplane. Imagine psychedelic skyrockets firing off in the darkness around you, leaving gentle trails and flares and flowerlike blooms of illumination—here for a moment and then gone so completely that you wonder how tangible they really were. It seems random, even dreamlike, to the human eye, like some whimsical, haphazard peyote vision; I have to struggle briefly to remember that I did not create this from my imagination. Despite my own indulgence, this is serious business for the animals who must live here. In a world where there is no place to hide, light takes on a whole new meaning for the viper fish and jellies and microscopic dinoflagellates around me. What is phantasmagoric to me is utility to them. Widder's voice crackles into my headset: "You're getting a fairly accurate view of what most of our planet is like."

In the deep sea around us today, critters use light in three major ways, Widder explains: to find food, to attract mates, and—most commonly—for defense. As a defense mechanism, bursts of light are sent out to blind or distract predators, while less intense glimmers are used to let others know they are poisonous—what Widder calls "conspiratorial whispers." In some cases, an animal under attack can flash great bursts of light "like a burglar alarm." These frantic alerts serve to draw larger predators into the action, thwarting the attack by making the smaller predator who initiated the assault far more visible—and thus, eatable. Finally, and perhaps most spectacularly, the luminescence is manipulated as camouflage. In this way, critters—say, a decapod shrimp—turn light into a "cloaking device," says Widder. If they can't be transparent, they'll fool others into thinking they are. They do this by using sensors to read the scant light coming down from above and then refiring it back out below at the same intensity using their photophores. When seen by predators from underneath, their silhouettes become invisible.

Unlike firefly light, which is green, or nearshore bioluminescence, which is blue-green, deepwater light is cold blue. Each natural biolight, Widder explains, is designed so it can be best used in its localized environment. In the ocean, blue light travels greater distances through clear water than any other color. In coastal waters, by contrast, sand and other particulates scatter the light, making blue-green the better color for the animals that live there. Both the starfish and the sea pen shell use blue-green. On land, where the absorption qualities of water don't come into play, fireflies—which are actually beetles—flash yellow, while the Malaysian land snail glows greenish-yellow, and the railroad worm of Central and South America burns red and green-yellow. Given the number of species that use it, says Widder, bioluminescence may be the most common communication technique on earth.

A small squid soars by my window, leaving a trail of dark liquid in its wake. "He thinks our lights are very rude," says Widder. "So he tries to ink them out." Liberatore tries to follow him so we can film the action, but the squid makes a nosedive into the abyss. A member of the class Cephalopoda, the squid, with its eight arms and two longer tentacles, is likely the most intelligent of all the invertebrates. Certainly, it has the most highly evolved nervous system, including eyes not dissimilar to those of us who wear a backbone. By expanding or contracting specialized pigment cells called chromatophores, squid can also change color swiftly and dramatically, for camouflage or to display feelings—hunger, fear, comfort, rage. "How does he know what our depth limits are?" says Widder, only half kidding. The thought of a giant version of this small, intelligent animal once fascinated Verne; today the possibility of a big brother of the squid we've just seen also fascinates other scientists, like Dr. Clyde Roper. At this same time we are roaming the Cuban sea, Roper is preparing to cruise to New Zealand to find a giant squid larger than the JSL somewhere there in the depths.

After our squid disappears, we turn off our exterior lights and hover at eighteen hundred feet. As we do, we are totally surrounded by what seem to be millions of fireflies, all flashing their tiny lights in the water. I ask Widder what this is, and she says it's an *unknown*. They are, effectively, the undersea version of astronaut John Glenn's fireflies, sighted in the darkness of outer space.

"Watch this," she says, as she asks Liberatore to turn the lights back on. With the bright camera lights now ablaze, the water seems abruptly empty of all life, save for a few specks of sediment. What has happened? "My theory is it's a form of bacteria, too small to see," says Widder. "We've tried to collect it and come up with nothing. There's been no scientific paper done on it yet."

One of the great tragedies of political isolation is that scientists, who may probe the same seas, using similar methodologies, are often unable to share their work. For instance, the Soviet oceanographic ship *Rift* visited Cuba in 1985, making a series of dives with the submersible *Argus* off Bahía de Matanzas, around Isla de la Juventud, and outside Havana. In fact, we are now following a portion of its same route, west from the Canerreos, up and around Cape Antonio, until we reach Havana. A primary goal of that trip was to survey the geomorphology of the Cuban coast; a secondary aim was to collect fish and inverts. For the latter purpose, both Claro and Alcolado were along. A paper published in Spanish in an issue of *Bohemia* revealed that they retrieved, among other things, a deepwater sea cucumber (*Holothuria lentiginosa*) at 1,650 feet, found a sea star (*Nymphaster arenatus*) at 1,050 feet, and even recovered an ancient ceramic bottle in deep water off Hicacos, east of Havana. I wonder if we are not acknowledging the *Argus* work because the Russians sponsored it—or because it invalidates Discovery's claim of underwriting the first high-tech oceanographic expedition here. Either way, it is a glaring omission.

But there is more at stake than the *Argus* dives. Mesopelagic science, performed down here outside the glare of politics, might help show that the biological "marvels" of the deep are universal; the siphonophore that just moved past my port was not wearing national colors.

As we continue the dive, I divide my time between the port window and my technician duties as record keeper, stopping to jot down a few personal observations in my notebook whenever I get a chance. Widder advises me of any collection going on up front and alerts me to anything glowing that might have crashed into the screen. As she does, I dutifully write it down on the "Dive Log" on my clipboard. On the log, I note that we have deployed at 9:29 A.M.; that a comb jelly splatted into the screen at 10:08 at 2,000 feet; that a ctenophore was collected and put into one of the rotary vats under the pilot sphere at 10:27 at a depth of 1,960 feet; that an unidentified fish with a strange fin swam by vertically in the water at 10:49 at 1,900 feet; that a siphonophore was collected at 11:16 at 1,935 feet; that a ctenophore crashed into the screen at 11:44 at 1,955 feet. At one point, I look outside the port and get a start as the tethered Styrofoam head—crushed down by now to the size of a softball—bobs up against the glass, its cheeks sunken and its lips as puckered as a parrot fish.

In comparison with other regions in the world, like Ecuador's Galápagos or the Gulf of Maine in the northeastern United States, the sea off the shore of Cuba is startling clear, Widder tells me. With fewer nutrients to cloud the water, not only is the visibility better, but there are also far fewer critters, which are normally sustained by the nutrient-enriched food chain.

"Food is manufactured at the surface," Widder says. This includes leaf and plant detritus, as well as the living free-floating plankton of plant and animals trying to tough it out until they grow big enough to metamorphose, so they can swim or hide. Some of this surface fodder rains down, and the mesopelagic animals eagerly glom it as it does. But the mother lode stays put near the surface, and the deep-sea denizens swim up to pick it off at night—regardless of what mechanism they use to detect the arrival of the cover of darkness. For instance, little crustaceans called copepods migrate vertically to eat dinoflagellates, and larger animals follow to feed on them. Taken wholly, this nocturnal journey includes tiny shrimplike crustaceans called euphausiids (commonly referred to as krill), siphonophores, copepods, cephalopods (including squid), and even small fish. "Every single day, in all the oceans of the world, the most amazing migration of the planet takes place, as the midwater animals move up towards the surface," says Widder, who sounds a bit amazed herself with this knowledge. "And most of us are blissfully unaware of this." Indeed, this upward migration is so thick that marine biologists know it as the "deep-scattering layer" because sound impulses from sonar are scattered by its density.

At 12:27 P.M., we prepare to begin our gradual thirty-minute ascent back up to the surface. I record the time on the log, pause, rub my eyes, and then turn to my own personal notebook. It may be the last time I am ever at two thousand feet under the ocean, and I want to connect with something that is more than just an inventory of sea animals. I search my mind until I remember a few fragments of a favorite Tennessee Williams poem. And, as dutifully as I recorded the harvest of a ctenophore, I jot them down:

> I want to go undersea in a diving bell
> and return to the surface with ominous wonders to tell . . .
> where the action is slow
> but thought is surprisingly quick.
> It's only a daredevil's trick
> the length of a burning wick.

I start to close my notebook, and then, inspired by the lyric, write: "The exhalation of the whale; the dreams of the dolphin as he sleeps; the gleam of desire in the eye of a squid. This is where they all coalesce. It is the repository for the ocean's alchemy—a place most humans could barely imagine."

Widder's voice startles me from my reverie. "Let's go up with our exterior lights off," she says to Liberatore, excitedly. As Liberatore starts to empty the ballast, we begin our slow rise back to the surface, returning to our own geological time. It is all astounding stuff, this starlight under the sea. And it has been especially so for me, at this time of the year, a season when miracles are celebrated. As we ascend, bioluminescence disturbed by the movement of the JSL fires around me, as magical as lights on a Christmas tree I once knew as a little boy. As we near the surface, the water outside us is now full of air bubbles from the ballast—big bubbles, little bubbles, a dense curtain of bubbles, all rising now, faster than us. Illuminated by the surface light, they seem to shine individually from within, traveling through water that has again become lime green. The forbidden ocean has become a giant spritzer, effervescing around us. "I love these bubbles," I hear Widder say, to no one in particular. "Aren't they beautiful!" As we finally hit the surface, I half expect us to keep going, to fire ourselves up and out of the water, like a leviathan, breaching itself in celebration of its return to the light.

Monday, December 22

Sambo Head

Sambo Head is unmapped, a no-man's-land of shallow reefs just south of Cayo Avalos, adjacent to the Aguardientes. From our ship, the closest islet is little more than a mirage of treetops, five or six miles away. Up on the bridge, the captain shows me where the sprawling reefs of Sambo should be, tapping his finger on the chart to indicate where they rise from the water at low tide. Sambo Head mortally snagged an ocean-going freighter some three months ago, and we can see the foundering, abandoned ship today from our vista on the bridge, less than two miles to the north. It is a vessel larger than our own. "This reef isn't even on the map—but it has been grabbing ships for a long time," says Seiler. "This is as close as I want to get to it."

If Cuba is taboo to most Americans, then a treacherous uncharted reef that has been puncturing ship hulls for centuries seems even more so. It is worth a visit, and both scientists and filmmakers load up for several runs to the site. As usual, Giddings goes first, offloading his crew in the shallow waters around the wrecked freighter. The Whaler returns to pick up those who want to dive on Sambo Head or visit the wreck, for whatever reason. Along with us today is José R. Larraldo, a local Cuban guide who just came aboard yesterday from The Colony resort on the nearby Isla de la Juventud to help us locate good dive sites in the area. He says we should call him "Larry." Larraldo, a dark-skinned, stocky, bullnecked man who speaks no English, seems vaguely familiar. McCosker says "Michael Spinks," referring to the American boxer. "Dead ringer." He tells Larraldo this in Spanish, and Larraldo laughs. Larraldo will spend a few days with us, sleeping on the floor of Ricardo's already cramped cabin. For his guide expertise and the six-hour boat ride that brought him here from The Colony, the producers have agreed to pay $440.17 in U.S. dollars.

Our Whaler skims over clear water, atop underwater ledges that climb, one shallower than the other, as we near the wreck—from nine hundred feet to the thirty-foot-deep bank where Sambo hides. As we approach, I can see the top of the reef, just below the surface. As I do so, I better understand the dilemma of the freighter's captain, as well as that of all those who came before him: one minute, you are in the safety of deep water; the next, your hull is impaled on a pinnacle of coral. The grounded *Spyros* looms just ahead, a tragic sight to any mariner. Two battered Cuban fishing boats are already moored to it; aboard, workers from a local fishing cooperative are removing bags of powdered cement from the hold of the *Spyros* to share with their village, along with anything else they can salvage. We pull alongside, and Marrero hops on a ragged rope ladder and pulls his way up the side of the behemoth freighter to see what he can find for himself. Lipscomb takes the topside film crew aboard to get some footage of McCosker and Pomponi poking around on the ghost ship. Later, McCosker will describe the experience as a "ridiculous" waste of time. In his journal, he writes: "This is a Panama [flagged] freighter laden with Mexican cement, made in Germany and previously owned by Russians. . . . I got a Russian flag and a plastic door sign that read [in Cyrillic] 'Women's Toilet Room.'"

Straus, Fagen, and I are the only ones left on the Whaler, and Conda drives us a couple of hundred yards away. Here we put on our scuba gear and flop overboard. We sink over a shallow, scarred reef crest in less than fifteen feet of water, a place where the surge is moving everything back and forth metronomically in the water column—sea fans, tropical fish, divers. Stands of branching elkhorn and staghorn surround me, interspersed with cannon-shaped hunks of more coral. As I look closer, I see that the hunks, with their squarish trunnions still clearly defined, are indeed cannons, and they are scattered here like giant pickup sticks. Elsewhere, under me, coral appears in suspicious forms—the barrel of a musket, the blade and handle of a saber, scores of "bar shots" and "chain shots"—softball-sized cannon balls hitched together in pairs by bars and chains. Coral grows slowly—an average of an inch a year. Under the ever growing reef, other wrecks could be hidden deeper—who knows?

I fin away across the field of cannon with Straus, stopping to watch a small blue and gold cocoa damselfish flit about the barrel of one of the large guns. The once fearsome breech is nearly sewn shut by coral and algae; a hole the diameter of a pencil is all that remains. As we go, a large, territorial barracuda escorts us, reasserting its claim to this warship and the ecological food web it now sustains. Suddenly, the coral bottom drops out from under us, and we are finning over a white, sandy gully between reef heads. Something large and wooden seems to be underlying much of the sand, and I reach down to fan the heel of my hand over it to get a better look. It is wood—the structural ribs of an old wreck?—and it is punctuated with the tiny holes of wood-boring toredo worms, as if it has been shot repeatedly by a shotgun.

Straus moves deeper, and I follow. As I watch, she points her camera toward a dark hole under a rocky ledge. There, just a few inches away, is a five-foot-long green moray—its pelt smooth as velvet, its toothy slit of a mouth in slow undulation. I think of one of my favorite movies, *The Deep*, in which Nick Nolte and Jacqueline Bisset struggle with bad guys over two tropical wrecks—a modern ship sunk over a historical one. In it, a giant green moray bites Lou Gossett soundly in the head. Here, in real life, there are some of the same eerie coincidences at this site—including the presence of documentary producer Giddings, who did the underwater work for *The Deep*. I look over my shoulder to make sure Giddings isn't around today, giving stage directions to the moray. From the sand gully, we follow a gigantic anchor chain of the *Spyros*. As it first ran aground, the captain must have thrown the anchor out in a futile, last-ditch effort to stop his collision with the reef. The chain soon leads us to the ship, which had been nearly hidden in the white silt stirred up by the surge. It is massive, a grayish leviathanlike structure that stretches for several hundred feet. Under it are acres of bleached white coral—the living polyps crushed by the original collision of the hull.

I fin into one of the sandy swales under the hull where thousands of fish are stacked up like cordwood in the protective darkness—French grunts and schoolmaster snapper and something else, silver and long and quick. Farther back, at the stern, the sea courses through the gigantic prop blades and around the rudder, frothing and foaming. The aerodynamic of the prop seems to be activated by the upwelling of the surge, from the deeper waters surrounding the reef. I swim over and, grasping the edge of one blade, hang there, testing the edges of this strange dynamic. Suddenly, an unexpectedly strong swell crashes me into the steel rudder like a rag doll, ripping the regulator from my mouth. I swallow a gulp of seawater and reach out for the hose, pulling it back to me. As I do, another surge sends me flying into the prop blade configuration, bashing me into the rudder's hard metal and tumbling me over on my back before it spits me out on the other side. Oddly, the image of a tiny goby being sucked sideways up into the collection tube of the JSL flashes through my mind. When I finally recover and right myself, I am glad to find that I have only a few slices in the shoulder of my wet suit from the collision.

I surface to get another tank of air, and as I am changing gear, I chat with Fagen, who has just finished his first dive here. He shows me a map he has drawn of the area, based on a chat he had with Roger Dooley back in Fort Pierce and fleshed out with his own dive on the site. The wreck with the cannon, says Fagen, probably dates from the early 1700s and may be British. Given the presence of what is—to me—the more captivating wooden wreck and cannon, I wonder why so much attention is being lavished on the rusting hulk that is the *Spyros*. "Jesus Christ, man," says Fagen, pointing to the *Spyros*. "Look at that thing; it's like a frigging skyscraper."

I study Fagen's map and see that it shows an astounding total of forty-four cannons and five anchors scattered over a football-field-sized area of reef and sand. The multiple anchors are a strong clue that there is not just one vintage wreck here but several, suggesting a historical range from the 1700s to the early 1900s. Fagen, as excited as I have seen him, plans to see what he can discover here. As he plunges over the side for the next dive, he carries a hammer and a small rock-breaking chisel.

"I had dreams of discovering doubloons, heavy archaeological treasures," Fagen later writes, his wistfulness to be more than the shipboard intellectual becoming tangible. But the surge in the shallow water is not friendly to such activities. "I lost the chisel and was reduced to banging on the coral encrustation with the hammer," Fagen reports. "We loosened a couple of cannon balls (which we took) and I knocked away at what seemed to me a musket, a cutlass, and a flat object of iron that seemed a heavy sheet or plate of some sort." Dooley had advised that bronze "slave bracelets" were common on the site, but none were found. "Who knows what's under the wreck from the 1700's," writes Fagen. "It could be anything."

A combination of growing surge and the machinations of other divers on the site have stirred the water so that the visibility on my second dive is only a few yards, making the experience far less rewarding than the first. I do make it a point to stay clear of the prop, though. After I surface for the final time, our boat putters over to the *Spyros* to retrieve Marrero and the others. Marrero makes two trips down the ship's ladder, his free arm carrying the booty, including a large telegraph and a handful of light fixtures. "That's what happens when you set a Puerto Rican loose with a screwdriver," says Marrero, good-naturedly.

Back on the *Seward*, Fagen lays out his finds on the deck, and several of us begin to take photos of the haul. Although all is heavily encrusted with coral, each artifact seems to bear the outline of the object inside: chain shot, bar shot, a musket barrel, a saber. Several of the crew gather around to take photos of the "treasure." But once Ricardo learns what is going on, he quickly intervenes. Apparently, we have no permission to salvage anything from the colonial era, and Ricardo—although he seems not to mind personally—is anxious to keep our salvage work a secret. I am asked not to write anything about the incident for the Web site, and those who took photos are asked not to publish them anywhere later. Romance has run head-on into reality: although operating in the best of intentions, our expedition has been performing archaeological brain surgery with a chain saw. So far, this appears to be the only major political blunder we have made on our journey, but considering all that Norteamericanos have taken from Cuba over the past century, it is not a small one. I go inside the cabin to answer some incoming E-mail inquiries, and when I again emerge, the artifacts have disappeared, and no one seems to know their whereabouts.

By dinner, our fully recuperated cook has prepared a fine meal of ostrich steak, and I welcome the change in cuisine. McCosker gives me a small plaquelike label he has taken from a control panel on the bridge of the *Spyros*. Written in Cyrillic, it translates to "Silhouette," says McCosker. At dinner, I learn that Dick Robins and Gilmore finally cornered the illusive *Verilus* from a late-afternoon sub dive. Indeed, Gilmore still seems elated by it. All was captured on camera, including an interview with Claro, who emphasized the value of *Verilus,* especially in that "Cuba has very few specimens in its collection; we have given most of them away to Harvard."

Off camera, Gilmore provides me with some more background on the mysterious *Verilus*: "Its ancestry doesn't rival the coelacanth, but it does represent the first of the spiny rayed fishes which radiated substantially after the cosmic collision at the Yucatán caused the extinction of the dinosaurs. Its lineage gave rise to nearly all of the shallow-water reef fishes, most estuarine fishes and the percids (perch, darters) and centrarchids (bass, bluegill) that dominate the catch of freshwater sport anglers. He may not look the role, but this guy is very important in so many respects."

After dinner, I walk back to the aquarium to see the celebrated fish in action. It is a small, modest-looking perchlike fish, and it is scuttling along the bottom; a look of bug-eyed amazement is locked on its face, as if it has betrayed all of its kind by allowing itself to be sucked out of the sea and into this odd predicament. There is no sphincter factor, no melodrama, and for all but the ichthyologists aboard, it is a fully inauspicious moment. Indeed, Fagen writes in his journal: "Grant brought up an ordinary looking little (ten inch) fish with bug eyes that sent him into a transport of joy. This is a known 'prehistoric' species which has been seen many times but NEVER captured alive. Grant has been chasing it for 17 years! He and Dick Robins were literally dancing on the aft deck. It should play very well on film."

I go to Gilmore to get some perspective on his obsession with *Verilus*, which the Cubans call *pargo chino*, Chinese snapper. He explains:

> Imagine that everywhere you go in the Caribbean Sea and tropical western Atlantic, this fish is laughing at you—it just lies on its side, daring you to suck him up, squeeze him with a manipulator arm or poison him. He is in the Florida Straits by the thousands on all the [deepwater] Lophelia banks. Every well-respected ichthyologist that has been down in a sub has had the opportunity to capture the little beast, but no matter how close, he escaped every time. At least twelve sub pilots have done their best to outsmart the critter from 1982 to 1997.
>
> Now, you have to also realize that there are only two specimens of this fish in existence in any museum on the planet—both are said to be in the Harvard Museum of Comparative Zoology, given as a gift by Louis Agassiz, from Felipe Poey, who first described it. It was brought to Poey by a Chinese fisherman, using a hand line in fifteen hundred feet of water near Matanzas—hence, the common name, *pargo chino*. We are not even sure if the original "type" specimens even exist anymore! If not, our *pargo chino* would immediately be placed into a neotype category, to be as revered and protected as the holotype should have been.

The ichthyological bonus of this catch is that the original drawings and description made by Poey of the fish are said to still exist in Havana, at the home of Dr. Dario Guitart Manday, an esteemed Cuban scientist. A visit to Guitart's home would allow Gilmore and Robins actually to verify this specimen as *Verilus*, using original work done 140 years earlier. "The thrill of being able to actually see these books—as yet unpublished over a century of Cuban revolutionary history, war, death and destruction—is overwhelming," says Gilmore.

Later at night, we fish for shark with our deepwater downrigger, baited with live menhaden and a piece of leftover ostrich meat, dropped to a thousand feet. Earlier, Gilmore had seen a six-foot silky shark swim by the JSL's bubble when he was on his deep *Verilus* hunt, and Liberatore reported seeing a nine-foot hammerhead at two hundred feet. Someone spots a shark fin circling behind the ship, and Jay Grant hooks up a live ballyhoo he has caught with a hand net and casts it from the stern. I lean against the waist-high starboard bulwark of the *Seward*, panning from the water to the sky. Needlefish dart about at the water's surface, and overhead, the stars burn like pinpricks of light in a velvet cloak. I watch the sky more closely and in three minutes spot three meteors, slashing through the night.

I hear a shout and look over to see that something very powerful has hit the downrigger bait, bending the metal arm impressively with its force. Gilmore cranks the reel with both hands, and finally, up comes a 125-pound deepwater species of grouper—*Epinephelus mystacinus*, the "misty" grouper. The grouper lives at depths of 1,000 to 2,000 feet, far beyond the normal range of local fishing lines—which helps explain how it was able to grow this large. Once it is onboard, McCosker lies down on the deck next to it, to give a perspective of size. The side-by-side disparity of fish doctor and fish creates an out-of-body moment for me, as if both have been hooked and boated, and now they lie next to each other like specimens in some alien seafood market.

By now, everyone not on duty is on deck admiring the giant grouper. The misty is not rare enough to preserve as a specimen, and even if it were, it would be difficult to figure out how to do so. Using a scalpel, McCosker removes an otolith for later study and takes some tissue samples. Then the fate of the misty becomes clear: Cook Grant unceremoniously fillets it for tomorrow's dinner.

In the dry lab, Alcolado is working late, sitting on a stool and looking into a scope. He explains that he is examining the tiny spicules of sponges we have collected to make a positive identification of each—not unlike how ichthyologists count and compare spines of a fish. Already, he says, we have some sponges aboard he believes may be new to science. Although often mistaken as plants because they are rooted to the bottom, sponges are the simplest of the multicellular animals—grouped in the phylum Porifera. Surface perforations called "incurrent pores," or ostia, draw in seawater, filtering oxygen and microscopic food, and then pump it back out through larger "excurrent openings," or oscula. I have hovered underwater next to sponges before and, with my bare hand, felt the gentle outcurrent sweep of seawater, the exhalation of a sponge.

Some sponges may be half an inch across; others, like the giant barrel sponge, may be six feet high and wide, says Alcolado. Many take on easily identifiable shapes and colors—like the pink vase sponge and the orange ball sponge—but others change color and shape depending on water chemistry, light, depth, and age. All these variables make lab examination, like Alcolado is now performing, critical to description. "There are so many, you would not believe," says Alcolado, in awe of the diversity of the animal he studies. "We count three hundred [species] just here in Cuba." He turns away from the scope to show me a folder containing hundreds of pages of tissue paper, with pencil drawings of individual spicules. "I brought this back from Russia when I studied in Leningrad," he says. "I could not bring the book, but they let me trace the pictures!"

Alcolado asks if I want to look through the high-powered scope. There, I see crystal-like structures of the spicules in the shape of rods and branches and even icicles. "Looks like icicles," I say, wondering if Alcolado saw such things when he was in Russia. "Yes," he says, "like on our tree," and then I remember that our tiny artificial tree in the galley has been hung with foil icicles.

This night Fagen has a long private conversation with Lipscomb, ostensibly about collaborating on another film on the rich cultural history of Cuban limestone caves. But in the course of the chat they stray into the complexities of social psychology. Fagen later writes of it: "Jim is the only one on the ship with whom I could have such a discussion. Clearly, he cares about ideas. And he also understands *narrative*, something that Al really does not 'get.' . . . It's images that count and Al is so good underwater that he can find images almost anywhere—but from a more systematic point of view, I feel we are missing *mucho*."

Fagen also notes what everyone else is thinking but no one has yet mentioned: "Although the crew is very disciplined and good natured, there is a strong feeling that we absolutely MUST get off the ship soon—no later than Xmas day. The most likely place is The Colony Hotel, which will soon be within easy steaming distance. Taima [Hervas] seems to take this seriously as—I hope—does Al."

9

Isla de la Juventud,

Ensenada de la Siguanea,

and Punta Francés

Wednesday, December 24

Isla de la Juventud

Today we are riding the southeasterly trades to Isla de la Juventud, out here at the lip of the Golfo de Batabanó. Last night, the misty grouper was baked for dinner, and the fillets of the big fish were much tougher than I'd imagined, almost like pork. McCosker noted that no one was showing any signs of ciguatera—a food poisoning common to larger reef predators—and I took that as a good omen. Afterward, fishing from the stern with a sturdy fishing rod, using the head of the misty as bait, the cook caught a small, four-foot-long silky shark. The silky, which roams deep water and is among the few sharks known to attack divers, was a sleek, beautiful animal, and it writhed on the deck in anger and pain. The plan was to clean it and eat it as we had done with the misty—shark meat can be quite tasty if it is bled as soon as possible to eliminate the ammonia scent from its blood. But no one was assigned the task of butchering it. As a result, it lay on the stern all night, and by morning, its flesh useless, it was tossed over the side, a terrible waste.

The wind continues to blow out of the southeast, and given the vast fetch of the southerly sea, it is packing a wallop this morning. An early sub dive off Isla de la Juventud was scrubbed as a result. Despite the wind, the air temperature is in the low eighties, and the sun is warm enough so that it is comfortable wearing shorts and a T-shirt out on deck. Later today, if the wind cooperates, we hope to put ashore at a century-old sea turtling village settled by English-speaking Cayman Islanders who sailed up from their homeland, some 180 miles to the south, in the early 1900s. They named it Jacksonville, in honor of the Jackson family, who helped lead them here. During that time, just after the War of Cuban Independence, the island was known as Isla de los Pinos, Isle of Pines, for the forests of pine trees that dominated the landscape. (It was renamed Isla de la Juventud, the Isle of Youth, in 1978 in honor of the "International Work Brigades" of young people who were recruited and trained here in agricultural schools. During the peak of the Brigade movement, students from Nicaragua, Africa, Yemen, and North Korea joined Cubans in studying in sixty different schools and working in citrus groves on the island.)

At the time of the revolution, Americans owned nearly 90 percent of this island. In fact, the Platt Amendment (1902) even forbade Cubans to hold title to land on Los Pinos. Under those circumstances, a new settlement of English-speaking foreigners on Cuba's largest satellite island didn't seem particularly out of place. After the revolution, Jacksonville was renamed Cocodrilo for the endemic Cuban croc (*Crocodilus rhombifer*). The Cayman Islanders, who had long severed ties with their own homeland, were assumed to be assimilated—or were they? I am eager to find out.

By 9 A.M., we are about a mile south of land, as close as the *Seward* itself will get to the shore. The village is mapped at the tip of the southernmost coast of the sprawling 1,180-square-mile Juventud, just beyond the light at Punta del Guanal—inside enough of a lee, I hope, to give us some relief from the steady line of rolling breakers. From the ship, the light beacon appears as a sharp point on an otherwise low horizontal island of limestone, beach, and mangroves. In the distance is a bathtub-sized rowboat, about as far from land as we are, and it bobs precariously in the rough seas. The two men on it are standing up, fishing with seines.

Alcolado edges next to me on the rail. Since neither he nor Claro has been certified by HBOI to scuba dive, they are spending most of their time collecting specimens from the JSL or helping to identify and preserve critters others have found by sub or scuba. Although neither is getting much on-camera time, both are valuable resources for the American scientists, Claro for fish and Alcolado for invertebrates. The Cuban scientists are pleasant and companionable, but Alcolado is a bit more jocular, and I look forward to having a few minutes now and then to chat. Once, he told me that as a youngster he attended an elementary school for children of Americans stationed in prerevolutionary Cuba at Gitmo. His first "puppy love" girlfriend, he said a bit wistfully, was an American. When he went to the cinema on the base, it was segregated by color, with blacks up in the balcony. This strikes me as unusual for a Caribbean nation, but then again, Gitmo has always been an American fiefdom.

Once I asked Alcolado about his habit of carving a slice out of his pencils and inscribing "Pedro" on them, thinking it might be a grim sign of the Special Period, perhaps only one pencil per scientist. His answer reminded me of how we Americans are prone to pigeonhole Cuban nationals. "It is not because of money," said Alcolado. "It is just something I have been doing ever since I was a young boy, something I learned in school. Pencils are cheap. We have lots of pencils." And now, today, out of the blue, comes this: "Do you know the Cubera snapper?" I think for a moment. Thick lips, deep reef dweller, looks a bit like the gray snapper? He smiles, nods. He is clearly proud of what he is about to tell me. "It was first identified in Cuba!" If there is any one way to define the Cubans I have met, it is not by the common media slang of despair. More than likely, they are *conflicted*, at odds between their own strong sense of national patrimony and the frustration at the jerry-rigged nature of their country.

Of all the islands we have seen on the southern coast, Isla de la Juventud has been populated the longest, with the most people. Today, some 100,000 Cubans live here, most on the northern shore, sprawling out from

Nueva Gerona. The central core of the island rises up from the low flood-plain to nearly one thousand feet. Citrus is grown on irrigated flatlands to the west. The island is old enough to have large deposits of *mamól*, gray marble, a rock quarried for both structure and sculpture. Most of the southern shore is consumed by the Lanier Swamp, with only a few villages at its edge. Alcolado tells me that almost all of Lanier is also designated as a Military Zone—which requires a permit to enter—thus helping protect the swamp by restricting access. Rare critters live here, as they do in the Zapata: the diurnal Cuban pygmy owl; the bare-legged owl; the blue-headed quail dove, considered the most handsome of Antillean pigeons; and the butterfly bat, a three-gram lightweight that beats its wings so fast that it sounds like a tiny motor when it flies.

Indians once called this island Camarcó and also Sigueanea. But after landing here on his second voyage in 1494, Columbus named it La Evangelista. Along with a number of other isles I have visited in the tropics—Costa Rica's Isla del Coco, Grand Cayman, and the Bahamas' New Providence—Juventud stakes its claim as the real-life setting for Robert Louis Stevenson's *Treasure Island*. Indeed, during the seventeenth century, it was briefly mapped as "Isla del Tesoro," and the shape of the island roughly resembles Stevenson's sketch map. Today, a ten-mile stretch of beach on the southwest shore, between Punta Francés (named for French pirate François Leclerc) and Punta Pedemales, is still known as La Costa de los Piratas.

Near Punta del Este, there is a wild beach flanking a series of lime-stone caves where, according to local legend, the pre-Columbian Indians known as the Siboney (also called Ciboney) left behind pictographs—a three-thousand-year-old series of arrows, triangles, and odd snakelike lines. Among other things, the cave art represents a lunar calendar, populated with humans and animals both real and magical. The caves themselves were sacred places, natural cathedrals where the spirits of ancestors and the gods of nature lived.

Taino scholar Irving Rouse says that the Siboney actually lived in the central part of Cuba and that a more primitive tribe called the Guanahatabey colonized this western region, living in caves, hunting game, and fishing for conch and turtles. Rouse speculates that the ancestors of the

Guanahatabeys could have paddled either out from Central America, taking advantage of the easterly North Equatorial Current, or up from South America, hopping from one island to the next until they reached Cuba, taking advantage of the westerly South Equatorial Current. However they got here, only time separated them from the Taino, who later paddled large dugouts up from South America after first migrating over the North American and Central American land bridges.

Both Claro and Dooley had earlier described Isla de la Juventud as one of the most popular sport-diving destinations in all of Cuba for foreign scuba divers. Some fifty-six dive sites between Cocodrilo and Cabo Francés are buoyed, not just to mark them but to encourage dive boats to tie up to a floating mooring rather than damage the coral with a dropped anchor. The sport of free diving, the traditional fins-and-mask skin diving, has also been obsessively practiced in this region of Cuba, with teams of Cuban free divers learning the Zen-like, energy-efficient methods that would take them far below recreational scuba diving limits. Certainly, expensive scuba gear and air compressors have been beyond the reach of average Cubans for years. Those who wanted to experience the underwater world of their island nation had to learn the mastery of breath-holding techniques, and they excelled at it—routinely diving to 150 feet and more.

Yesterday, we made an exploratory scuba dive near Cayo Matias just off Punta del Este, the remote southeasterly cape of the big island. A couple of the scientists wanted to see what they could find there, and Giddings's team wanted to test the water for later filming. The seas were high and the current swift. I finned down to ninety-eight feet, where a series of striking erosional features were cut into the sand bottom, mostly covered with soft corals—sea whips and rods and fans. The individual polyps on the soft corals were extended to feed, giving them a fuzzy, carpetlike appearance; by night, the hard corals—the stars and brains—would do the same. Schools of giant predatory tarpon roamed in midwater, shards of sunlight ricocheting off their scales, and a pair of queen triggerfish wove in and out of arches of coral, their graceful swirling fins and puckered mouths giving them a slightly operatic look, as if they were preparing to wail an aria or two. Toward the end of the dive, I had watched as McCosker collected a blackcap basslet from inside a coral overhang, using rotenone. At depth, the little fish appeared all black, washed clean of its primary colors by the layers of seawater. But back on the surface, the sunlight restored its stunning hues, and I could see it was magenta and indigo, with faint lines of gold on its head. I marveled at its beauty, but it was bittersweet; I knew its destiny as a specimen would mean that its colors would soon fade for good.

I surfaced then after using most of my air, expecting to be the last aboard the Whaler. But camera assistant Wimberg and Larraldo, our guide from The Colony, were nowhere to be seen. After a few more minutes, we became concerned, especially because the seas were by now three to five feet; the pair could be hidden in the wave furrows—perhaps even flushed into the vast Caribbean south of here by the strong surface current. Conda turned off the engine so we could listen for shouts, but we heard nothing. He cranked it back up and drove around a bit, following the current, which likely carried them away. Finally, several hundred yards off our stern, we saw what looked like a slender red balloon poking up just under the wave crest. Looking closer with binoculars, we saw Wimberg and Larraldo at the surface, Wimberg waving a four-foot-long "sausage," an inflatable rubber signaling device he kept rolled up in his BC. We zoomed over to pick them up. "Man," says Wimberg, "I'm glad I brought that thing along." Larraldo smiled and shook his head, mumbling something about *perro*, and I finally realized he was referring to the sausage as a large dog penis. Back on the *Seward*, Giddings was impressed with our description of the site, but given the increasingly rough seas and the potential of what lay ahead, he decided not to film here.

Instead, we will use the dive boat to run a topside and underwater crew ashore to Cocodrilo. There is also a turtle farm somewhere nearby, so the symmetry is profound—a turtle farm next to a village of old turtlers. The Whaler, heavily loaded with crew and gear, plows through the waves for its first run. It will return and pick up those of us, like Fagen and me, who don't have the priority of the filmmakers. In the meantime, I use the sat phone and laptop to download some incoming E-mail inquiries to the Discovery site. Many are full of effusive holiday greetings, reminding me that today is Christmas Eve. Despite our little tree and scattered hints here and there, no one has much talked about the season—certainly, there is none of the giddiness that relentless advertising, office parties, television pro-gramming, and repetitive radio-play Christmas carols might arouse back home.

Pomponi and Liberatore have taped a large Santa face with a "Happy Holidays" slogan to their cabin door and set up their own little artificial tree under the stairwell. Someone secured a magazine page of a half-naked Cindy Crawford—embellished with a drawing of a holly sprig—to the door of the cabin I share with McCosker.

Fagen pokes his head in to tell me that Conda has finally returned with the Whaler; we climb aboard for the bumpy run to shore, over a steady roll of whitecaps. By the time we arrive, the underwater film crew is busy shooting half-grown hawksbill turtles swimming in a clear pool chipped and hewn from the sharp "iron shore" at the edge of the sea. Conda eases the boat in carefully near a ledge, flipping agilely between forward and reverse to keep our bow from colliding with the jagged rock edges. With the swells of waves rebounding from the shore, the surge carries us back and forth a yard or so, regardless of what the motor does. Finally, Conda advises us to jump from the bow to the ledge, one at a time, at the exact moment when the surge brings us to within a few feet of the rock. This works, and finally we are all ashore, and Conda quickly backs the boat away into deeper water.

At the tidal pool, I see Giddings lying under three feet of clear seawater with his huge Betacam shooting the turtles as they flipper about. When they manage to move out of camera range, Larraldo and government ob-server Ricardo, who are standing in thigh-deep water, push the turtles back into the frame. The hawksbills, once hunted relentlessly as a species for their handsome olive-colored shells, are about the diameter of a large dinner platter. The turtles swim a few feet and then poke their heads up out of the water for a gulp of air, looking around as they do. Since they have spent almost all their lives in tanks at the nearby farm, the experience must be a confusing one for them.

Lipscomb's topside crew is about forty yards away, at the top of a bluff overlooking the pool, filming Giddings filming the turtles. Nearby several villagers have gathered, mostly kids but also a few men and women in their twenties and thirties. They are watching impassively, squatting down on the limestone or standing and occasionally chatting with one another. There is none of the awe-struck frenzy that Americans usually display when they stumble across an event being filmed—whether it's the local nightly news or a feature movie. It's a bit of an odd tango, this two-step of science and art, and the visual impact may often be more Fellini-esque than not—the sight of Betacam-wielding filmmakers in Nikes mingling with unassuming villagers for whom television is more rare than the local endemic crocodile.

Giddings rises up out of the water, clearly not happy with the extra boatload of people who might possibly stray into his shot. It is one of the filmmaker's greatest concerns, and I have even seen him snap at Straus—his girlfriend—when she strays anywhere near the critical area. "Go back to the ship now, or stay until dark!" he shouts. A few who don't want to spend another six hours here choose to return immediately; I have a canteen of fresh water and a few granola bars in my backpack, so I walk away from the water, up to the bluff where Lipscomb and his assistant Hervas are breaking down their gear.

A few hundreds yards away, at the edge of a steep limestone sea cliff, is the low-tech "experimental" turtle farm, its turquoise-colored rooftops gleaming against the monotone of gray like the sea itself. Lipscomb's team is headed there, and I tag along. At the dirt path leading to the farm, a maintenance man is cutting a thin strip of grass with an old electrical lawn mower. He is slight, almond-skinned and by far the oldest human I have so far seen in the village. It is hot under the December sun and he is covered with sweat, but he waves a friendly greeting. Since there are no handy outlets for his mowing device, he has run the already low utility line down to a four-foot-high pole, and from there, stripped back the insulation around the wires and spliced them onto his lawnmower cord. The farm is a collection of a few small concrete block buildings next to a series of concrete vats. The vats are covered with the bright blue roofs but otherwise open on all sides. Each vat contains hawksbill turtles (*Eretmochelys imbricata*) in various stages of growth. A wooden sign with a painted picture of a sea turtle reads "Cuba los Protégé."

Pomponi, the sponge expert, has been brought along to be the "character" in the segment. She will ask questions about the turtles and the farm as Lipscomb's camera rolls. The matchup of an American sponge specialist with sea turtles is daunting logic for me. I wander from vat to vat, watching the young turtles and asking a few questions in broken Spanish. A young biologist named Carlos Rodríguez Castillo tells me that eggs laid by the sea turtles are dug up and brought here—in the manner of the work the boys from the Manzanillo fishing school perform back in the Laberinto. In the wild, predators—from raccoons to humans—often get to the nests first. Of those eggs that hatch, up to 70 percent of hatchlings are eaten before they even reach the water. The incubation here and the "grow-out" of the vats provide a valuable jump-start for the sea turtles, which are released after they grow to the dinner-plate size of the specimens back in the lime-rock pool. Each long rectangular vat here is devoted to a different size turtle—from perfect miniatures the diameter of a drinking glass to prerelease size adolescents. The biggest, I am told, are four years; the smallest are not long out of their eggs. Of the six species of sea turtles that roam the Caribbean, the greens—prized for their meat—and the hawksbill are most likely to nest on Cuban shores, says Rodríguez.

Although most of the turtle eggs hatched here were dug from beaches in the Laberinto, some are transported overland all the way from the province of Camagüey, which encompasses Cayo Coco and hundreds of smaller cayos on the middle northern coast. Farms like this are gaining popularity within the wider range of the Caribbean—from Los Roques in Venezuela to the Cayman Islands. Rodríguez tells me that nine thousand turtles were hatched at this farm alone last year and that there are three other such "research stations" for turtles in Cuba. I bend over to look at the vat with the smallest turtles, admiring the tawny, remarkable shells of the forty or fifty hatchlings. As I do, the entire population of the vat suddenly beats a mad thrashing dash to me through the water, moving like plastic bath toys wound up way too tight. Rodríguez laughs. Conditioned by daily feedings, the turtles have come to associate any human bending over their tanks with food.

Sea turtles, as American herpetologist Archie Carr first found, migrate thousands of miles during their lifetime, using one site to nest, another to breed, and still another to feed. Their sense of navigation seems to be a miraculous synthesis of genetic memory, an ability to sense the earth's magnetic fields, and some ancient alchemy—perhaps even feeling the currents and reading the stars. If there is ever a barometer of the health of the seas, it is the sea turtle, the canary in the ecological coal mine of our oceans. Regrettably, they are closer now to annihilation than they have ever been, threatened not by hunting but by a decline in water quality and the loss of traditional nesting beaches to affluent tourist resorts.

From the little village, I hear the distant clanging of a bell—perhaps from a schoolhouse. Leaving the camera crew behind, I shoulder my backpack and tread off toward it by myself, down a worn single-lane road with a thin veneer of asphalt, stepping around potholes, stopping to rest under the welcome shade of a clutch of fig and mango trees. As I do, a man on an old bicycle pedals past, carrying two live roosters by the feet, dinner on the hoof. Another cyclist negotiates the potholes with a stringer of marine life he has caught on a hand line from shore—a slender hound fish, a plate-sized sting ray, and a tiny grunt. For most fishermen, seafood like this would be considered incidental nuisance fish too bony or hard skinned to make them worthwhile to clean and eat. But as I have been seeing, the coastal seas around Cuba are heavily scoured for food, and larger, meaty fish like grouper and snapper are virtually absent. The subsistence fishermen appear to be working their way down the food chain. One aged Russian truck rumbles by, then a lone man with a straw hat driving a rusty tractor, then the street is empty again. I stand in the middle for several minutes and look around. In this village of 400, I see or hear no other vehicle. I figure I have been in the middle of Cocodrilo's version of rush hour. Roadside, I walk past houses cobbled together from wood, tin, or roughly mortared brick—sometimes all three. Roofs are metal or thatched palm, and windows are covered with shedlike wood shutters instead of glass. In the heat of midday, nearly all shutters are closed. I pass one little bodega with an exterior wall stenciled with the likeness of José Martí. An electrical power line sags low between poles, which seem roughly whittled from tree limbs. Behind the row of houses is a thick canopied forest, and behind that is the vast Lanier Swamp, which isolates Cocodrilo from the rest of the island.

Young children in blue-and-white uniforms fan out over the street. Like everyone else I have met on the dirt main road, they seem shy but friendly.

I speak to a trio of them in my rudimentary Spanish, asking if I can take their photographs with my digital camera; they say yes and immediately line up in a row. When I play the digital image back for them in the tiny monitor, they giggle and smile at the pictures of themselves. Then, the novelty over, they shoulder their books and walk away.

The bell I heard must have been rung to signal the end of the school day, and a bit farther, I see the low-slung school, built in a U-shape around a modest courtyard. The school, with no glass in its windows and its doors left open, is empty. I walk inside and see that the classrooms are spartan but neatly kept. In the courtyard is a lone bust of José Martí, a light cover of dust on his eyelids. Back out in the street, I walk up to the only building with glass in the window. It appears to be a bodega of some kind, and the glass is used not for luxury but as a display case. Indeed, this bodega seems to be a supermarket in miniature, the mercantile reflection of the reef's biodiversity, albeit with a low inventory—a can of beans, a bottle of shampoo, a pair of baby shoes, a wrench, a plastic mermaid, a Barbie knockoff with unworldly green hair, and the lone sign of Christmas, a trollish sort of doll with big starbursts painted around its eyes and a red Santa stocking on its head. I try to walk inside, but can find no door.

Although it is clear I am not a Cuban—and, with an English inscription on my T-shirt, may even be an American—I sense no hostility from anyone. At what must be the end of the town, I see the "Puesto Fronterizo" with its high wooden guard tower overlooking the shore. This is the Guarda Frontera, the Frontier Guard, and it maintains posts at all "ports" to regulate the comings and goings of all ships and boats. As there are no docks or marina services here for boats, and as entry for even our small launch was clearly a tricky proposition, I can't imagine there is much port traffic here in Cocodrilo. I take a photo of the installation, focusing on the two camo-wearing soldiers armed with rifles at the top of the tower. They casually look at me and then look back to the large telescope, which I notice is pointed offshore, toward the *Seward*. Alcolado had told me that the Guarda Frontera is trained to be ever vigilant for invasions—after all, both Castro's rebels and the CIA-funded Bay of Pigs invaders assailed the coast in such a way, at different times.

Walking back into town, I see Larraldo and Ricardo sitting with several locals in a rough-hewn patio in front of a local house, surrounded by a low fence of chicken wire. Several reddish-brown chickens are pecking at the dirt. Then I realize that the patio doubles as a chicken pen. The men are drinking coconut water from the shell. I stop, thinking maybe they might want to talk a bit, but they virtually ignore me. Patronization, common to tourist-driven economies, seems not to be practiced. They continue speaking to one another in rapid Spanish; I catch enough to hear that "all gringos are crazy." At first, it startles me a bit. Then I think of the recent scene of grown men lying in a tidal pool to film turtles with a camera that costs more than the entire village makes in a year. If the roles were reversed, I might be thinking the same thing.

A few hundred yards away, associate producer Hervas is chatting up a maintenance man at the edge of the road. I walk up and listen. He is speaking in English, with a light Antillean lilt, a distant echo of his ancestry apparent in each softly delivered vowel. His name is Henry Jackson y Tatum, and his father sailed here from Grand Cayman as a little boy, the leader of the family that founded "Jacksonville." He has lived all his life in this village, he says, working as a fisherman until recent years. His skin is finely sun-etched, as if each voyage on the sea left its memory clearly imprinted on him. Now, Jackson makes a meager living by helping to maintain the turtle farm for a few pesos. We stroll in this December Caribbean afternoon to the weathered house where Jackson was born some sixty-seven years ago. Slowly, with a quiet dignity, he reaches for an unfiltered Cuban cigarette in his shirt pocket, pulling it from a pack next to his red plastic comb. English is his second language, he says, and he apologizes for it, but he speaks flawlessly. As a young man, Jackson fished for lobster, shark, and turtle. As he got older, he fished for snapper and grouper. Now, barely a dozen fishermen here in Cocodrilo are left, and they must spend a great deal of time at sea to catch anything at all. Most villagers gather timber from the thick forest to sell as building lumber or, more often, to turn into charcoal. They trade the charcoal with one another or sell it to passing fishermen, who use it to cook aboard their boats. They do what that can to survive, says Jackson, because they always have. Turtlers, during the heydays of Jackson's forebears, were among the most affluent and respected people in the Caribbean. If the equation that puts turtles in the sea has changed, so too has the prosperity of the culture inextricably woven into that same resource. Of all the original Jacksons, only he is left.

Hervas tells Lipscomb about Jackson, and Pomponi is quickly enlisted to walk down the middle of the dusty street with the old turtler. As they go, Lipscomb crouches in front of them with his camera on his shoulder, backing away as they move toward him. Camera assistant Jon Dodson, who usually works with Giddings's crew, has been assigned to walk slowly behind Lipscomb and, holding on to the belt of the producer, keep him from toppling over. It is a sight to behold here on this modest Cocodrilo street. Crazy gringos.

Overhead, the wind wafts through the palms, and the sun edges down close to the horizon. The film crew packs up to head back to the launch. I hang around, waiting until the last minute, when they are ready to cast off. A small group, maybe a dozen people, begins to assemble at the doorstep of the bodega with the Martí image stenciled on the side. The bodega, which has nothing to sell, is closed. Someone takes out a machete and slices the top off a green coconut and hands it to me. I finished my luke-warm canteen water long ago, and it is a welcome treat, cool, sweet, with shards of white coconut. On the stoop, an old man sits and plays a guitar and harmonica at the same time, and a couple on a nearby bench move their shoulders along to the rhythm, singing softly in Spanish. I am the stranger in their midst, come here from the big white American ship that is setting off in the water, but that seems not to bother anyone. When I leave, a few people wave goodbye, no big deal, just an adios to the gringo, like I might be returning in fifteen minutes or never.

It is Christmas Eve in Cocodrilo, Cuba.

Thursday, December 25

Ensenada de la Siguanea

I studied the nautical map of Isla de la Juventud more closely up on the bridge early this morning. As I did, I realized that if the island ever came to life as a sea creature, it would be mostly head—sort of like the coffin fish (*Chaunax pictus*) caught by our sub the other day. There would be just enough left over to make a tail, and that tail would be squeezed tight by the Caribbean into the shape of a tapering caudal fin. Wrapped inside the western lee of the caudal is the massive Ensenada de Siguanea, a vast lagoon with channel creases just deep enough for the draft of the *Seward*.

Lipscomb and Giddings have finally caved in to the pressure to take at least part of a day off for the holiday. We will make a sub dive at Punta Francés at 8 A.M. and then head deep into the mouth of the Ensenada to set anchor. Later in the day, everyone will have the chance to go ashore for the holiday.

As I clank down the stairs to the galley for breakfast, Ricardo is the first to wish me a Merry Christmas. It catches me a bit off kilter, since as a Communist and atheist he doesn't believe in Christ or Christmas, but I figure he is just being polite. I make a cup of espresso and join Ricardo at a table. I have been curious about a few things, and now is as a good time as any to ask him about them. Ricardo may not be a true believer when it comes to Christmas, but he fully believes in the potential of the Castro regime to help the country realize its destiny. In contrast to the Batista era, he says, medical care is now widely available for all Cubans; so is education. As a result, literacy has soared. I tell Ricardo I understand the theoretical aims of Castro, to empower his people by better education. But I find the conflict between increased literacy and censorship—including imprisonment for criticism of the regime—to be a gaping contradiction between theory and practical life. "This is important," says Ricardo. "Wait a minute, and we will talk." He then makes another espresso, pulls up a chair, and gives me a shorthand briefing on the revolution. "The media— as well as the church—were owned or controlled by the people Fidel was trying to overthrow, the people who supported Batista. They were all corrupt, all in his pocket. They had the money and the power, so why did they care if the people had none?" The reason Castro has outlasted so many American presidents is that he has come out of the Cuban people; he did not arrive from outside. "Because we have been compromised by foreign powers for so long—first Spain, then the U.S.—we had to erase all signs of foreign influence before we could even begin to understand what was the Cuban destiny." Activists planning sabotage were sentenced to death, but saboteurs are generally treated in such a manner, even in the United States, says Ricardo. That may be true, I argue, but they are sentenced after due process of law, and not by one person's sanction.

The buzzer announcing the imminent sub launch rings, putting an end to the discussion, and we file out to the stern. Giddings will ride up in the pilot sphere this morning, and it turns out that the dive will be mostly devoted to setting a buoy along the plunging wall at seventy feet. Tomorrow night, the underwater dive crew plans to return to that same spot to film the sub with its lights ablaze in the dark sea. From the stern, I can see a crashing surf line where the cape of Isla de la Juventud tapers into a point to the east. I point my binoculars toward the inside of the lagoon, where a tiny white splotch materializes into a series of buildings. No other built structures are visible anywhere within range; this must be The Colony, the old hotel originally built for the exclusive use of the wealthy Americans who once controlled Isla de la Juventud. It is said to be near the site of one of Columbus's landings in Cuba. Once built as a private investment by Fulgencio Batista, it even had its own abortion clinic for visiting Americans. During the peak of the Americanization of Cuba, ten flights a day from Miami landed on this island.

With the sub down and no scuba dives planned, I dither around half-heartedly in my work station, writing a short essay for the Web site. Alcolado brings by a computer-generated print of a graphic he has made of a Santa Claus. Santa is an assemblage of finely detailed circles and lines. In pen, Alcolado has written "To Bill" and "From Pedro." On the graphic, Santa is speaking in a cartoon quote bubble: "The most invaluable virtue of every person is respect and love to others." It is the highlight of my morning.

A Christmas dinner has been planned for 5 P.M. today. But with little to do underwater, the sub makes an early return, and I learn that the dinner has been moved up to 1:30 P.M. A huge bowl of eggnog made from scratch using a Lipscomb family recipe—embellished with several bottles of hard liquor—suddenly appears. It is a wondrously rich amalgam of cream and eggs and booze. The ambience magically changes. Tiny red-and-white felt stockings have been hung along the wall shared by the galley and the day room, each with the name of a crew member on it—even one for dive guide Larraldo, who is still aboard with us. Presents have been stacked under the tiny tree. Hervas and Straus seem to be behind this celebration, and the generosity of their spirits definitely lightens the mood of us all. Ichthyologist Robins, with his white beard and substantial gut, makes an appropriate giant elf; he appears in a Santa hat and begins to hand out presents. We all get little fishing lures, polo shirts with the HBOI logo, some candies, and gold-embossed Christmas cards. I give McCosker a copy of the David Quammen book *The Song of the Dodo,* and he gives me a little plastic case of hand-tied flies. Fagen is wearing a shirt covered with a print of colorful fish; on seeing the shirt, Larraldo remarks in Spanish: "Man must have a lot of cats in his house to get a shirt like that." We eat a huge dinner of turkey, ham, stuffed pork tenderloin, key lime pie, and apple pie. After dinner, Giddings stands to say how happy he is to be in Cuba, especially with our gracious Cuban hosts aboard. He reminds everyone that Fidel has "sent word he'd see us in Havana." The politics of individual expedition members lean heavily toward the live-and-let-live approach to life. While they may not agree with the opinions of El Jefe, most seem to admire his perseverance and survival skills—and as a result everyone seems to be looking forward to meeting him in person.

Fagen then gets up and reads a poem that he said he "found in the aft deck." He said it was entitled "Christmas at Sea":

We're anchored, I think, or perhaps we are docked.
It's Christmas at sea, and the whole gang is crocked.

The telly is silent, no gunshots, no crying.
No murder, no mayhem, no bodies left dying.

Edie has cooked us a jellies soufflé
And Tammy is out trawling Batabanó Bay.

John's flat on the deck; he's hugging a snapper.
Richard's dead drunk, down stuck in the crapper.

Grant's trying to draw Karen (he thinks she's a fish)
While Dick's tickling gobies awash in a dish.

The Cubans look on and quietly give thanks.
That the ship they are on has no CIA tanks.

"I've 12 million pixels," brags Al as he shows
The newest from Sony, "It bolts to my nose.
Resolution's just great, resolution to spare—
See every damn molecule, even in air."

The festivities move from the galley to stern, where the captain has arranged to run a launch to and from The Colony, every hour on the hour,
until 11 P.M. Most of the off-duty crew, except for Fagen, who actually
got sick from drinking the rich eggnog, and Terry, the dour chief engineer, load up on successive runs to go ashore. McCosker and I, joined by
Gilmore and Wimberg, climb into the Baby Whaler to see what we can
scare up in the way of bonefish in the mangrove flats a mile or so away
from the shore of the hotel. The ride in is exhilarating, wind blowing in
my face and the expansive, warm Cuban sky seeming to stretch overhead
forever. For me, there are few experiences more comforting than to be
in a small boat, headed for a line of mangroves on a remote island I've
never visited before, in the company of a few guys whose trust you can
count on.

We anchor and fly-fish for three hours, wading up to our waist in the
soft sand bottom, spread out from one another over the shore for nearly
a mile. Although I occasionally see large single fish swimming away just
under the surface, I get only a few hits and no strikes. McCosker, the best
fisherman of the bunch, catches a snapper and a small barracuda. But the
tally of fish doesn't matter. It is simply a glorious day to be immersed in the
ensenada, a wild place with a quiet so consuming that it seems to absorb
sound. Just the slightest hint of a breeze is wafting over it all, bringing
with it the newness of something exotic and unseen—burning tropical

wood scented like incense, the blossoms of wildflowers, dried salt, and sun-warmed mangroves.

Twilight approaches, and I slosh up onto the thin rim of sand beach just beyond the mangroves to make the half-mile walk back to the Baby Whaler a bit easier. As I do, I see that there is another shallow lagoon behind the beach line. I run across Gilmore, who said he tried to fish it but the bottom was thick with deep mud, and it was impossible to wade. As we walk to the skiff, we pass a sandy beach studded with shells—most prominent are the thin, turbanlike domes left behind when a sea urchin dies and sheds its spines. Several little yellowish birds known as palm warblers flit in the mangrove branches; fishermen here call them "sea canaries"—*canerreos*—and Gilmore and I wonder if the archipelago is named for them.

At the Baby Whaler, we board, haul anchor, and drive back to the ship, intending to get cleaned up for a later social visit to The Colony. By the time I am finally ready, it is after dark, and Gilmore and Wimberg have already ridden the shuttle in. McCosker and I are joined by the off-duty captain for our ride. The Whaler deposits us at the end of a long unlit dock, and we must carefully pick our way over it—stepping around piles of construction materials—to get ashore. Given the obstacle-course nature of the dock, I am figuring that we may lose a few crew members on the walk back. Above us, there is no moon, and the black night sky is so full of constellations that it seems to be more given to starlight than to darkness.

The patio restaurant of The Colony is open on two sides over a lavish floor of *mamól*, edged with a long bar counter. Unlike the bodegas of Cocodrilo, this bar is well stocked. A few Italian dive tourists are drinking here, but otherwise the room is given over to our expedition. A small Cuban band is playing bongos and string instruments and shaking castanets; Wimberg is doing a sort of spirited jitterbug with Pomponi, and Alcolado is dancing with a stunning Cuban woman with skin the color of *café con leche*. I order a Hatuey beer, which costs fifty cents American and is named for a fearless Guanahatabey chief long ago slain by the Spanish. Dehydrated from the fishing outing, I gulp it down, and the whole scene acquires a nice shimmer to its edges. Gilmore appears beside me. "Want to try a *mojito*?—it's the national drink." I say sure, and the bartender pours clear rum over a tumbler full of ice and adds a dash of sugar and crushed mint, one for each of us. I take a sip and realize that it is potent stuff; then I notice that most of the other crew have been drinking *mojitos* since they arrived four and five hours ago.

The band, back from a short break, launches into a salsa tune, and most of the assembled Americans and Cubans unaccountably form a conga line, a ragged, mindlessly happy group of filmmakers, scientists, ship's crew, and, at the very end, sub tech Jim Sullivan carrying a small brown mongrel dog. I, too, am somewhere in this line, swept along by the immediacy of the moment, performing an odd, arm-thrashing, leg-twitching two-step that ordinarily would make me feel like a buffoon, snaking around the edges of the bar, weaving through tables and atop overturned chairs. It is like a scene from the novel *Don't Stop the Carnival*. Colony employees are standing by in awe, perhaps never having seen Norteamericanos this convivial before; the Italian tourists watch wide eyed, as if some mutant American sitcom just erupted before them. After the conga line dissolves, a dazzling brown-skinned woman in a skin-tight black-and-white outfit of shorts and top—looking not unlike a soccer referee—appears and dances with several of the crew, her inspired gyrations soon becoming the center of attention. At one point, our cook is down on his knees, putting his hands together in front of the referee in a mock marriage proposal. She says in Spanish that it will cost him, and he asks if she takes credit cards (she doesn't).

I go to the *baño*, and when I return, Sharky Martin tells me that the cook had just tried to play harmonica with the band. I ask how he did. "Okay," says Martin, "except for two things: he didn't know the songs, and he was slobbering drunk." McCosker tells a joke about a man who, inexplicably, has eaten his pet parrot. The parrot eater is driving his car when he is pulled over by the police and given a breath test. At this point, McCosker blows heartily, and tiny puffs of Styrofoam fly from his mouth, looking—during this singular moment in time—like tiny parrot feathers. I catch the next shuttle back and, holding on to the center console,

watch in amazement as the *Seward*, now brightly lit, seems to float between ebony sky and sea, no defining line of horizon to keep it anchored
to the earth.

Saturday, December 27

Punta Francés

The topside crew was rousted early on Christmas Day to go ashore for
planned filming of the petroglyphs and graphs at the caves in Punta del
Este. Claro, who knows a bit about early Siboney history, was along to
narrate. Of all the biological science he has done during the expedition,
little will be shown in the documentary; instead, what will make it into
the final film is the footage of the ichthyologist describing the cave art.

The caves were first explored by Cuban anthropologist Fernando Ortiz
in 1922. Their walls hold some 238 separate drawings dating from around
800 A.D. At least one account describes them as a "Sistine Chapel" representing the cultural and spiritual mother lode of Indian life. Like the Maya
in Mesoamerica, the aborigines who lived here paid close attention to the
sun, the moon, and the seasons. On the day of the Spring Equinox, the
morning sun penetrates the exact center of the cave entrance, creating a
light beam that moves across a wall of concentric circles—an intimation
of nature's phallus honoring procreation and life.

Today, some filming has been planned for the lobster *acópios*, the aquatic
holding pens to which local fishermen bring their live catch. From there,
the spiny lobsters (*Panulirus argus*) are sent ashore to processing plants.
Fagen, who a few years ago wrote a magazine article about the lobster fishery in Cuba, says he has learned that the holding pens are almost empty—
and also that we have not been authorized to visit them. But we can spend
time with some local lobster fishermen he spotted on a scouting run yesterday. I load into a weathered local cabin cruiser we have chartered for
the day from The Colony. From the decals stuck to its windshield, I see
that it is used mostly by Italian and German sport divers. Our cruiser is
named—with no trace of irony—after Captain Jacques Cousteau's globe-
roaming ship, the *Calypso*.

Off we go, around the *punta* and across open sea to a place where a single large fishing boat and two tiny skiffs are working. Before the revolution, the plight of independent lobster fishermen was not a happy one, Fagen tells me. Using three-pronged spears, they harvested as many of the shellfish as they could for the then booming local tourist restaurant trade. But with piles of dead lobsters on their hands, spoilage was high and bargaining leverage low. Yet conditions were desperate, creating a short-term response to the dilemma. To make more money, the fishermen aggressively took even more lobsters, including females heavy with eggs and immature juveniles. Local populations of the spiny began to plummet, threatening to end the fishery entirely—especially here in the shallow Golfo de Batabanó, where 70 percent of all the spiny lobsters in Cuba are harvested. "When the Cuban economy was tied to the U.S., the fishing industry was of little importance," explains Fagen. "Fishermen were among the poorest and most neglected groups in Cuba."

American naturalist Barbour, writing in 1945, said the that "spiny rock lobsters," sold at five and ten cents apiece for years, were becoming scarce even during his time in Cuba. As a result, the genesis of lobster conservation biology was quietly launched in pre–World War II Cuba, with Dr. Isabel Pérez Farfante de Canet, a Cuban-born Guggenheim Fellow, studying the crustacean "with the intention of recommending legislation to determine when the season should be closed for the protection of the propagation of these species." Despite the biological realities revealed by such early work, conservation laws paled next to the massive influx of foreign investment—mainly by Americans earlier in the century.

Fagen tells me that Castro converted what was a "dead tail" lobster fishery run by independent fishermen—all who were at the mercy of buyers—to a series of some thirty-odd cooperatives. With support from the government, the cooperatives built icehouses and processing and quick-freeze plants. Fishing schools, like the one supporting the boys we met back in the Laberinto, were established. The basic design of the new boats was said to result from a series of meetings between Castro and some fishermen near Cayo Largo—hence the names of the standardized lobster boats as "Cayo Largos." Built of native woods, beamy and functional, the fifty-five-foot-long boats can carry as much as ten thousand pounds of ice, accommodate a crew up to ten, and stay out on the coastal banks for up to twenty days or more. The centerpiece of the boats is the live wells, which extend under a good portion of the top deck. A few feet of fresh water in the wells keeps the lobsters alive and kicking until they can be transported ashore to a co-op plant. In addition to jump-starting the prosperity of the lobster fishermen, the cooperative strategy transformed a sorely overharvested fishery into one that was sustainable. Even the technique for capturing lobsters, as we will soon see, changed to ensure that the crustaceans with the white, meaty tail would be taken alive. In this way, egg-bearing females as well as smaller, immature specimens would be returned to the sea. The cooperative for Golfo de Batabanó, with its fleet of two hundred Cayo Largos, is one of the largest in the country. As lobster landings elsewhere in the region declined, they stabilized and then increased in Cuba. Lobster products, now delivered fresh-frozen to Europe, are among the most valuable of Cuban exports. Those who harvest them earn several hundred pesos a month—plus what amounts to a bonus paid in American dollars, making them among the most prosperous of all Cubans. Ricardo, who is standing nearby on the stern of the *Calypso*, adds that the lobster fishermen earn more than he does. "But," he says in a bit of honesty uncharacteristic of a bureaucrat, "they work much harder." We near the Cayo Largo boat, which is anchored in the lee of a slender cape near Punta Francés. As we pull alongside, both Fagen and Larraldo holler greetings. The tanned, muscled lobster crew look at us curiously at first but then welcome us aboard. Overhead, the southeast winter wind has streaked the billowing cumulus, and here at sea level, the tropical ocean sloshes blue-green with a steady turbulence.

This Cayo Largo is the *Coloma*, named for a nearby port on the main island. We moor next to the *Coloma* and climb onto its deck, one at a time. The boat sports a thick wooden mast, a boom with a block and tackle to transfer boxes of live shellfish from smaller skiffs, and a canvas awning over the stern. Boxes of limes, manioc tubers, and plantains and a crate of charcoal are stored in the shade for cooking. Atop the pilothouse are boxy palletlike contraptions of chicken wire and thin, split logs. These are *jaulas*, cages. Scads of others like them have been placed on the fifteen-foot-deep sea bottom, providing the illusion of safe shelter, a dark place for the gregarious spiny lobsters to congregate. The practice is wondrous in its simplicity: the *jaulas* are dumped into the water, lobsters take up residency there over a period of several days, and then fishermen return to shake them loose. Unlike traps, no bait is required. Originally, the *jaulas* were buoyed to mark them. But a disturbing side effect of the new capitalism Cuba is trying in the wake of the Special Period is that hard currency has bred greed among some lobster fishermen. Trap robbing is common. As a result, buoys, which would give away trap locations, are no longer used.

One of the lobstermen offers me a cup of espresso, cooked up over a charcoal fire and served in a small ceramic cup. It is syrupy, sweetly pungent, with a welcome jolt of caffeine. I thank him and then ask how the cages can be found if they are not marked. The lobstermen know generally where the traps are, he says, by watching for nuances of shape in nearby mangroves. But more important, when a cage is first put overboard, a free diver goes into the water and clears a halo of sand around the *jaulas* by yanking out the seagrasses at the edge of the cages. From the surface, the halo can then be spotted if the fishermen know what to look for.

I walk with my espresso to the edge of the *Coloma* to watch as a small skiff prepares to harvest the contents of a *jaula*. The skiffs are tiny affairs with narrow sterns. The operation of them in tricky seas like this is an art to behold. From the bow, one fisherman alternately works two oars to move the boat atop a *jaula*, while the captain—an agile barefoot man wearing a straw hat—leans overboard. First, he sets a buoy-held seine with a tapered end around the *jaula*. Then, having lifted or jostled the cage with a long pole to scare out the lobster, he goes to work capturing the "bugs." Bracing his knees inside the narrow stern, he leans over with his head pressed against a glass-bottom bucket, which he holds in one hand. In the other, he uses another long-handled pole with a small net at one end—a *chapingorro*. Beneath him, some of the lobsters beat a hasty retreat into the end of the seine; the rest get snatched up by the *chapingorro* and pulled over the transom. Topside, the balancing act is quite spectacular— especially in that the oarsman must periodically put down his navigational tool to bail after a wave washes over the tiny boat. I watch all this in amazement, even as the small boat pulls up next to the gunwale of the *Coloma* and its wooden crate of lobsters is lifted aboard. Into the live well they go—except for the undersized or berried females, which are tossed back to the sea. Down in the live well, Giddings is lying amid hundreds of squirming lobsters with his mask pressed up against the viewfinder of his underwater Betacam housing, new arrivals being dumped on top of him as they are hoisted onto the *Coloma*. Along with the live lobsters, I also see a box fish—an odd rectangular little guy who looks like a papier-mâché version of a fish—along with a grouper and a flying gunnard, sitting quietly on its pectoral fins as his world thrashes around him.

There are two Cayo Largos working this area, and the captain says they will harvest twelve hundred kilos of lobster in one day. (Fagen figures that at current wholesale rates in Florida of four dollars a pound, this would be worth ten thousand dollars, American.)

I climb back aboard the *Calypso* to prepare for our extended, wave-rattling ride to the *Seward* across open seas. Lipscomb has joined us from the Whaler. Giddings is by now up out of the live well and seems in good spirits from his lobster encounter. Unaccountably, he tosses an expensive walkie-talkie through the air to Wimberg, who is aboard the *Calypso*. Giddings laughs in anticipation of his co-producer's response. Predictably, Lipscomb crosses his legs and puts his hands over his privates, as if the random act of carelessness has struck his very manhood. Wimberg smiles as if he's in on the joke, but then he turns to me. "Man, I wish he wouldn't do that. . . . If I dropped it, I'd be the one to get blamed." The producers offer the fishermen a hundred dollars for accommodating us for the afternoon, but the proud captain repeatedly refuses; finally, he accepts the money and gives us twenty large spiny lobsters in return.

Ricardo joins us, and I ask him what the lobstermen thought of having a camera crew on their boat, crawling about in their live well with the lobsters. He shakes his head. I know the answer. He looks over his shoulder, as if he is talking to someone else besides me.

"Crazy gringos."

10

Cabo Francés and

María la Gorda

Monday, December 29

Cabo Francés

By 9 P.M., Cuba has vanished, consumed in the black night—all gone except for a distant flicker of a lighthouse marking the exact place where the mainland has been squeezed into a point of treachery at Cabo Francés. Off the stern of the *Seward*, large red squid—perhaps two-pounders—have been darting about at the surface, invertebrate bodies constantly reforming themselves, as if free-associating not with thought but with form. I put on my wet suit and join McCosker, Giddings, and a few of the underwater crew in the Whaler for a night dive here.

In the heavily loaded boat are a Honda generator to power Giddings's underwater lights, three hundred feet of heavy insulated cable, and the two eighty-pound Betacams with their housings. Add eight people and their dive gear to this and you have an unstable craft with very little freeboard.

A new winter front has again cooled the air, corrugating the sea into small waves. As the Whaler prepares to push away from the *Seward*, an entire school of flying fish—giant pectorals spread like wings—pull from the water, glide fifty feet over the surface and then disappear almost soundlessly, as if they are being stitched in and out of invisible seams of the gloomy sea. The rebreather tech, along to schlepp gear, makes a gratuitous comment about how the colder night waters are perfect for an encounter with a great white shark. This particularly bothers me because I know he is right. After all, the Monstruo de Cojimar was—at twenty-one feet and seven thousand pounds—the largest great white ever caught in the world, and it was hauled ashore near Havana.

We have been here for two days now, delayed not by the weather but by Lipscomb's concerns that if we were to arrive in Havana by New Year's Eve the entire crew would go ashore and run amok. "Everyone liked the 'referee' and that was a lot of fun," Lipscomb had said, in reference to the Christmas night of debauchery at The Colony, "but we need to get some film in the can." Fagen writes in his journal: "Jim fears that our crew will get in trouble on New Year's Eve and queer Castro's visit." Underwater exploration that could have taken place off Havana can as easily be done here, Lipscomb reasons. But we need some science to perform. When McCosker suggests that the availability of deep water and a late-rising moon will allow us to hunt for the elusive and peculiar "flashlight fish" at scuba depths, Giddings seizes it as an occasion for a night film dive.

The map shows a sudden drop-off here, marked as La Furnia, where the shallow platform holding Cuba does odd things—first plunging steeply into nothingness, then sending up tall pinnacles to within fifty and sixty feet of the surface. I had asked Alcolado for a meaningful translation of *furnia,* and he says the closest it comes in English is "drop-off," although "abyss" might also work. Earlier today, I watched the wind pick up, tearing apart the high clouds like shredded Cuban flank steak, *la ropa veija* in the sky. Ashore, I could see the low coast restructure itself into a series of arid escarpments, announcing the arrival of the isolated westerly peninsula of Guanahacabibes, the place where the Taino known as the "Guanahatabeys" made their last stand.

And now here we are, preparing to penetrate the Taino's black sea. As we gear up on the bucking Whaler, McCosker tells me a bit about the fish we will be searching for—*Kryptophanaron alfredi*, the Latin genus name for "hidden lantern" and the species name for Alfred Mitchell, who originally collected a dead specimen off the coast of Jamaica. Our quarry, one of four known species of flashlight fish in the world, is the only one found in the Caribbean. "It has a set of bright bioluminescent organs under each eye— and when it needs to 'turn off the lights' to avoid predators, it retracts them by rotating the organ downward . . . like the way the headlights of a 914 Porsche retract." Adults, which max out at four inches, spend their days inside caves and crevices at depths of three hundred feet or more. At night, they emerge and can be found skittering along in water as shallow as ninety and a hundred feet—if you know where to look. Although the fish was first discovered from a dead specimen in Indonesia in 1781, little was known about it until later in the twentieth century. McCosker said he first stumbled over a related species during an expedition to collect the coelacanth at Grande Comore Island in the Indian Ocean. He returned to the California Academy of Sciences with several specimens, some preserved and some alive. Later, at the Steinhart Aquarium, he was able to observe the fish more closely in captivity. "It's a classic synergistic relationship between the fish and the millions of tiny bacteria that live in organs under each eye. The fish provides the bacteria with housing and nourishment, and the bacteria provide light." The luminescence is notable because— unlike many of the jellies and other inverts that use light only for one specific purpose—the flashlight fish alternatively uses its "headlights" to find and attract prey, communicate, and confuse predators. McCosker says that, despite the abundant life glowing in the night sea, it should be easy to find because it will be one of the brightest lights of them all. In context, several of the little fish together will look like "a rally of little Volkswagens on a dark country road."

Surely there is great novelty here. But McCosker says *Kryptophanaron* also has biomedical promise because competing bacteria aren't able to invade its light organs—indicating a very effective immune system that can ward off unwanted foreign attacks. And certainly, no species has ever been recovered live off Cuba. If we can collect several healthy specimens, we can even donate them to the National Aquarium in Havana in a great public display of international fish diplomacy.

McCosker and I drop overboard, at the point where the sonar shows pinnacles rising from a steep bottom, and begin our descent. We are both carrying lights; I also have a large glass specimen jar under my arm. The Whaler putters a few hundred feet away to where Giddings's crew will set up their bright HMI underwater lights near a shallow ledge at a depth of about sixty feet. The dive plan is for McCosker and me to free-fall in slow motion with our lights off until we sense we are close to one hundred feet, an act signaled by the constant clearing of pressure on our ears from the increased depths. At that point, we will search for the fish, and once we spot it, we will turn our lights back on. "It'll be blinded by the light," McCosker has promised. "You can literally pick it up and put it in the jar." We will then capture the fish and take it over to the impromptu underwater film set, where the klieglike illumination will turn the little unassuming fish into a documentary star. That was the plan, and it sounded reasonable at the time.

Down we go in the dark, bioluminescence flashing around us everywhere—blue light in tiny muted fire-fly blinks, in long exploding skyrocket trails, and, occasionally, in distinct outlines marking the silhouette of a large fish or sea turtle swimming past us. McCosker, a slow breather, only reveals himself to me by the exhalation of his scuba bubbles, each flush of air effervescing as miniature sapphire spheres. McCosker has assured me that the light of the fish will make my jar glow like a lantern, once we herd it inside, and the notion is both exciting and vaguely nostalgic. It reminds me of summer nights I spent as a child in lonely country fields collecting lightning bugs to turn other jars into lanterns. Between my eager anticipation, the sparkling luminescence, and the nitrogen in my system from the depth, I am no longer an impassive observer of the sea—I have become a living part of it, as inextricably woven into it as the school of flying fish.

The weight of the sea pushes more firmly on my body, and my exhaust actually sounds different, somehow tinnier, both signs that I am in deep.

Finally, I turn on my light to read the digital computer gauge on my wrist. The numbers that show depth are scrolling rapidly as I continue to drop: 100, 104, 108. I shine my light down and see that I have missed the edge of the cliff for which we were aiming. Below me, the beam of my little light seems pitifully meager as it disappears into the quarter-mile deep void of La Furnia, down into the everlasting veil of infinity.

This is definitely not a good thing. I splay out my fins to stop my descent and then raise my light to where I think McCosker ought to be, but he is not there. Slowly, weightlessly, I rotate 360 degrees in the water with my light and still I see nothing—no McCosker, no pinnacle, no bottom, and, sure as hell, no *Kryptophanaron*. A shard of logic in my brain tells me that McCosker may have descended on another side of a pinnacle earlier in the dive and that now, with the current, I likely have washed somewhere away from that rock, into deep open water. I remember my sub dive with Widder, recall her telling me that by night the primitive ancestors of life living much deeper in the sea—the mesopelagics—rise to the surface to feed. I wonder what else could be there among them, beyond the siphonophores and the ctenophores and the medusae, animals millions of years older than my own puny mammalian form. The warm fuzz of the nitrogen meets head-on with a strong surge of adrenaline, creating a sort of midroad psychic collision. A tiny voice informs me that I am somewhere off the coast of Cuba in the middle of the night and that I am likely as lost as I have ever been. It suddenly occurs to me that I am in dire need of a new plan. I hold on tightly to my glass jar, figuring that if I drop it, it will signal the end of my presumptive role as a cine-science explorer and reinsert me directly into the food chain.

I switch my light back off and rotate once again, this time looking for the scantiest sign of light from Giddings's HMIs. The incandescence from the plankton in the water is so rich that each time I exhale, my own exhaust sends an upwelling of tiny blue aureoles across my mask, obscuring my vision. Widder's magical cool blue light, seen so safely from the dry interior of the JSL a few days ago, has now swallowed me whole.

I turn once again, this time more slowly, trying to control my breathing so that I don't panic. I am at least a hundred feet beneath the sea. High above, the surface is choppy, and if I surfaced, I could be lost in the wave gullies and carried off by a current to God Knows Where. Merchant ships, which might offer some random downstream hope of surface rescue, are virtually absent because this, after all, is Cuba and political voodoo has kept the country poor and the wave troughs free of such vessels. I am left to fin through the ocean at fifteen fathoms, hoping ardently for some faint trace of dead reckoning to kick in.

At last, I see a glimmer of light slightly brighter and steadier than the natural blue flashes around me. I check my air and see that, even though my initial adrenaline rush sucked up more than usual, I have enough for another ten minutes if I ascend to sixty feet. Up I go, my eye on the distant light. At sixty feet, I level off and then start to swim carefully toward what I most earnestly hope is the film crew and the safety of the boat. After finning in that direction for five minutes, the light doesn't seem to be getting any closer. It dawns on me that maybe the moon has finally risen and what I am seeing is its reflection in the sea. I try to get my mind to focus on some real questions: Have I been actually swimming in the wrong direction, away from the boat? Is my dive buddy spiraling below me somewhere in the abyss? And what previously extinct apparition from some distant geological epoch is preparing to rise and feed? When you are lost and alone under the sea at night, your mind can imagine you as a gulp away from most any reality—up to and including any sea monster Odysseus may have encountered. An odd trinket of memory settles down on my consciousness, reminding me it was McCosker, after all, who cowrote a book on the great white shark. In it, he suggested that if the *Carcharodon megalodon*, a ferocious ancestor of today's great white, still existed today, it would likely be somewhere in the abyss of the ocean—in the same sanctuary where the "extinct" coelacanth was found living back in the 1930s. Fossilized seven-inch-long teeth of *Carcharondon* have been found, big enough to support a shark that stretched sixty to eighty feet from end to end—as long as a line of ten Volkswagens on a dark country road. It would be large enough to open its mouth and simply inhale me without missing a stroke. Were it not for the cobwebby comfort of the nitrogen buzz, the bold hope that I will actually find my way back safely might also vanish into infinity.

I promise to give myself another five minutes' worth of finning toward the distant light at depth, and if that source does not then prove to be real, I will at last surface and from there take my chances. On I go, with my light still off and the jar still clenched tightly under my arm. Although this is the tropical Caribbean Sea, it is December, and at this depth, it is cold. Despite my quarter-inch-thick wet suit, I am shaking, but I don't know if it's because of the chill or the grim realization of my condition. Just as I figure my final five minutes are about up, the light becomes markedly brighter.

Soon I find myself at the edge of an aura of HMI-induced sunshine. Several divers with the underwater film crew are moving slowly, dream-like, as if navigating through syrup. My heart pounds. My relief is clearly visible—I exhale into my regulator with a great sigh. I see Giddings fiddling with his camera, and I fin over to him. I feel like Odysseus just returned from some horrific mythological voyage. Giddings looks up and points to the jar, which I am still cradling under my arm. I realize my entire life-and-death quest is unknown to him, and he is simply asking where the flashlight fish is. I shrug—who knows?—and ascend to the decompression line trailing from under the Whaler. There I am elated to find McCosker, who apparently has been hanging on to the rope for some time now. We both blow off nitrogen on the line until our air is almost gone and then fin up twenty feet to the surface. I take off my fins and weight belt and tank, hoist myself over the side, and then help McCosker in. He had made two deep dives earlier today, and tonight's dive with its unplanned meanders may have pushed him to the edge of decompression sickness. He doesn't look well.

Finally, Giddings and crew are all aboard, and we are headed back to the *Seward*. As we climb up onto the larger ship, I see that McCosker is now pale and shaky. He sits on an overturned PVC bucket on the stern, and one of the crew brings him a small tank of pure oxygen, a treatment for the bends. After a few minutes, he begins to look better, although he still seems a shadow of his spirited self. One of our first rebreather dives is slated for an underwater film session with Pomponi and McCosker in the morning. Nearby, I hear the rebreather tech expressing alarm about tonight's incident, but the concern is not about McCosker. "The rebreather dive tomorrow won't be scrubbed—right? Right?"

Back in our room, getting ready for bed, I see that McCosker is looking much better. It was his fearless attitude about diving into the abyss with our lights off that helped convince me of the relative wisdom of such exploration.

Unable to sleep, I stretch out on my top bunk and read a reprint of an article McCosker wrote about flashlight fish in *Scientific American*. In it, he observes, the fish are very seldom seen—even by diving ichthyologists—for a good reason:

> The rarity of these fishes must be attributable to the habitat they
> presumably prefer, namely reefs that are below the depths where
> most scuba divers go and rocky areas that are relatively inaccessible
> to collection with nets.
>
> I might add on the basis of personal experience that for sane biologists
> deep diving in tropical seas on dark nights with one's diving light turned
> off is rarely-practiced and never enjoyed.

I roll over, switch off my reading light, and shut my eyes. The last thing I remember before falling sleep is an emotional shrug of expeditionary proportions: *Now he tells me.*

Wednesday, December 31

María la Gorda

The peninsula of Guanahacabibes arches out from our starboard this morning, magnificently flat and forked, the twin capes of Corrientes and San Antonio finally giving Guillén's lizard of stone and water its cleft tail. Inside the cleft is the Ensenada de Corrientes, a large protected bay. I am anticipating what is reported to be the best diving in all of Cuba—clear, sheltered water, healthy corals, and lots of marine life. The underwater terrain is so diverse that a sport-diving resort ashore at María la Gorda has identified fifty different dive sites, from plunging vertical walls to coral canyons, tunnels, and caves. We will launch the sub barely half a mile offshore, and it will track down the outside edge of the wall as it slopes into the dark void. Inside the wall, divers will have a chance to get a close look at the shallow labyrinth of coral arches and canyons that prosper in the shallower surface light.

Topside, the low and geologically young peninsula is a thin layer of limestone capped with sand and maritime shrub, rimmed with deserted slivers of beach. Inland, there are oceanic blue holes dotting the terrestrial landscape, classic, symmetrical faults in the topography where land has caved in to underlying caverns below. With labyrinthine veins of the caves now filled with seawater, these holes may be linked laterally to similar faults in the sea, as they are in the Bahamas. In fact, of all we have seen along the southern coast, this region looks most like the Bahamas. Claro tells me that a large chunk of the peninsula has been designated as a Biosphere Reserve since 1987—part of a worldwide program supported by UNESCO for areas exceedingly rich in biodiversity, with great conservation value. There are five other such reserves in Cuba. This 398-square-mile protected area, however, is also bounded on three sides by water; the lone terrestrial entry through a single gate can be more closely controlled.

Although Pinar del Río Province is only 180 miles from Havana, the overland road from the capital winds patiently through the province's spectacular hilly karst terrain, from which buttelike mogotes rise like abandoned temples. When it reaches the deserted, rock-strewn reserve, the path quickly turns coarse—what one visitor has described as "like driving on the moon." By spring, great legions of land crabs, *cangrejo de tierra*, will migrate across the isolated roadways here, answering some ancient genetic call to procreate. When I think of land crabs and Cuba, it is hard to forget the scene in Hemingway's *Islands in the Stream* in which expatriate artist Thomas Hudson used a .357 pistol to shoot a land crab between the eyes, simply because he could.

Between its biosphere designation, the ten-dollar entry fee, and its lack of accessibility, Guanahacabibes is considered the only place in Cuba where rare and endemic species of plants, including orchids, are safe— from both collection and destruction of habitat. Rimmed with dense woodland to the south and red mangroves to the north, this peninsula also supports 12 amphibian species, 29 reptiles, and 147 birds, including 9 of the 22 endemic to Cuba. There are also a number of the wildly colorful tree snails, speciated by the narrow biological range they inhabit, grouped into either the genus *Polymita*—the Cuban painted tree snail—or the genus *Liguus*, its own cone colorized and striped by the palette of its tiny geographic territory.

Of all the birds, perhaps the most distinctive is the 2.5-inch-long bee hummingbird, *zunzuncito*. The male is so variously colored that he is said to be the organic, winged actualization of the colors of the Cuban flag. Silva Lee reports that, centuries ago, the striking little bird ranged throughout the country. But it requires old forest growth with a dense network of lianas and branches saturated with orchids and bromeliads—habitat like that found only in the Zapata, Cuchillas del Tora, and here. It is a recurring theme, not just in Cuba but worldwide—fauna and flora being pushed into secluded little corners or ceasing to exist at all, as a result of the intrusion of humans. The magnificent four-hundred-pound giant land tortoises, like those that still live on islands in the Galápagos and the Indian Ocean, once thrived throughout Cuba, as they did on the peninsula of Florida until being hunted to annihilation. Certainly, extinctions occur naturally when the wick of a particular life form burns out. But the depletion rate caused by humankind is—by the most conservative estimate—one hundred times that of nature. The impact on islands is greater and more obvious because of their strict geographic limitations: beginning with the early arrival by humans here some seven thousand years ago, the Antilles have lost up to 90 percent of their land mammals. The later immigration by Europeans continued that trend: since 1500, from one-quarter to one-half of all extinctions of mammals worldwide have occurred in these islands. As Edward O. Wilson astutely points out in *The Diversity of Life*, unless reversed, the trend revealed in island biogeography will be repeated on a larger global scale, as clear-cutting, conversion of land to monoculture, urbanization, and road building continue to fragment forests and other natural lands on the continents.

The beginning of Guanahacabibes signals the end of our westerly journey along Cuba's southern shore. Except for plans to send down the sub at the deep mouth of the harbor in Havana after we round Cabo San Antonio, this peninsula is the final stretch of our high seas expedition, the de facto culmination of a month-long exploration. If Castro does visit us in Havana, his presence will surely provide drama of another sort—indeed, Havana itself will prove to hold its own cultural surprises. But Guanahacabibes is our last big chance for real oceanographic exploration. All aboard will be astounded—and shaken—by what we find here.

Since expectations here are running high for this site, a second dive boat has been charted from the resort at María la Gorda, *La Gaviota*, the seagull. Although not really needed here in the relatively shallow waters, the rebreathers will be used today, with Pomponi wearing one. McCosker, whose dislike for the rebreather tech intensified after his incident at La Furnia, now sees even less benefit in the clunky, high-tech gear.

With two boats, nearly everyone who wants to dive in the calm bay of Corrientes can do so today. Giddings hopes finally to find the large animals—the "charismatic megafauna"—that have charged the drama of undersea documentaries since Cousteau first began to make them. Claro has advised that there is a sunken wreck here but that sometimes currents cover it over with sand. He suggests looking for the anchor, as it is more likely to be exposed when the sand ebbs. A sport-diving guide notes the presence of a colonial wreck it describes as the "Ancla del Pirata"— pirate anchor—found in fifty feet, encrusted with corals and sponges, and I wonder if these two are the same ship.

It is a radiant morning, with a robust new Cuban sun cooled by a light land breeze, making the world seem fully lustrous and wild and inviting. We are close enough to shore that I can see the old metal lighthouse on a spit of white sand at Cabo Corrientes, shimmering itself and the land on which it sits into a mirage.

I rest my haunches on a gunwale near the stern of *La Gaviota*, leaning backward as we drive toward shore, spindrift spraying into my face. After my late-night blundering in the black confusion of La Furnia, it feels great to be alive, inhaling the fresh sea breeze, my skin warmed by the sunshine. I imagine the strongest fishermen of the ancient Taino paddling dugouts here on these same waters under the same tropical sun, a thousand years and more ago. It is not a stretch to think I am riding off the shore of a coastline that looked much the same as the one they saw from their own boats. If so, it is also similar to what Columbus first saw when he cruised the coast, describing the Indians and their seaworthy skills in his journal: "They have very many canoas like rowing fustes, some bigger and some smaller, and some are bigger than a fusta of 18 benches. . . . Some of these canoes I have seen with seventy and eighty men on board, each with his oar." Despite their strength, vigor, and "handsome stature," the early explorer reported that the Taino are also "wondrous timid." On being reassured that no harm would come to them, the native inhabitants showed a selfless grace the Europeans found hard to understand: "They are so artless and so free with all they possess, that no one would believe it without having seen it. Of anything they have, if you ask them for it, they never say no; rather they invited the person to share it, and show as much love as if they were giving their hearts." Until he put a halt to it, Columbus's men traded broken crockery and glass for gold and bales of spun cotton.

Soon we are anchored, and each of us is overboard, on the descent into the Ensenada de Corrientes. I am again partnered with Straus. She has been a tough read—handsome and bright, quiet and reserved. I first took her to be aloof, but I now realize there is something more complicated going on, and I am simply not astute enough to figure it out. Certainly, I have come to admire her resolve. She has proved to be one of the best dive partners I could have hoped for—staying close when the viz is bad or the conditions unknown, or splitting up as veteran divers often do to explore on our own when, on days like today, conditions are optimum. We sink together into clear shallow water, the bright sun overhead stronger than I have ever seen it from depth and I more fully relaxed than I have been on any dive here. Within minutes, Straus gives me the "okay" sign and then ducks behind a massive stand of pillar coral with her camera. I go my own way, head poked down, examining the macroworld embedded in the minutiae of a single square meter: the shrubbery of the bryozoans waving in the light current, the balletic slow-motion dance of the calcareous tube worms, and the encrusting sponge, working its way over a slab of brain coral, traveling a fraction of an inch in a month. When I look up, Straus has disappeared, and I won't see her again until near the end of the dive. Around me, there is healthy coral everywhere, little of it affected by the fungal-like malaise of anthropogenic diseases (like white- and black-band) that are increasingly killing reefs in the heavily populated

Florida Keys. It is a simple equation: where there are fewer people living ashore—upstream from the ocean—there are fewer problems with corals in that same ocean.

And can there be anything more magnificent on earth than a healthy coral reef! As naturalist Silva Lee observes: "The outer limit of the personally visible and tangible Cuba is marked by a collar of almost pure coral; about four dozen species live here, most of them colonial. Day after day, the polyps of each of these colonies deposit a thin layer of mineral, which by the end of the year translates into an increment of an inch or so. . . . A result is an annular metropolis of overwhelming architectural complexity, one that provides a foothold and haven to thousands of other creatures, and which marvels, every single time, those who have taken the minor daring step of putting on their backs a tank of compressed air."

Today I also have time to examine more fully a phenomenon I had seen earlier, one I thought was random and isolated when it occurred in other parts of the coast. Two scarps are found here, the first beginning in 35 to 50 feet of water, and the second—separated by a plateau of coral and sand—plunging down sharply in 85 to 120 feet. I realize that they are not random but rather more representative of how the edges of the island are configured underwater.

Later, I will learn that Silva Lee has not only identified these scarps but has also explained the geomorphology of these ancient submerged coastlines: "The regularity of these two scarps is astounding. . . . Fishermen call these declivities *veriles*. . . . [They] represent the levels where the ocean stopped its ascent or descent long enough to carve these two cliffs" from the prehistoric edges of an exposed shore. But Lee points out that there is also a third scarp, far beyond my own diving level: "Some 200 to 300 feet under the waves there is still another veril, this one corresponding with the sea level some 17,000 years ago, when the last great glaciation stole about four percent of the oceans' waters." It is not surprising that fishermen would come to understand the ecological utility of such places, as radical changes in underwater topography—represented by the veriles—provide the same bioabundance as the confluence of rivers and streams in the terrestrial world. Where there are verils, there are likely to be more fish, for they are living aquariums, walls of thriving marine life, visited by yet more marine life, swimming, darting, crunching, feeding.

Underwater, I fin out across the flat sand pasture and then watch a bluff of living reef as it rises up and away from me like a wave of calcium, creating a series of porticoes that open to the deep blue water beyond. I swim down to a small canyon of coral at sixty feet that leads to one portal. I think of Cousteau's visit to Cuba and of his own description of the coral reef system: "The reef . . . was an intaglio structure with porches of coral, winding colours, and countless narrow cracks aswarm with beings waiting in the wings like walk-on players at the opera." As I go, I fin past giant boulders of brain coral, punctuated with steeples of pillar and steps of star coral, an astonishing miasma of subdued color and form. Every last bit of the surface is wiggling with something alive—feather duster worms, reclusive bug-eyed blennies, territorial hamlets and damsels. A few feet above the corals, a pair of giant barracudas—five feet each—hover, chomping seawater with their stilettolike teeth. Although I was headed for the portal and the deep sea beyond, I am slowed down now, breathing deliberately in time to the slow pant of the nearby barracudas, becoming more fully in this moment. Looking around, I see the spiny antennae of a lobster waving out from inside a dark crevice, something I would have missed if I had been moving too fast. I fin over to it, reach down, and touch the brittle tips of its antennae. As I do, it seems to spar with me, twitching them across my bare fingers, rough at first and then, finding no aggression on my part, more gently. They are horny, rough like raw, unspliced wire.

I look up in time to see an octopus dragging itself along the bottom, carrying its head. I move toward it, and as I do, it changes color almost instantly, moves up off the bottom, inks to obscure itself, and darts away as if it is fired by tiny jet engines. This octopus is an enormously intelligent animal, one that, if it had a backbone, would have likely ruled all of the sea, and perhaps even beyond. Naturalist Gilbert Klingel, once shipwrecked on Inagua Island just north of Cuba in the early twentieth century, also wrote in *Inagua: An Island Sojourn* of his own fascination with the octopus and its evolution over millions of years in the ocean: "They were [at first] like man, puny and fleshy, without protection, and had to develop intelligence to survive. . . . Alone among the mollusks they have acquired by concentration of their chief nerve ganglia what may be truly considered a brain. With the casting aside of their shell, they have also gained their freedom, speed and mobility." Wistfully, Klingel wrote: "I feel about octopuses—as Mark Twain did about the devil—that someone should undertake their rehabilitation."

This is by far the best that the 1,128 miles of coral reef along the southern coast have offered up so far. Up I finally go through an archway and beyond the sea fans, whips, and rods lining it, out to the deep slope. Suddenly, the warm color of the reef is gone, replaced by an endless blue, dropping beneath me for thousands of feet. I hover over it, feeling as if I am at the edge of eternity, and that eternity is tinted a perpetual, shimmering cobalt. Oddly, it seems to pull at me, wishing me to go down, down, down with it until I become consumed by its own energy and can no longer return to my own world. I have stared into the abyss, Nietzsche once wrote, and the abyss stared back. That used to sound very glib and remote and metaphoric. But now, I finally have a visceral taste of what he meant.

I hang here until my tank is nearly empty and then find my way back to *La Gaviota*. When I climb aboard, Giddings and his crew are already here. Despite the lack of megafauna or pirate anchors, the Alpha filmmaker is effusive. "I've just made the best dive I've ever made in the entire Caribbean!" he says, and he is so convincing that not only do I believe him, but I feel the same way.

Back on the *Seward*, I shower and put on a worn pair of old jeans and a T-shirt. In my rabbit warren, I work on an essay about today's events, download some digital photos from my still camera to the laptop, and then field some E-mails forwarded by Discovery. One is particularly disturbing:

Dear Dr. Gilmore:

I wish you and all the crew a Merry Christmas. I would one day like to dive the waters of my native land. I am a diver and I have been diving in the Florida Keys and the Bahamas for many years. It is beautiful there, and often, lately, I wonder how great diving the reefs in Cuba might be, especially the abundance of food and game fish (since Cubans don't have pleasure boats).

I cannot help to think though, that as you dive the depths off the coast, does the sub pass perhaps by the wrecks of sunk would-be escapees from the island, like the tug boat "13 De Marzo" sunk by the Cuban coast guard, its crew (mothers and children on board) still lying in the silence of their underwater grave? Your expedition of course is extraneous to what happens on the beautiful Island paradise, but as I browse through this inviting and exiting web page it is to me like something out of a Sci-Fi short story about some alien world where unsuspecting astronauts study the land while inhabitants enter daily rituals of slaughter but they pass oblivious to it all.

Tony

I track down Gilmore, show the E-mail to him, and ask if he would respond. He hesitates for a moment, says yea, this really needs a reply, and then goes to the galley for a cup of coffee. Returning, he sits down at the laptop and writes:

Dear Tony,

I appreciate your interest in our expedition around your home country. I grew up in Florida and with many close Cuban friends. Two of my closest colleagues in the U.S. left Cuba in 1960–61. I also have close colleagues in Cuba today. One is on this ship now. They, like all my Cuban friends, are warm, generous, industrious and intelligent humans. There is music and charm in the blood and the smile. I love Cuba and Cubans just as you do. As a concerned scientist I can only support collaboration and understanding in a search for truth. Whether it is in Florida or Cuba we need to bring that truth to the surface. Then I believe understanding and collaboration will prevail.

Cuba is without question a biological paradise and has not received any of the rampant coastal development and pollution that you see elsewhere in the Caribbean and in Florida. We are bringing to the surface many new records for the Cuban fish fauna. Our studies demonstrate that there is a great connection between Cuba and Florida through shared faunas. Much of this is due to prevailing ocean currents which take larvae from Cuba to Florida. Undoubtedly the viability of the Florida lobster fishery is due to the vitality of the Cuban lobster population. They regulate their lobster fishery much better here than in Florida.

I know you will have the opportunity to dive the beautiful waters of Cuba one day. You will see a marine world that far surpasses the Florida keys. You will also see that Cuba still consists of the wonderful people I know so well in the states.

Sincerely, R. Grant Gilmore, Ph.D.

Gilmore's answer is earnest and complex. But a similar issue—regarding Castro's upcoming visit in Havana and how it should be handled—is faring less well in on-board discussions between Giddings and Lipscomb. In his journal, Fagen summarizes the conflict: "Taima [Hervas] had cornered me asking 'Why should we put Fidel in the film at all? He's killed thousands (quoting Jim).' I patiently explained: 1. Because every aspect of what we've seen on the coast bears the stamp of the Revolution, and Fidel is key to the Revolution; and, 2. Because we will see him in Havana and he is a part—a key part—of that landscape. I told her I had trouble discussing that question in the abstract. It depends on the quality of footage you get. Look at it first. Then, you can decide how to use—or abuse him. But don't write it off categorically without even *thinking* about it."

Later, I ask Giddings how he perceives Castro, and he tells me: "I've known him for about eighteen years. I've been to Cuba about five, six times. Each time, he's hosted me and helped me with different projects. . . . He's an avid diver, a wonderful conservationist, and our common ground has never been political, it's been ocean ethics and aquaculture and those sorts of things. If it wasn't for Fidel, we wouldn't be here." I ask Lipscomb the same question, and he shrugs off Giddings's convictions: "Al sees Castro as a good guy because he's his 'friend.' The man's a killer, but Al doesn't acknowledge that. Al sees what he wants to see."

But there is more than just reactionary politics at work here in regard to simplifying issues, and it is creating an omission commonplace enough to be regarded as a trend. As Fagen observes: "Although Jim's [other] documentaries suggest he is good on the 'people' side, very little effort has been made to get to shore and capture the coastal fishing side of the story. . . . The rebreathers are a case in point: instead of being used as tools, they are being treated as supporting stars of the show. And of course, the submarine is star par excellence." Later, in an impromptu shipboard meeting,

Fagen suggests we try to track down Juan Alvarez when in Havana—as Alvarez is an older Cuban who dove for coins before the revolution, taught Castro to scuba dive, and generally personifies the rich maritime culture of the Cuban people. But the trend of omission again reemerges—and I finally realize it is a paradigm shaped not by Lipscomb, who is indeed a talented storyteller, but by the demographics of corporate broadcasting. It is a mind-set that began to take hold during the bizarre shipboard visit by the Discovery Channel producer, weeks ago. Cuba, if seen as a "Marine Marvel," will not be the political hot potato that Cuba, the "Forbidden Waters," would be. Within that cartoonish approach to reality, the only way to produce a film on Cuba is to do it without Cubans. Or as Fagen writes: "It soon became clear that 'folkloric' Juan could not easily be fit into the quasi-MTV format that the boys are thinking about."

The JSL has just broken the surface and is lifted up and over the stern of the *Seward* by the **A**-frame crane. There seems to be a routine collection of sponges and sea squirts in the rotary plankton collector under the pilot sphere—but there is something else here, too, something that seems startlingly out of place. It is a second stage of a scuba regulator, white with encrusting marine growth. Sub pilot Liberatore said they came across two complete sets of dive gear as they were working their way back up the deep slope, the first at eight hundred feet and the second at six hundred feet. Both sets included tanks, buoyancy compensator vests, and regulators. As Liberatore attempted to recover one set with a claw arm, the regulator hose snapped off from the heavier assembly. It is that regulator that sits on the wet stern of the ship today, crew now gathered around it, puzzled by its presence but clearly expecting the worst. Back in the dry science lab on the ship, the videotape shot by the sub on that dive is closely reviewed. As I watch, it reveals both sets of dive gear lying two hundred feet apart on the slope, no signs of a diver anywhere. Although I have often stumbled over fins, weights, and even dive masks before, it is strange to find entire rigs like this.

Back at my workspace, I review some of the reference books I have brought along on Cuba. In one, a *Cruising Guide to Cuba*, author Simon Charles reports that there is a large bronze monument at the dive resort at María la Gorda. The marker honors "Ludo," who was a young dive master and the son of the French operator of the resort. Ludo, accompanied by a buddy, attempted to set a record for diving on compressed air some four years ago. The attempt was made at the edge of this deep slope. Ludo was wearing one set of gear and carrying another, planning to switch at depth when air in the tanks of the first was exhausted, so as not to bother reconfiguring the snaps and belts of the entire rig by transferring tanks. I tell Lipscomb about this news, and Ricardo calls the dive resort on the phone to confirm it. A boat is dispatched and makes ready to go ashore to the resort. Lipscomb invites me to go, but I decline. Given the high drama of the story, I know it's an activity that will surely make it into the final cut of the documentary—Solemn American Divers Visiting Memorial of Dead Counterpart. But the whole business is just too morbid for me.

My concern is compounded by the fact that I have trouble understanding the motives of those who risk their lives for the sheer thrill of it. It is the difference between expeditionary discovery, even adventure travel—which yields information to the person and perhaps the world at large about the nuances of the journey—and an "extreme" sport, which does little except to challenge and satisfy the personal obsession of the participant. I think of philosopher Joseph Campbell's concept of the heroic traveler as one who risks his or her life to journey to a rare place—but who then brings back something of that experience to share with the world. However stilted or restricted this final documentary may be by its ultimate corporate demands, it is far more than a cheap thrill. Indeed, the members of this expedition—including the filmmakers—have surely worked very hard to bring something of value back. Clearly, they fulfill Campbell's definition of heroic travelers.

When the boat returns a few hours later, a thirty-something French national is along with them. His name is Nelson, and he was the dive buddy of Ludo, the buddy who survived the aborted record-setting attempt at deep diving. I stand next to him in the dry lab as he reviews the underwater video taken by the JSL of the discarded scuba gear at depth. As the first set of tanks appears on the screen, Nelson exhales sharply from his lungs and puts a hand over his mouth. Those are the tanks Ludo was wearing, Nelson says in Spanish. And then: "We were there together at three hundred feet, and when I turned around, he was sinking far below me."

Most deep diving is accomplished by a complicated mixture of gases, usually helium and oxygen, the chemistry of which compensates for the rigorous physiological demands of breathing at extreme depths. Compressed air—like that which fills most sport-diving tanks—is seldom used. Narcosis is much harder to control; and oxygen toxicity may often occur, leading to a condition that causes sudden blackouts and death. Ludo's body was never recovered, and the implication was that he was blacked out and was literally consumed by the depth—or more literally, by the marine life that lives in it. Despite the foolhardiness of what Ludo and Nelson tried to accomplish, I feel bad now just watching the survivor of this dive, here on this strange American ship, finally learning what had happened to his long-departed friend. There ought to be some satisfaction in piecing together the puzzle of the abandoned tanks, but I take little solace in it.

Later, in postproduction back in the States, the sub's footage of the tanks, the visit to the bronze memorial at the resort at María la Gorda, and the somber voice-over narration will eat up a big piece of documentary. At last, not only will the abyss have the chance to stare back, but it will be able to do so on national TV. As a result, the depths of Cuba can now be safely labeled as "forbidden," rendered so by the act of being excised from the arena of political reality—and placed into the realm of melodrama and human mortality.

11

La Habana and

Anticipation

Thursday, January 1

La Habana

New Year's Eve was spent rounding the horn of Cabo San Antonio in the dead of night, sneaking out of the lee where we have spent most of the last month and, with our 204-foot-long oceanographic ship, breaching the wide open sea. Since we were navigating the narrowest point between the mainland of Cuba and Mexico's Yucatán Peninsula, we were also smack in middle of a channel where much of the water flowing north from the vast Caribbean gets squeezed into a narrow conduit. Factor in some converging countercurrents and a dose of southeast wind, and waves were piling up in eight- to twelve-foot-high ridges, pounding the hull of the ship democratically on all sides. No wonder the Spanish annotation on the nautical map here at the cape shows "Perpetua Rpte"— Always Breaking.

This strong north-flowing current confluxes with another that swells up and out of the Gulf of Mexico, together creating the five-knot-per-hour Gulf Stream, a warm and powerful "river" that flows through the sea, transforming all it touches. Although the Taino surely knew of it, Ponce de León was the first European to "discover" the Gulf Stream on his first voyage. He found that it was not just another temporal, regional current but one that had the capacity to carry treasure-toting vessels out of Havana, across the Florida Straits, and north toward South Carolina, finally spitting them out into the east and back toward the Old World. The Gulf Stream became the Carrera de las Indias, the Life Line of the Indies, the northern maritime route from Havana to Spain. Hammered by the rough seas, I tossed in my bunk and, sleepless, tried to imagine the early Spanish riding this same current into Havana on their wooden sailing ships, assembling here with their plunder—ingots of gold and silver, as well as indigo, tropical hardwoods, and casks of tobacco—from Central and South America, before rigging their sails for their final journey home across the Atlantic.

Like other remarkable natural forces, this Carrera de las Indias has gripped the imagination of many, even long after its glory as a maritime treasure route dimmed. It was where Hemingway went to fish for marlin and swordfish on his *Pilar* from the little fishing village of Cojimar east of Havana. In Ernesto's literary world, the Gulf Stream became a serial character, reappearing in many of his own stories, novels, and articles, including those he contributed to American fishing magazines to make a few bucks. In his novel *To Have and Have Not*, Hemingway fictionalized his experience of approaching the current from near Havana: "By then we had passed the smacks with their fish cars anchored in front of the Cabanas and the skiffs anchored fishing for mutton fish on the rock bottom by the Morro [Castle], and I headed her out where the gulf made a dark line. . . . The stream was in almost to soundings and as we came toward the edge you could see her running nearly purple with regular whirlpools."

This morning, I awake to gray skies, great blue-green waves crashing against portholes, decks heaving fiercely, chairs and computers overturning, unsecured sponge and fish specimens and cameras indiscriminately tossed to the floor by the raging sea. Morning becomes mostly a function of trying not to fall into things. I attempt to write, my laptop still safely Velcroed to the counter, but twice, heavy lists knock me off my stool, and finally I give it up. At one point, I open the door to the stern, where a monstrous wave has just hit, knocking the rubber Tuffy cans of scuba gear over and scattering BCs and regulators and fins on the deck. I run out quickly, gather up as much as possible, and stuff it back into the containers. By the time I nearly have the lids all roped back together, another, less powerful breaker washes over the bulwarks, soaking me and knocking me off balance. Not worth it, I figure, and I lurch through the sloshing water still undrained by the scuppers, making it back to the safety of the cabin over the heaving deck. Sometime later, a mammoth wave will envelope the entire stern, nearly snapping the sturdy iron downrigger in two with the force of its weight. I am grateful I was not out gathering gear when that one hit.

I go up on the bridge with a set of binoculars to survey the shore. For most of the morning, we have been running parallel to the northwesterly coast of Cuba, just off the islands of the Archipiélago de los Colorados. Farther inland, two mountain ranges crest the horizon for most of this distance, first the Sierra de los Oacuterganos and then the Sierra del Rosario. Both ranges rise into a mist of spindrift and smoke from land fires until they disappear entirely into a low cloud cover, distant images that could be faded background scenery in a stage play. Rosario is another UNESCO Biosphere Reserve, a midelevation montane forest that had been historically worked over by logging since the earliest colonial days. A reforestation program has been under way for years, and now there is enough natural woodland in the 96-square-mile preserve to support six hundred endemic plants, providing habitat for Cuban trogans, nightingales, parrots, and the national bird, the *tocororo*. Somewhere here is the smallest frog in the world, *Sminthilus limbatus*.

We pass *cayos* mapped as Buenavista, Rapado Grande, and Levisa. Like those on the southern coast, these *cayos* represent ancient ridges of coral or colonies of mangroves, many large enough to support sugar white beaches. Only Levisa seems inhabited, with a dive resort to take advantage of the nearby reefs. Beyond Levisa, a *cayo* named Paraíso was a favorite of Hemingway's. In 1989, the government placed a monument there in commemoration of Papa's affection for it. It reads:

"From the beginning of the 1940's, this place was the refuge of the great North American author Ernest Hemingway, who visited it assiduously, sometimes remaining on the cay for up to 20 days at a time. Here, he wrote, rested, roamed the beach, swam and loved it so much he used it as a base for submarine operations from his yacht the Pilar during the Second World War."

Indeed, in *Islands in the Stream*, Hemingway described Cayo Paraíso: "There was a long white beach with coconut palms behind it. The reef lay across the entrance to the harbor and the heavy east wind made the sea break on it so that the entrance was easy to see once you had opened it up. There was no one on the beach and the sand was so white that it hurt his eyes to look at it."

By its description, Cayo Paraíso could have been hundreds of other untamed islands we have passed on the coast—I think of my own afternoon fishing on Cayo Rosario and how strongly it has been imprinted on my mind. Cayo Paraíso was made iconic by its celebrity, an odd characteristic distinguishing it from all others by words written by a famous dead North American writer.

By noon, we have passed Mariel, the port known for its notorious boatlift in 1980, and the upscale Marina Hemingway with its fancy Club Nautico Internacional Hemingway, a squeaky-clean, sterile place that is the antithesis of all that the rough-and-tumble outdoorsman represented. The new skyscrapers of western Havana's Vedado district first appear as sharp geometric angles on the soft horizon, and as we move in closer, they give way to Habana Vieja, the old colonial city with its waterfront boulevard and bulkhead, the Malecón.

I leave the bridge for an espresso, and when I return, I find Alcolado, Ricardo, and sub pilot Santos there, standing next to Captain Seiler at the wheel. Ricardo calls the port authority on the ship's radio and asks for a harbor pilot to come out to lead us in, as Diogenes did back at our first landing in Santiago.

Alcolado is plainly excited. "We are seeing Havana! You should be on the phone [intercom] telling everyone we are seeing Havana." This is an unusual burst from the mild-mannered Alcolado, who throughout the entire expedition has made virtually no demands on his American hosts. Captain Seiler suggests that Alcolado himself use the phone to broadcast the visual alert, and Alcolado gratefully complies. His voice rings throughout the ship, barely able to contain his enthusiasm. "Havana is in sight. Havana is in sight!" Then Alcolado turns to me and points off in the distance. "That is my neighborhood," he says, proudly. Pedro Alcolado, one of the most renowned invertebrate specialists in all the Caribbean, is as happy as a boy to be coming home.

Finally, the turreted fortress of Castillo de los Tres Reyes del Morro looms, marking the entrance to the natural harbor of the city, and we enter through its deep and narrow mouth. Once we are inside, the seas turn calm. With its jet thrusters, the *Seward* agilely edges up next to the Avenida del Puerto, an extension of the bulkheaded Malecón, just inside the protective watch of the old fort, which seems to be a twin of the weathered stone edifice we first passed back at the harbor mouth at Santiago. As we snuggle in to the bulkhead, I see that the ship's deck is nearly level with the Malecón. When we are fully tied off, a small gangplank is set down between the *Seward* and the sidewalk. After a month at sea, the idea of walking right across the Malecón and into a five-hundred-year-old city, with its outdoor bistros and its narrow colonial streets and its rare time-stuck panache, is so palatable I can almost taste it. A shark-finned American car from the 1950s clatters by, then another—vehicles imported before the U.S. trade embargo was launched in 1961, not unlike cars I rode in as a little boy. These *cacharros* are held together by body putty and baling wire and Cuban ingenuity. The juxtaposition of the forty-year-old American autos, our space-age ship, and a city first founded by conquistadores in 1519 is mystifying. I think of a line from Cuban novelist Alejo Carpentier: "The furniture was growing taller." It is as if someone hit the "pause" button on reality; nothing seems preposterous anymore.

Before we go ashore, Fagen gives us a quick briefing on what we can expect here, handing out little photocopies of maps of the old city, so we won't get lost. We are reminded not to get into trouble in Havana, because we don't want any bad publicity. Despite how odd our ship must look next to the colonial waterfront, we have attracted little attention and certainly no media. It is too late to expect a visit from El Jefe today, so we can leave the *Steward* and fully immerse ourselves in Havana without having to worry about anything else but the experience of the moment. It is by now late afternoon, and the low tropical sun is casting a soft, golden light on the old buildings. Habana Viejo seems luminous, almost as if it is glowing from all the energy that has passed through it over the centuries.

Most of the crew crosses the gangplank and, after poking a bit at the edges of the old city, reassembles in a houseboatlike bar about three hundred yards away from where the *Seward* is berthed on the Malecón. McCosker, Dick Robins, Grant Gilmore, and I head deeper into Habana Vieja. It is like walking inside an old stereograph. Encircled by walls until the 1860s, this district known as the Old City has languished, while the nearby district of Vedado has been modernized, its original structures demolished and replaced with skyscrapers. But it is expensive to reshape the skyline, and renewal—or restoration—clearly gets less attention than education, medical care, and rural development in Cuba. With little money available for such architectural reconstruction, Old Havana has remained largely as it was built, without suffering the Disneyfication of, say, San Juan, Puerto Rico, or the skyscraping blight of Caracas and Mexico City. There are some eight hundred buildings in this district, many dating from the 1500s; together, they represent a UNESCO World Heritage site. Old Havana is shabby and peeling, as many left-brained, traditional travel writers have noted. The right wing pundit P. J. O'Rourke once described it as "1960 Cleveland after a 37-year-strike by painters and cleaning ladies." But this Havana is also authentic and visually lush. Certainly, it is the largest and most integral colonial city I have seen anywhere in the Western Hemisphere, a place that still has its original sense of scale. Noted architect and designer Andres Duany calls it "the last great Latin American City," one with its architectural integrity and Latin soul still intact. With little street crime, I feel safe here, much safer than I have ever felt in Kingston or Port au Prince, Haiti—or parts of Miami, for that matter.

Around us, elegant old mansions with their intricate stonework and iron filigree have been turned into tenements, often one family to a room; laundry flaps from upper-story windows like banners. Balconies and turrets and towers rise, fold in, and meld together. The street itself has become a giant front porch, where everyone gathers to talk, play hopscotch or dominoes, or tinker under the hood of the vintage American cars. We walk down a series of narrow streets, once designed for horse-drawn carriages, and emerge in a large square, the Plaza de Armas, the city's oldest. I am immersed inside a work of art—Doric columns and cornices, balustrades and archways with most anything you can imagine jumping out at you in bas-relief—little seraphims and gargoyles and what seem to be sea serpents.

I look closely at the building blocks and see that many of them reflect the imprint of long-dead corals. Like the Morro Castle, the oldest buildings here seem to have been mined from the sea itself. A million years or more ago, the materials forming these buildings were organic, glowing with color, just like the living reefs and walls we have seen during our underwater explorations. The delicate lacework of metal over windows and on doors reminds me of the texture of the sea fans, finely woven strips of iron imitating the embroidered fibers of calcium. If this island is from the sea, so too is its architecture, its rhythms, even the disposition of its people and their internal landscapes. As José Lezama Lima wrote in *Paradiso*: "For him, every awakening was a discovery of the infinite expansion of each one of the starfish's radiations. . . . On each of its plates, a fish appeared, its face enlarged and corroded by the beginning of sleep." And so it is with this city, a vision radiating out from an ancient dream.

Street vendors are selling all manner of goods, many of them handmade from natural products—castanets from gourds, carved wooden boxes, bamboo gewgaws, cowrie shells incised with the iconic images of Che and José Martí and Fidel. I buy a marvelously stylistic swordfish of papier-mâché, a happy ten-inch-long fish with a blue-trimmed dorsal, a red body, and a set of green and yellow pectorals. Its body is covered with bright white spots, and under its pointy "sword," it has a big grin on its face. It costs fifty cents. I ask McCosker what the species of this fish could be, and he says, "Cuban." Other vendors are selling what appear to be their entire personal libraries—exquisite hardbound copies of everything from Spanish translations of William Faulkner's *Absalom, Absalom* to Che's nonfiction treatise *Guerrilla Warfare*. Apparently, the underground economy of private capitalism has become less so and is now out in the open and available to anyone ambitious enough to participate. Patrons are indeed tourists, although almost all appear to be Europeans. I hear no English spoken. There is also none of the hyperactive and congested frenzy that accompanies the disembarkation of thousands of American cruise ship passengers, vis-à-vis Nassau. Although there are scores of people here in the plaza today and the ambience seems somewhat festive, it also remains untarnished by pushy, demanding American visitors—the sort of people who make me not particularly proud of my country.

There may yet be a sane, midroad approach to mass American tourism to Cuba in the future—and in the best of worlds, to the larger notion of sustainable development here. But without such a strategy, when the embargo against U.S. trade is lifted, Old Havana, this plaza, and all the people in it will never again be the same. Last year, tourism surpassed sugar as the top income earner in Cuba. In fact, this country has led all Caribbean tourism in its rate of growth, from 600,000 a year in 1994 to 1.2 million in 1998. Even if the embargo remains in place, tourism is expected to continue to increase by such proportions in the years ahead. Once regarded as a neocolonial malaise by Castro, tourism is now aggressively courted via Canadian and European investment partners.

None of the foreign visitors combined, however, will do as much damage as a flood of happy-faced, *hamburgesia*-chomping Americans strenuously intent on a Cuba they can digest, an accidental-tourist version of Cuba accessible via cruise ship gangplanks. Without a plan to sustain the environment and the related culture, Old Havana will likely become a giant modern Key West without the trawlers and bohemians and artists, an upscale heartless imitation of the reality it displaced.

If Santiago was more of a Caribbean city, this Havana is a large Latin American one. The stew of the two million *habaneros* who live here is highly seasoned and dynamic, and as I walk down the cobblestone streets, son music from radios and rich smells from kitchens and laughter from courtyards swirl in gyres about me. It is simply sensory overload, and it would take a couple of weeks just to start sifting through things, trying to put them all in order, as we Norteamericanos like to do. McCosker and I stop to buy a couple of berets with the image of Che on them. Robins is wearing an old fashioned pillbox-style military cap, not unlike a hat a soldier might wear, and a vendor selling *Granma*, the party-run newspaper, sees him and in passing asks, "*Comunista?*" and Robins says, no, biologist. We stop in a sidewalk café, order some *café con leche*. A young man walks over, quickly sketches a caricature of me, and then asks if I will give him a dollar for it. I have spent my last cent on the coffee and apologize that I have no more money with me. He smiles and gives me the caricature anyway. The *café con leche* is smooth and rich, the day glorious, and the moment rare and fleeting. I think of a description Hemingway used in *Islands in the Stream*, in which Thomas Hudson referred to a painting as *nostalgia hecha hombre*—nostalgia in human form—and that is how I think of this instance in time.

From here, we head into the nearby Museo de la Ciudad, which now commandeers the grandiose 1780-era mansion where a long line of powerful Spanish governors of Cuba once resided. After the Spanish-American War, a U.S. governor actually lived here for several years, picking up the trappings and power of colonial rule where former Spanish autocrats had left off. On the walls, there are hand-painted floral designs, a framed quote by Cuban writer Carpentier, and a broad table of rich tropical hardwood, covered with a silk cloth and rimmed with plush leather chairs, trimmed in silver. Glass cases exhibit the trappings of the vanquished Spanish sugar dons: an ornate cane of hawksbill turtle shell and mahogany; another trimmed with amber and the vertebrae of some animal—which McCosker identifies as a shark. On a shelf is a revolver with a handle of pearl, inlaid with more hawksbill shell. Under glass are a first edition of José Martí's *Obras completas* and a book by Guillén open to the page with the famous stanza: "Yo soy un hombre sincero/de donde crece las palmas." Giant double doors are large enough for horse-drawn surreys—or a '57 Chevy—to enter. We exit through one and find ourselves in a courtyard, with Doric columns supporting the edge of the inner rooftop. The carved columns are composed of more sea grit: fossilized coral polyps and shells and tube-worms embossed on the surface of each.

Robins and Gilmore leave for a visit to the Catedral de La Habana, and McCosker and I walk down Calle Obispo to the Ambos Mundos, a five-story peach-colored hotel edging a corner. Before moving outside town into the Finca Vigía, Hemingway roomed and wrote here. Among other things, he much appreciated the prevailing northeastern trade winds—La Brisa—which waft over Havana year-round. Havana, he wrote, "is cooler than most northern cities in those months [July and August] because its northerly trades get up about ten o'clock in the morning and blow until about five o'clock the next morning." Some six decades before our own ship launched an exploration into these waters, Hemingway performed his own version of fish collecting in the nearby "great blue river" of the Gulf Stream. Offshore, this great blue river is a conspicuous link between our time and his; here on land, I wondered what other nuances of Papa's day might still be left.

We enter the Ambos, walking up the five flights of stairs to visit Hemingway's old room, which, like the Finca, is memorialized as a museum. But when we reach it, the room is locked. McCosker finds a maid and speaks to her softly in Spanish; she smiles and produces a key to the room, opens the door, and then leaves us there alone. There is a bed, an antique typewriter on a small desk, a display case of shoes and glasses, and a few copies of American magazines, dating from the 1930s. A set of shuttered windows open to the old city, and I pull them back and look out, enjoying the same view Ernesto once knew. When Hemingway first arrived in Cuba in 1928 as a twenty-nine-year-old correspondent, he had one published novel to his credit. He was headed to Key West, easily reached by direct steamship then, only ninety miles away. After returning in 1932 on a marlin fishing trip, he began traveling back and forth between here and his home on Whitehead Street in Key West. During his early years in Havana, he booked this same room at the Ambos Mundos. In 1938, he started *For Whom the Bell Tolls* here.

Later, his then wife Martha Gellhorn found the Finca Vigía, a twenty-one-acre farm in the suburb of San Francisco de Paula, and they soon bought it. Unlike Key West, where the writer's image and name are peddled unmercifully on T-shirts and in bars he never frequented, Cuba played ed a much more important role in influencing Hemingway's work. He lived here for twenty years—longer than anywhere else in his adult life. Six books were written in part or in their entirety at the Finca or here in the Ambos Mundos. Most biographers, like Cuban Norberto Fuentes, agree that Hemingway moved to Cuba to escape his growing fame in Key West, but once here he fell in love with the land and its people. The complex depths of his affection can be felt in *The Old Man and the Sea*: "He was an old man who fished alone in a skiff in the Gulf Stream and he had gone eighty-four days now without taking a fish. . . . He always thought of the sea as *la mar* which is what people call her in Spanish when they love her. . . . The old man always thought of her as feminine and as something that gave or withheld great favours, and if she did wild or wicked things, it was because she could not help them."

Hemingway's fondness for Cuba and Cubans was not unrequited. His works are required reading in school; his novels best-sellers here. Castro—citing Hemingway's condemnation of economic and political injustice in many of his novels—has claimed Papa as his favorite writer. Indeed, there is nearly a Hemingway cult here, the likes of which aren't matched in North America by any Latin writer. The main Havana marina is named for him, a special rum (El Ron Vigía) was distilled to celebrate his ninety-fifth birthday on July 21, 1994; he's even been honored on a postage stamp.

We close the door to the room and find our way back down the stairs and out into the street, which by now is in twilight. As night falls, candles and lanterns and oil lamps flicker in windows, augmented by single low-watt incandescent bulbs here and there. The old colonial cobblestone avenues and alleys glow in this timeless light, and as I walk over them, it is not hard to imagine that I am no longer in the present but have slipped through a worm hole in time, emerging some five hundred years ago.

Our visit to the Ambos Mundos seems to have jump-started us onto the unofficial Hemingway Trail. Huddling on a street corner, we decide that the next obvious stops would be two of Papa's favorite drinking spots, El Floridita and La Bodeguita. We head out for them, asking directions along the way, blundering down streets that seem to lead nowhere until we finally get our bearings. Not only did Hemingway drink at El Floridita, so did his characters—most notably artist Thomas Hudson. But as we stand just inside the doorway of El Floridita this evening, I quickly see that the place looks expensive, contrived, and crowded, with a bright phony luster that comes with too much money and the wrong kind of celebrity. El Floridita is the Havana version of Key West's Sloppy Joe's, albeit with a more extravagant facade. We leave without even bothering to sit on a stool and have a drink.

Down the street, Hemingway's other "favorite" bar, the bistrolike La Bodeguita del Medio, is far more to my liking: cluttered and cozy, walls jammed with memorabilia and faded signatures of patrons, it seems more like Old Havana itself, unrestored and tattered and genuine. It was made popular by its location, near a print shop frequented by writers like Guillén and Carpentier. We walk up to the top floor, where we sit outside on a rooftop at a table next to a crown of palm fronds. We order some fried plantains and espressos. The tropical January night air is scented, refreshing, heady. Hemingway was said to have written on the wall downstairs: "My Mojito in La Bodeguita/My Daiquiri in El Floridita," thus providing some immortality to both the *mojito* and the bar. Although the slogan has been repeated fondly by travel writers over the years, biographer Fuentes and others confirm that the quote was manufactured by the bar's owners after the revolution. At any rate, La Bodeguita at least *seems* like the place where Papa may have made such a claim. It is widely accepted, however, that Guillén, the national poet, actually did write a poem in honor of the Bodeguita. Reprinted on the bar's brown paper placemat, it reads in part:

Brindo porque la historia se repita
y porque lo que es ya la bodegona
nunca deje de ser La Bodeguita.

Friday, January 2

Anticipation

I am up early enough this morning to catch the new sun rising over the old city of Havana. Today is the day, Ricardo is telling everyone, that Castro is most likely to visit, probably sometime this evening. We are all excited about that. But there is still a last bit of expeditionary work to be done: the *Seward* moves away from the Malecón, just out to the edge of the harbor mouth. There is said to be a six-hundred-foot-deep gully here, scoured by the tides through the bottleneck created by the mouth. Giddings, who calls it the "bone yard," suspects that nearly every ship that ever sailed into this historic harbor has left something behind—an anchor, a discarded rum bottle, a dropped sextant, maybe even some lost treasure. After all, Spain's Philip II, who ruled from 1556 to 1598, decreed that all treasure *flotas* returning from the New World to Spain must first gather in the natural harbor of La Habana. Once the ships were safely inside the harbor, a thick metal chain would then be pulled up and across the narrow mouth each night.

Earlier in our voyage, Giddings described all of Cuba as a Pandora's box, but he may well have been speaking of this harbor, for most anything could still be hidden in its murk. While CaribSub has begun to excavate wrecks under the clear seas of the coast, this harbor is deep and muddy, with strong currents and poor visibility. Some hardy sport scuba divers over the years have brought up relics from depths of two hundred feet, but no one has ever been deeper.

The JSL prepares to dive to gather what it can from the harbor floor, and there is little pretense of science on this single exploration—just the hope that something mysterious will emerge to provide some intriguing footage. Mate Sharky Martin jokes that the sub may return with Jimmy Hoffa. The JSL descends in a slight current, and near the sloping wall next to the bottom, it begins to pluck whatever Liberatore can find protruding from the mud. But within minutes, a deeper and more powerful current pushes the JSL into a tangle of thick cable, and the sub is briefly is ensnarled there at 320 feet. Libertore does a masterful job in freeing the sub, but a decision is made to surface immediately, while we are still ahead of the game.

Up on the stern deck, the booty is examined: an old woven hemp rope, five ceramic and glass bottles, something metallic and rusty with no discernible form, and several sponges that were growing atop other debris. The dive has been a wash—the most it has accomplished is to provide a bit of drama during the time when it was briefly snagged on the bottom rubbish. Biology-wise, the sponges may be the last chance to prove that there might be some biomedical merit to our expedition, via Pomponi. But initial examination proves that—like other sponges we have recovered over the past month—they, too, have no new miracle drug potential.

There is still a big chunk of the day left, and after the *Seward* travels back to the Malecón, I join some of the biologists for a pilgrimage to the home of a venerated Cuban ichthyologist. On the way, we stop by the Instituto de Oceanología located west of Havana near Vedado, on the edge of the sea. This is one of the most prestigious ocean science institutes in all of the wider Caribbean. Some seventy doctorate-level scientists work here, along with seventy technicians with graduate degrees in biology. Despite its esteemed repute, the institute looks like a very cheap one-story motel that just washed up with the flotsam. McCosker describes it as a "tragic wreck." Two wings of the institute face each other across a scrubby field of sand and weeds. There is no running water. We stop by Claro's tiny battered office, and while the scientist is searching through a rusty file cabinet for some piece of information, I notice McCosker and Gilmore looking at each other with barely disguised anguish. Under the glass over the desktop, there is a map of Cuba in Russian. Nearby is a broken glass beaker and a badly corroded scale. Outside the window is a small cove, its beach covered with driftwood, empty rum bottles, children's lost toys, a rusty hatchet. McCosker tells me that the institute produces many important studies, but because of the political problems with the exchange of information with the United States, they are seldom seen by American scientists. Later, Gilmore says the entire $1 million annual budget for the institute would barely pay for grounds keeping back at the fancy Harbor Branch campus. Both institutions have about two hundred employees each, but the similarities abruptly end there. "We have seven doctorate-level marine scientists at HBOI," says Gilmore. "They have seventy Ph.D. scientists and seventy master's level people. Their budget is around $1 million annually; our is $35 million, and most of it goes to activities other than marine science. At Harbor Branch, the ratio of accountants to scientists is about 1:1."

Until two years ago, the annual budget of the institute was funded by the Cuban government; but now the government provides only $100,000, with the rest coming from foreign corporations, which are now required by a new Cuban law to provide environmental impact studies for their resort developments. The new law, effective in 1995, created a Ministry of Science, Technology, and Environment, replacing an agency (Comisión Nacional de Protección del Medio Ambiente y del Uso Racional de los Recursos Naturales) that seemed to lack real authority to enforce environmental laws or to penalize violators—relying instead on voluntary cooperation.

"They [the new ministry] pay us to do assessments of impacts," says Claro, "and we can recommend 'yes' or 'no.'" There is now a strong push to develop the wild *cayos* of Cuba, Claro explains. Already there are three constructed causeways leading out to the Archipiélago de Sabana-Cama-güey at Cayo Coco in the north, where forty-eight bridges and smaller causeways link islands there to support future tourism development. The longest bridge-causeway system, at forty-eight kilometers (twenty-nine miles), spans Bahía de Perros from the mainland. Claro hedges on how much clout the institute's recommendations actually carried in the past. "We have been able to get them [the ministry] to build bridges whenever possible [instead of bermed causeways], so that the tide waters can at least pass under them." Certainly, having any bridges at all was a victory—albeit a compromised one. Any bridge to an island will allow that island to be developed, forever changing the natural landscape. While the new ministry may have more clout, I am guessing that Claro and his colleagues face the same dilemma of staff members of environmental agencies back in Florida. There, public officials, compromised by their connections to real estate development, routinely grant exemptions to ecologically sound management plans, overstressing fragile environments like the Florida Keys, polluting nearshore waters, and destroying coral reefs. I wonder if the Keys and their declining reef system have any value at all as an object lesson.

Back in the car, we zigzag through the suburbs, down a broad boule-vard shaded with a canopy of mango and fig and banyan trees, until we reach the home of Dr. Dario Guitart Manday. Guitart, a former professor of Claro's at the University of Havana, is one of the most eminent marine sci-entists in all of Cuba. In the post-Batista years, when Cubans were gaining a sense of their true national identity that transcended colonization, Gui-tart was pivotal in helping to organize a marine biology department at the University of Havana, as well as to establish the Instituto de Oceanología. In addition to helping design the national aquarium, he has written more than sixty scientific papers on ichthyology and marine ecology as well as *Sinopsis de los speces marinos de Cuba*, a four-volume illustrated book with keys for the identification of Cuban marine fishes. Dr. Guitart also has in his possession the bound—but never published—original manuscript of Poey's definitive description of Cuban fish fauna, with forty-one full-size ink drawings. More than just a guide to Cuban fish, it also describes many new species found throughout the entire Caribbean. We hope to find the illustration of *Verilus*, rendered in 1868, in order to compare it with one Gilmore has drawn.

Guitart, a kind, soft-spoken man now in his seventies, welcomes us graciously. We sit in his sunroom, unscreened jalousie windows open to the trade wind breezes, over a cool floor of terrazzo. I notice there are no bugs, odd for the tropics. Potted ferns and succulents and cacti crowd into every corner of the patio. A handmade wind chime of seashells shivers, gently. Guitart was the first to describe the long-fin mako; Gilmore had corresponded with him over the years about such things, quietly conducting his own exchange of information with this embargoed country. Gilmore shows Guitart his own sketch of *Verilus*, and Guitart counters with the original Poey drawing from the large bound book of time-yellowed pages. The accuracy of both sketches is uncanny: the two renditions of *Verilus* are nearly identical. Guitart said that Poey put the fish on top of paper and then outlined it for better precision. Indeed, a great barracuda is illustrated on a fold-out page, to actual size. Many of the specimens he sketched no longer are kept in Cuba; they now reside in collections of holotypes back in the United States. Gilmore shows Guitart sketches of the four other "new" fish we think we have discovered, and Guitart says that those are fish he does not know.

We sit and talk, drink some espresso in demitasse cups, and snack on tiny fried pieces of plantain. Gilmore tells Guitart of Florida's problems with overfishing, that his state once allowed long lines—giant trot lines baited with hooks—that stretched for fifty miles, strung out offshore for swordfish but also killing much more as "by-catch" on the lines, including makos and even sea turtles. In order to examine pregnant females of the great pelagic fish, Gilmore would routinely visit local Florida fishhouses, where the "specimens" were being gutted and cleaned. Gilmore and Guitart lament that deep-sea fish—indeed, all fish with spawn dispersal sharing the geographic waters of the United States and the Caribbean—aren't managed by a broad regional marine plan based on ecology but are assigned odd little artificial twelve-mile territories dictated by politics.

McCosker, who coauthored a book on great white sharks, asks Guitart about "El Monstruo de Cojimar," a seven-thousand-pound twenty-one-foot-long great white said to be caught in 1945 by a fisherman out of the village of Cojimar and reported to the world at large by a Cuban ichthyologist named Howell-Rivero. If it was true, it would be the largest great white caught anywhere in the world. Guitart says yes, it is true; he has a tooth from that shark, given to him by his teacher Professor Luis Howell-Rivero, who saw it. And with that Guitart brings out a single giant 2.8-inch-long shark's tooth, about half the size of fossilized teeth from the extinct Megalodon. McCosker recognizes it as the "fourth upper lateral tooth." This could be the shark that ate Santiago's marlin (in *The Old Man and the Sea*), says McCosker, only half joking. The Monster of Cojimar was caught with a huge baited hook attached to an oil drum. Guitart said another great white, closer to five thousand pounds, was also caught off northern Cuba in 1975, near the surface. I flash back to my night in the abyss at La Furnia and, just for a moment, I feel the memory of the adrenaline surge.

We wander over to the adjacent parlor to examine rare first-edition books in Guitart's library. On the wall, I notice a large colorful poster replete with hundreds of fish: "El Mundo es un Acuario," The World is an Aquarium. And in English, there is a framed "Angel's Prayer." It reads: "Lord, give me the grace to catch a fish so big that even when telling of it afterwards, I may never need to lie." On a shelf is a trophy for soccer achievement, left from Guitart's undergrad years. Robins walks back to the porch, shaking his head. "For an ichthyologist, this is like the Gutenberg Bible," he says, referring to Poey's original work. "I feel like I've just touched history."

Suddenly, it occurs to me that Guitart may be old enough at least to have met Hemingway, who probably frequented some of the same waterfront hangouts, and when I ask him if he ever did, he says yes, once. I ask what Hemingway was like; Guitart pauses, thinks, and then says in English: "Big."

We thank Guitart for his hospitality and walk to Claro's house nearby for a celebratory lunch. Claro lives in a modest one-bedroom apartment in a high-rise building, which he shares with his wife, his son and daughter-in-law, and their small son. Along with his twenty-peso-a-month salary, the apartment is provided by the government. As we approach, Claro's grandchild runs out to greet him, and Claro picks him up, the serious fish doctor turning into the proud and happy grandfather. Inside, there is a single black velvet tapestry tacked to the wall depicting a naked woman rising up out of a wooded stream. We meet Claro's wife and his son and daughter-in-law. As we sit at a dining table in one corner of the room, Claro's son and his wife sit to watch TV in the other. Out come shredded meat and onions, yucca and beans, and a little salad. A bottle of Cuban rum is passed around. Considering that food is strictly rationed—that each family, for instance, receives one dozen eggs a month—it is an extraordinarily generous feast. Claro says his institute is not able to buy many things they need, because now the United States imposes sanctions even on those countries that would sell medicine and lab supplies to them. But then, he brightens: "Do you know how to preserve many fish?" he asks. "You can use Guaro [a cheap clear liquor made during rum distillation]. It is very powerful!"

Despite the prosperity we know in the United States, Gilmore and McCosker have more in common with Claro than not—with budgets for marine science being slashed and ocean exploration largely going unfunded. And after all, it wasn't a scientific foundation that underwrote this exploration of fish diplomacy but an entertainment conglomerate. Clearly, the scientists who study the sea have a Sisyphean job on their hands. And it seems as if the wagons have encircled this tiny table in this modest, crumbling building. It is more than just politics that conspires against them; it is a one-dimensional worldview of the oceans. Terrestrial forests and rivers and fresh air are easily accessed; the sea is far more difficult to figure. As a result, the cues to its role as a pervasive life force are simply lost on most. But they are not lost for right now, for the people who are right here. "This is a very special moment, for us to be together here," Grant says, in a toast.

Rodolfo, ever humble, bows his head. "And for me, also."

12

Fidel,

Retrospective, and

Back across

the Florida Straits

Friday Evening, January 2

Fidel

I have been seeing a triumvirate of symbols over and over again since I have been in Cuba: José Martí, Che, and Fidel. We have been expecting to meet the only living member of this trio sometime after our arrival in Havana, and now Ricardo passes the word to everyone that El Comandante will visit the ship around 6 P.M. this evening. We change into the cleanest clothes we still have remaining and, by 6, assemble on the stern. Lipscomb has given us all blue T-shirts with "Discovery Channel Cuba Expedition" on them for Christmas, and many of us are wearing them. Ricardo briefs us on how to address the leader of Cuba: " 'Fidel' is fine; 'President' is all right. But don't call him Castro, okay?"

Depending on your point of view, Castro is tyrannical and paranoid, or paternalistic and brilliant. Perhaps he is some of each of these. Sympathetic scholars say no one else in Latin America since Simón Bolívar has played such a large role in helping a country break its yoke of colonialism; most Cuban exiles in America see him as the devil incarnate. As I soon find, he is nothing if not compelling—and enamored with the art of engaging conversation. As Latin American writer Gabriel García Márquez observed: "It is hard to find one more addicted to the habit of conversation. His devotion to the word is almost magical." This is, after all, a man who still gives speeches that are seven hours long.

We wait forty-five minutes beyond the appointed hour, and some crew members begin to grouse that Castro may not show up at all. Then, a local television camera crew arrives and trains its own Betacam on our ship—a good sign! A visit must be imminent. Yet, if this were our own president, buttoned-down Secret Service agents would be swarming everywhere to secure the area.

Suddenly, without warning, two black, sleek Mercedes with tinted windows zoom up to the concrete curb next to the Malecón, followed by several smaller Fiats and Ladas. Out come bodyguards in fatigues, armed with what look like automatic weapons—perhaps AK-47s? And then, from a back door of a Mercedes, Fidel himself emerges. He is in clean, well-pressed green fatigues with a shiny silverish buckle and combat boots, his now famous beard gray but eyebrows still black. For the rest of the world, the Cuban revolution and its costuming may be over, but for Castro, it is ongoing, and he dresses in this way to represent that ideal. "A revolutionary," he has said, "never retires." Not only does he not retire, but in this case he is transformed into the realm of living metaphor. Close at his side is a very serious young woman who will simultaneously translate every sentence—English into Spanish, or Spanish into English.

At seventy-one, Castro moves agilely, confidently toward the ship, and at the gangplank, producer Al Giddings—whose long relationship with Fidel helped engineer this entire project—rushes to embrace his old friend. To promote a "stop smoking" campaign in his country a couple years ago,

Castro no longer appears in public accessorized with a cigar, and its absence is glaring—sort of like José Martí without his mustache, or Che without his visionary glaze. The entire entourage moves aboard, and Fidel walks right past me; he looks up and nods. His eyes are intent, the gaze of a guy who doesn't miss a trick. Lipscomb and his crew have the cameras trained on every movement. In the limelight, Giddings comes to life; he welcomes Castro in inimitable fashion, speaking slowly and clearly for the translator: "We went to many places and have wonderful film. We had plenty to do here, more than enough." And then: "I would like to show you the submarine."

The men move toward the JSL, but Giddings pauses to introduce Castro to Captain Seiler and then, waylaid from the sub business, says to Castro: "Each time, I come with a larger ship. It has been a beautiful trip to your country."

"Let me take a look at the submarine," says Castro.

Giddings is undeterred. "Everyone knows of your love of the sea—these are Cuban scientists and American scientists and divers." He introduces Claro and Alcolado, and one of the first things Castro asks them is about the capture of the strange little fish known as the *pargo chino*. Gilmore thinks to himself: "How refreshing a major political figure and national leader is actually interested in fish." They discuss the uniqueness of *Verilus*, of how Poey was the first to describe it, and how that description—along with many others of Cuban marine life—still languishes in a single bound manuscript of sepia-colored pages. "Shouldn't this be brought to publication?" asks Castro, and heads nod, yes.

Giddings, who is basking in the attention of the cameras, is now modulating his voice so that he sounds as if he's talking to a small, very slow child. "These Cuban scientists, they are wonderful men; they spent many hours in the submarine."

"Are you going to show me the submarine?" asks Castro, equally as undeterred. With that, Giddings moves over a few feet to the JSL.

"This submarine is like a helicopter—it uses different motors to allow it to turn, go up or down, or rotate."

"What kind of glass is that over the front [pilot sphere]. Is it fiberglass?"

"That is Plexiglas," says Giddings. "Don, come here and explain this.

Don's our chief sub pilot." Liberatore walks over, and Castro points to one of the torpedolike thrusters: "What do you call this yellow thing?"

"An electric motor," says Liberatore. "We have nine of them. They make it go."

Castro's curiosity seems immeasurable: he wants to know what the sub cost, how deep it goes, how long it stays down, and what all the strange mechanical arms and tubes are on its front. Liberatore tells him that the claw arms can actually catch fish, which have been stunned by the bright lights of the JSL or numbed by the rotenone. Still, Fidel is unquenched. He asks how fast the sub can descend, how long the average dive is, and what the temperature is at depth. And this suction device, how does this work? And the power for the submarine, where does it come from? Oh, the batteries, and how long do they take to recharge? By now, most politicians would have stopped to soapbox, somehow linking this mission to their own ambition, but Castro plows on, ferreting out the details: "Now, at what depth do you lose the light of the surface? And how long do you take to descend? And what do you breathe inside the submarine?" Finally, he has gathered enough information to form a metaphor in his mind. He pauses. Then:

"So," asks the young woman, in translation for Fidel, "this is like a spaceship that can fly underwater?"

"It's an 'inner-space' ship," replies Giddings, not missing a beat.

"Ahhh," says Fidel, who opens his eyes wide and ducks his head, as if the inner-space ship is preparing for takeoff.

From the sub, the group moves into the dry lab, where the Giddings crew has prepared a series of rough video clips shot here over the past month—from the deep water of the sub to shallow scuba dives. Down the narrow ship corridor moves the entourage, stopping as crew member Ben Chiong presents Fidel with a small Styrofoam cup crushed by the depth of the sub. Nearby is Widder, whom Fidel quizzes about bioluminescence, her specialty.

And then, out of the blue, to Giddings: "What did you do with Miss Universe?"—an oblique reference to an earlier film mission Giddings made to Cuba when he was traveling to great dive sites around the world with a beauty contest winner.

"Last night, I went to La Bodeguita," says Giddings, "and everyone remembered her!"

Castro is introduced to McCosker, who, addressing him as El Jefe, informs Castro that the largest great white shark ever captured in the world was caught off Cojimar by a Cuban fisherman. This seems to surprise Castro. "Have any of those big sharks showed up again?" McCosker, referencing Guitart, tells him of the five-thousand-pounder that was caught a few years ago. Castro ponders this. "I thought Cuba was free of white sharks."

"No," says McCosker, "they are here. Another honor for Cuba."

Giddings leads Castro and his bodyguards down to the dry lab. "We have a hundred hours of material. I will show him some things." Giddings's syntax seems to have become yet more remedial by the minute. During the preview of the underwater clips, Giddings makes a point to explain the lobster fishing techniques to Castro in great detail from our visit to Punta Francés. "They have a wooden habitat on the bottom, and the lobsters go into this at night. Then the fishermen retrieve them in the day with a net. . . . It is one of the most efficient and considerate techniques I've ever seen! They release females with eggs and small ones." Oddly, Castro is reputed to have helped design the Cayo Largo boats as well as to set rules to keep the lobster fishery sustainable—yet he continues to ask questions about the techniques, rather than taking credit for its existence. At this point, I begin to wonder if Castro is asking questions to patronize us. Or if perhaps the hands-on retrofitting of the Cuban lobster fishery was delegated to others more versed in biology. Then again forty years is a long time—could El Jefe have forgotten something this important?

Macroshots of deep-sea fish swimming in the shipboard aquarium are played on the VCR, batfish and gobies filling up the entire screen. "Some of the scientists are working on deep-sea fishes," explains Giddings. "So we would bring these animals to the surface with the submarine, then they would go into small holding tanks like this to bring an imitation of where they live. For documentation and science, these animals are brought to the aquarium . . . to make details." Giddings now appears to be speaking in broken English. "I think the film we do will be fantastic for the Discovery Channel showing to this wonderful audience!"

After the "Best of" highlights are previewed, all climb the metal stairs to the captain's bridge, where Giddings will show Castro our route on a large map of Cuba. Before the map, though, come more questions, this time about Harbor Branch, addressed to Gilmore: "Is it a private foundation? Was it created by the government? Who funded it?" Gilmore explains the nature of HBOI to the satisfaction of El Jefe.

We turn to the map. "Many of the places you have visited, I have been scuba diving there. Later, we imposed regulations on spearfishing because it depletes the resource—by killing the big mother fish."

Castro moves his arm across the map, as if he is willing it to arise, and then finally taps his fingers on the Golfo de Batabanó. Here is the heart of Cuba's spiny lobster fishery, says Castro. El Comandante then goes on to describe the life history of *Panulirus* in great detail, from mating to egg hatching to larval settlement—even showing us the movement patterns of the floating larvae around the gulf.

Sometime here, McCosker reaches behind Castro to get Giddings's attention, and a Cuban bodyguard responds quickly, grabbing McCosker's hand, while another moves in defensively between McCosker and Castro as a shield.

And then, with no segue, comes this, addressed to Giddings: "What did you use to go into the *Titanic*? How deep is it?"

Giddings explains that, in filming a feature film with James Cameron last year, he used the Russian *Mir* sub to visit the two-mile-deep depths of the *Titanic* in the North Atlantic, making seventeen dives to that wreck.

On the map, Giddings points to Uvero, where we made our own visit to the wreck of the *Colón*. "We are very thrilled! It is beautiful material!" says Giddings, sounding like a football coach giving his halftime pep talk. Castro asks if this was a ship sunk in the "1898 war," and Giddings says yes, it was. "It's falling apart, disintegrating down there," he says.

Castro, undoubtedly used to hearing criticism of his entire country falling apart, seems truly to lament the organic disintegration of the *Colón*. "Yes—but there is no way to fix that, so many years have passed. There is nothing we can do." It seems he has taken the deterioration of the *Colón* personally.

Giddings, undeterred, presses on and introduces Shirley Pomponi as "another one of our lady scientists aboard. She is working with sponges and looking for medical cures." Pomponi is not only a dedicated scientist but also a gregarious woman, and Fidel cranks up the charm factor a few degrees, gesturing and sometimes reaching out to touch her arm to make a point. Later, McCosker writes in his journal: "He was really trying to charm Shirley, and was obviously great with women."

Pomponi said that a sea squirt found near Cayos Rosario and Cantiles in Los Canarreos is the same species as one found elsewhere in the Caribbean—one with a known anticancer compound that is now undergoing clinical trials with humans in the United States and Europe. If it proves successful, says Pomponi, there is not enough of this animal in the wild to supply all the raw biomaterial needed, and aquaculture would have to be used to farm the sea squirt for this purpose. Castro brightens noticeably at the mention of aquaculture—sea farming. It is something he hopes can be used to help feed his compatriots with cheaply raised, high-protein seafood. Already, there are conch and turtle farms on the island, and the lobster industry uses a sort of "ranching" technique to help stabilize the wild spiny stocks. Chile is farming salmon, and perhaps such methods can work here. (In fact, aquaculture has accounted for some twenty-five hundred metric tons of shellfish and mollusks alone this year. Farmed species include the freshwater tilapia, Chinese and common carps, giant prawns, saltwater white shrimp, and mangrove oysters.)

Freshwater eels, which would be worth much in export dollars as a European delicacy, seem a favorite topic. "We have tried in a closed cycle [farm] with eels but they are very complex—the eel spends part of its life in the Sargasso Sea, and there they spawn and die. It takes them three years to swim to Europe, to the Mediterranean and Baltic, before they return to where they were born." The success of sea farming, says Castro, astutely, is the low conversion ratio of fish food to farmed, high-protein food for humans—only about 2.5 to 1 pound live weight, compared with 8 to 1 with beef. "The fish, they need to be fed, and they compete with man for food. The better ratio for protein is with aquaculture."

Yet the eel continues to elude him, even when his researchers surf the Web for answers. "We have heard of closed-circuit eel farming. Where the eels do not need to go to sea. But our people go on the Internet to look for information about the farming of eel, and we cannot find anything about that."

Cures can be discovered in the sea for many diseases, says Fidel, and perhaps with enough cures, the life span of humans can be increased to 120 years. Now seventy-one, Castro might also be looking for ways to squeeze more out of the years he has left. "We haven't reached our potential, maybe with cloning to handle genes, man can live much longer—he would be like the sea turtle." There is much laughter at this, although it is not clear whether Castro is talking about cloning sea turtle genes onto humans or is just fantasizing.

"If we find ways to make man live longer," says Castro, "then he will require more food!"

"But," reminds Pomponi, "it is the quality of life that is important," regardless of how long we live, and of course, Fidel agrees.

There is more talk about the need for a conservation ethic to save an ocean we all share. With the population explosion worldwide—and the related impact—this ocean needs such help, says Castro, more than it ever has before. But there may be other ways to ensure the survival of humans, even in the face of global change and disruptions of ecosystems on the earth. "At the end of the century, there will be colonies on Mars," says El Jefe, confident of this. "Perhaps even Venus—the planet the Romans wanted—she was the goddess of love." With this, he pauses and turns again to Pomponi, and the scientist smiles in return. "Not me," she says. "I don't want to live on Venus."

But, oh, says Castro, there is a theory that life once existed on Venus or Mars. "Who is to say that is not where we came from, and that we destroyed those planets and had to come here, and now we are destroying this one?"

While on the subject of global transport, Castro says that he has just seen the French Concorde, which flies across the ocean from Paris to New York City for a fare of seven thousand dollars. It seems an extraordinary amount for a Cuban, for a scientist, for the people in this room. "It cost over one billion dollars to produce," says Castro, straying a bit from the topic at hand. "The most impressive thing is the engines, which are very small." And then: "With the cost of one of these planes, you can buy many ships like this . . . and many submarines like you have—and still have money left to buy stocks in New York Stock Exchange."

He continues: "There are so many things unexplored. But it is true that now the ocean needs to be rescued, to be saved, because it has been polluted . . . lead, mercury, whatever." And then the only zinger of the evening: "We are able to preserve our island, so that people can come and watch healthy corals. But if you Americans don't keep your rivers clean, in Florida and in Louisiana, they will bring contaminants to the ocean. It is affecting our island, and of course, releasing gases which go into the atmosphere all over the earth." Finally, the only real bromide of the evening emerges: "I will save a tiny island so you can come forever and film here."

And speaking of film, Castro had met Cousteau, when the French film-maker came to Cuba for his own documentary and later, at the Earth Summit in Rio. "They have all the heads of state lined up for a 'photo op' in Rio, and I pulled him up with me, and say, Captain, join this picture in the 'photo op' because most people here know nothing about the environment. And he came up and was in the 'photo op' with all of us."

Cousteau clearly was a big influence on Castro's own ocean ethics. "I read his book [Cousteau wrote several] many years ago, and I learned so many things. Do you know he did not allow people on the *Calypso* to eat fish? Do you eat fish on this ship? He says it was like a commandment. No Could Eat Fish While On Board. I guess he would prefer to eat sheep . . . and beef and poultry instead. He was a vegetarian himself—he wouldn't even eat eggs. He said: I eat nothing that is an embryo. But he ate beans. And I said to him: A bean is an embryo. And he told me, well, you have to eat something. . . . You know, he loved exploring Cuban waters because of our protection." Castro is one of the few politicians who can speak earnestly of actualizing ideals and pull it off. As Márquez says: "He has been one of the great idealists of our time and this, perhaps, may be his greatest virtue, although it has been his greatest danger."

Giddings then asks Castro to sign a map of Cuba, one that will hang in his office back in the States. All the marine scientists aboard will sign it, says Giddings. "You know," says Fidel, "I have the idea of suggesting to you in my mind, of offering you the first signature. I will sign it on the place where I was born." And he does, and everyone on the bridge applauds.

Taima Hervas then asks Castro in Spanish if he will sign a few older photos—some from 1959—of a much younger version of himself. A few pictures are taken of Castro signing the old photos, and he looks up and says: "Maybe thirty years from now, I will be signing those photos you have just taken. . . . Maybe this girl [Hervas] will the be secret of youth!" With that, he heads down from the bridge and to the lower deck.

Most American politicians, faced with a similar scenario, would have done a walk-through, asked a few cursory questions, posed for photos, and then made a quick exit. But even now, his diplomatic job here done, Fidel's engaging style doesn't waver. When he spots our cook, Jay Grant—clearly distinguished by being the only one on board with an apron—in a corridor, he hesitates for a moment. Up from the dredges of Castro's mind comes a favorite recipe for spiny lobster; it is something to do with wine and onion butter, and Castro seems pleased by the remembrance of it. "With the thick sauces, you cannot taste the lobster. This is just right: cook for ten or eleven minutes, only. It doesn't lose its tenderness or its juice and doesn't get hard." Later Alcolado calls this recipe "Lobster a la Comandante."

There is one last exchange with McCosker, who promises to send Fidel more information on the Monster of Cojimar. Very dangerous, that animal, says Castro, and McCosker says, yes, but sharks are not as dangerous as politicians, and Castro laughs.

Giddings extends a parting and official-sounding accolade to Castro for letting us explore Cuba: "I would very much like to thank you on the behalf of the contingent here to be able to work in this wonderful country."

And Castro responds in kind: "We are the ones who should thank you for the interest you have shown in coming here, for the research you are conducting here, such useful work for everyone, for the world."

Giddings gets in the last word, under the mantle of diver as diplomat, albeit one that still seems a bit afflicted by his new broken English: "Let us speak together through this film, about our concerns and ethics, . . . for it will be distributed internationally. . . . I have been very excited to come back and to work in this atmosphere with these scientists."

"Megalodon," says Castro to McCosker, in an oblique reference to the extinct giant shark. "I have a tooth in my office."

And then El Jefe and crew go out on the stern, across the gangplank, and into a Mercedes, which speeds off as quickly as it arrived. Moments later, a 1956 Chevy with fender skirts and a chrome hood ornament putters by, a mélange of metal putty and wire and patched balloon tires, following in the wake of El Comandante, chugging off into the cool Havana night.

It was a remarkable encounter, and while most of the crew head to the nearby bar for a post-Fidel celebration, McCosker first writes in his journal: "He is an extraordinary extemporaneous speaker—about 80 to 90 percent of which is quite correct. Aging, the problems of feeding the world, medical cures, transformation of food through pigs, chickens and fish. He had some of it wrong, but he couldn't be corrected. All in all, it was an astonishing filibuster and we were amazed. . . . A charming, charismatic bull shitter, but an impressive guy."

Saturday, January 3

Retrospective

The tangle of cables at the harbor entrance has kept the sub from being deployed today, and most of us are free to wander about Havana. Claro and Alcolado off-load five-gallon plastic buckets full of preserved specimens culled during our visit. The buckets were from our kitchen, emptied and cleaned after use as food containers of cole slaw and beans. Historically—during preembargo days—scientific specimens sailed home with the visiting expedition in the best imperialistic manner. Then, during the embargo, there were scant funds for such work. Today, there are better collections of Cuban fish fauna in museums in Harvard and Paris than in Cuba. The contents of our plastic buckets represent the heart of a new, more complete collection that will ultimately remain in Cuba. And those specimens, coupled with the intimacy and dialogue shared between Americans and Cubans during the trip, were most likely the heart of what the real expedition was about.

Lipscomb gathers all the scientists around the wooden table in the day room for a retrospective on the expedition. Everyone is here, and a map of Cuba is in the center of the table along with several of the finely detailed drawings Gilmore has made of deepwater fish we have captured. I hang back, just behind the cameras, and watch. There is much talk about the intact nature of Cuba's coastal environment and the need to protect it. "If they can do a sustainable fishery for lobsters, there's no reason they can't do it for the other fisheries," says Gilmore. "Certain key zones can be set up as marine reserves—for 'no take'—and it will help guarantee plenty of fish elsewhere."

The other scientists talk of bioluminescence, deepwater invertebrates, and the comparison between the barren easterly volcanic coast and the richer one of mangroves and coral to the west. There are an estimated 1,200 species of fish in Cuba; our visit added 34 new records of fish never before seen in these waters. In total, we made 50 sub dives over 700 miles, and collected or observed 476 fish specimens belonging to at least 110 separate species. Four may be new to science—including two new gobies, a member of the Brotula family, and a duck-billed little fish that may belong to the Chrionema family. And of course, we caught *Verilus,* a fish that, though long known, hasn't been seen for years in Cuba and has never been captured alive before. Some 146 invertebrates—including 57 sponges—were collected, representing 97 different species. Nine sponges and two gastropod mollusks are scientifically undescribed. Twenty-one species of sponges known elsewhere in the Caribbean but never before seen here were recovered. As yet no active biomedical compounds in the animals have been identified.

I had been looking forward to this meeting because it was the first time each scientist had a chance to reflect on the trip in the presence of all the others. Yet those reflections soon become circumspect: certainly, no one really wants to disappoint the expedition's underwriters by being frank about what he or she didn't accomplish and why. As the film session drones on, I head down to my bunk and stretch out. McCosker comes in an hour later, and I ask him how it went. He tells me it was like Dali's melting clock, an interminable dissecting of time and space.

After ranging out again through Old Havana, I drop by the waterfront bar next to the *Seward* before heading to my bunk. Tonight it is full of attractive young women, and by the time I arrive, in midevening, two-thirds of the crew seem to be sitting next to at least one or two of the women. I order a Cristal beer and edge quietly into a corner booth, where seconds later I am joined by a stunning brunette in a short black dress. Speaking in conversational English, she introduces herself as Ana María. I try my lousy Spanish with her, which she seems to appreciate. The jukebox is loaded with American songs—some current, others by long-gone rockers like The Doors. All the windows of the bar overlook the harbor, and a wooden deck out back sits right atop it. I watch as a ferry returns to the Malecón from the other side of this quay, reflections of its green and red lights dancing on the soft night water. Ana María asks if I will donate quarters for the jukebox, and I give her what I have. She plays "Lady in Red," comes back, snuggles up close, and sings all the words to the song out loud. "It is how I learn English," she tells me, "listening here to those words." When she comes to "Lady in Red / Smiling at me," she pulls back a corner of her top to reveal a red lace bra. After the song is over, Ana María puts her hand on my thigh and gets down to business. "You work on that boat over there?" she asks, pointing to the *Seward*, which by now is glowing like a big white incandescent bulb at the edge of the dark and moody Malecón. I tell her yes, for now. She asks me how much I make; I hesitate and then tell her that, too. I can see Ana María doing the math in her head; she is figuring a rate that is fair, based on my earnings. A true *comunista*. "For thirty dollars, I will be your girl, your lady in red," she tells me. Ana María, like her friends, is a *jinetera*, an amateur hooker, trading the chance to party and make some spending money for sex with a stranger.

Unlike prostitutes who appear desperate or hard-edged, Ana María in her exuberance seems more to want the small luxuries and excitement that hard cash will bring. "I like to party, and this is how I do it. I am taking nursing courses in college and have nothing left to spend. Here, I have money." Ana María and her friends appear to be a jolly bunch, or at least are pretending to be so, and it is not my responsibility to lecture that dignity and self-esteem may ultimately be at stake. Then indeed, maybe it is only at stake in my non-Caribbean, linear mind. Who is to say at what point our lives and visions become compromised by the money and power of others? I am tired now, and moral questions seem not as clear as they should be.

More professional prostitutes can earn two hundred dollars a night—more than a secretary makes in a year in Cuba. But clearly Ana María is not among them. Nonetheless, it all feels wrong to me, and I can only say no, *lo siento mucho*, not tonight. Ana María is not discouraged. "Okay, then, you are a nice guy. I will sit and we will talk. You can practice your Spanish, okay? Maybe later, you might want to buy some Cohibas?" I tell her that, maybe later, that would be a nice idea.

Ana María swirls the ice in her drink and wonders what it is that I am doing on the big white ship. I consider the full answer—our submarine, the *Colón*, Herrero and the fishing school, the near fatal flashlight fish chase, *Verilus*, Hemingway's room in Old Havana, El Jefe in the flesh, the documentary. I realize it is asking too much for even me to understand just now. Instead, I ask if she has heard of Jules Verne.

"Jewelburn?"

"No," I say very slowly, "Verne . . . Jules Verne. He wrote about . . . exploring under the ocean. . . . It was a long time ago." I realize I have also begun to speak in broken English.

"Oh," says Ana María, happy now with a killer smile. "I know this Burn! Dav-id Byrne. But there are none of his songs in this bar. . . . There is much other music that you could like, though." And with that she gets up and punches in some numbers on the juke, and Jim Morrison is suddenly singing to me, here on the edge of Havana's Malecón. The dead American singer wails about strange days finding him, strange days tracking him down. The meaning is not lost on me.

Sunday and Monday, January 4–5

Back across the Florida Straits

Just after dawn, we cast off the thick rope moorings that have tethered our ship to Havana—physically and symbolically—and ease away from the Malecón for the last time. Ricardo is the last Cuban to leave the ship. We saw the others off last night, after a wrap party at a local restaurant in Old Havana, Lipscomb quoting Masefield's "Going Down to the Sea Again" one last time. This morning, Ricardo stands with a small group of men at the edge of the dock and waves to us. Those of us up at this hour stand along the railing of our ship and wave back. We wave until Ricardo becomes a tiny stick figure on the distant bulkhead, dwarfed by the sprawling colonial assemblage of Old Havana.

And then we steam out through the harbor, past Morro Castle one last time, and into the windward northern sea that will batter us unmercifully for the next forty-eight hours as we head back to our Florida port.

As soon as we hit open water, the steep, wind-driven waves lash at the hull unceasingly. They will do so for most of the day and the night of the crossing. I spend most of the time in my bunk reading, resting, just trying to process what I have experienced over the past six weeks. A reporter from the States who has been reading the dispatches I posted on the Web calls on the satellite phone to ask me about the expedition. We chat. A reporter from the BBC calls, wanting more scientific information, and I refer him to Gilmore. Then it is back to the bunk.

By the morning, we are approaching U.S. waters somewhere off southern Florida when we get an urgent message over the public address system. Lipscomb, McCosker, Gilmore, and I are summoned to the bridge. The Discovery Channel producer, the Envious One, has seen the press that resulted from yesterday's media interviews. He is livid that no one has told him that Castro was aboard the ship and, worse, that the world will now know about it. He asks to speak to me. "Did you know Castro was coming aboard?" Yeah, I say, it was in the treatment for your documentary—don't you remember? There is silence on the other end. "We discussed this before we left Fort Pierce last month," I tell him. "Marine Marvels, Forbidden Waters, all that."

"There could be serious repercussions," says the producer, who, no longer under the guise of the Envious One, sounds very strident and harsh and dogmatic. "No one should talk to the press in Fort Pierce. No one but a Discovery representative. We have to control the flow of information." I tell him that information has actually been flowing from the expedition all month via the Web dispatches. There is more silence. At this point, it becomes apparent that he does not fully understand how the Web actually works.

The producer then orders the ship to remain at sea another twenty-four hours until he can fly down from Bethesda to field media inquiries when we dock in Fort Pierce. Those on the bridge—from the chief engineer to Lipscomb to the captain—are united in their rejection of this order, and one by one they tell the producer that this is not a good idea. Still angry, he finally decides that Gilmore, as the chief scientist, should be the only one to talk to the press, that all others should remain silent, and that no mention of Castro should be made and no personal photos of Castro released. Oddly, the producer is doing a far better job of acting like a dictator than Castro did. It strikes me that corporate environments—with their autocratic obsession to control individuals—may be the real despots after all. With our voyage coming to an end, I disassemble my "office"— a narrow shelf behind a bank of video terminals and computers. Down comes my map of Cuba, my photos of family and friends, the baseball cap with the fishing flies John McCosker hand tied, the postage stamps I bought in Santiago, the underwater map of Sambo Head reef that Richard Fagen drew for me, a proof of a children's book on bioluminescence by Edie Widder, the Santa that Pedro had drawn on the computer. It is a bittersweet moment for me, like taking the decorations off a Christmas tree when I was a little kid.

I go out to the stern deck to pack up my scuba gear, discovering that I lost one of my neoprene boots during one of the earlier wave hits. Oh well, could have been much worse. When I'm done, I stand at the edge of a gunwale and watch as a school of dolphins passes just off the bow, arching elegantly before being swallowed up again by the slate-gray sea. The sun is breaking through the clouds, and the low shore of southern Florida is materializing in a distant haze just ahead.

Epilogue

An Associated Press article appeared worldwide after we docked, with a photo—which I had snapped and posted to the Web site—of Giddings and Castro next to the JSL. Radio Havana later used portions of the dispatch in its own report. High-ranking Discovery programming officials were oddly nervous over the release of information about Castro's presence on the *Seward*.

When the *Seward* docked in Fort Pierce, Gilmore gave a statement to a small contingent of reporters there, a sort of executive summary of our trip over the past six weeks. He stressed, as he often does when speaking publicly, the need for more federal support for deep-sea marine research. Each time he has left the HBOI dock with a submersible, said Gilmore, he has returned with "fishes that have never before been seen by human eyes." Yet this type of ocean exploration is simply not a priority in our country. "It is ironic, considering that the health of the planet is largely controlled by the ocean and major food resources are derived from the sea." Just 5 percent of the sea floor is mapped—making it less known than our moon. The bells and whistles of space travel capture the lion's share of taxpayer money: the government spends a little more than $500 million a year on ocean science, in contrast to $13 billion given to the space program, says Gilmore.

The two-hour documentary produced by our expedition and narrated by Martin Sheen was broadcast on the Discovery Channel. The film was finally entitled "Cuba: Forbidden Depths." At the beginning of the documentary, Sheen intoned the seriousness of the mission: "A great research vessel on a historic voyage along the coast of Cuba . . . A state-of-the-art submarine . . . Top American and Cuban scientists plunge to the forbidden depths of inner space!"

The segment with Castro was entirely excised from the final cut, a decision that went beyond the Discovery producer, all the way to the upper echelon of Discovery Communications itself. After seeing the rough cut of the film, Gilmore wrote to John Hendricks, founder and CEO, to make a plea to reinstall Castro, as well as to use more of the Cuban people themselves. He was told it was too politically risky.

It mattered little that Castro himself said nothing political—indeed, much of what he did say was enlightening, or at least revealing about his own complexity. More to the point, Discovery officials were greatly concerned about anticipated protests from members of the anti-Castro exile community in south Florida if their former homeland—including its leader and its people—was portrayed with any sense of charity. In other words, any film that did not demonize Castro and objectify the Cuban people as desperate and miserable—the common mass media portrayal—was unacceptable. Gilmore's hope for fish diplomacy went down the tubes. The higher ideal of using a shared ecological resource to open the door to resolving political differences was shelved in favor of the white-bread corporate disdain for controversy. Censorship that was oddly reminiscent of media control practiced in Cuba clearly prevailed. As a result, American audiences anxious for real information about the riddle that is Cuba instead tuned out in alarming numbers. And, despite the stunning images and the well-known celebrity of the place, the ratings of the film were far below what was expected.

Both producer Lipscomb and scientist Alcolado were said to be so disappointed with the final cut that they did not watch the show when it aired. To this day, the documentary has never been broadcast in Cuba.

A final log of thirty-eight sub dives reveals that Giddings made a total of ten dives, while Alcolado made only four. Claro had nine dives, but five were in the aft compartment—where collection is nearly impossible. Of Gilmore's twelve dives, half were to the aft. "This is not a very good record and would certainly have been otherwise had I really been a chief scientist on a voyage of discovery," Gilmore told me afterward. On a pure science cruise, twice as many sub dives would have been made, and each working scientist would have been supported by up to four research assistants, resulting in a body of new information so profound that it would have been a "magnitude more" in comparison with the film cruise. "I would give anything to repeat the voyage strictly for the benefit of scientific discovery." Oddly, Gilmore—a veteran scuba diver—never participated in any of the underwater filming dives during the cruise, and I wondered why. "I am a careful diver and deemed much of the macho dive antics Giddings required as not only dangerous but foolish," Gilmore said. In reviewing the dives of the expedition with HBOI dive master Liberatore afterward, Gilmore learned that there was "more than one close call that could have easily spelled disaster."

The Discovery Channel Web site, once bold and innovative, has been downgraded into a program guide, designed almost exclusively to promote upcoming shows. Its new incarnation virtually eliminated "real-time" expeditions. Once ignored or regarded as competition for viewers' time, the Web site has since been fully commandeered by its television programmers specifically to promote and advertise Discovery products.

Al Giddings and Jim Lipscomb continue to produce high-quality documentaries on contract, as they have throughout their careers, although they have no current plans to collaborate on other projects. Gilmore, who had worked at Harbor Branch since his days as a grad student, left HBOI almost to the day of the broadcast premier and is now directing a marine science program at the Kennedy Space Center. Many of the crew of the *Seward*—including Captain Vince Seiler and cook Jay Grant—have also resigned or retired.

On our return to U.S. soil, Gilmore was debriefed by a team from the CIA. The agents were particularly interested in Castro's health—how he walked and talked, the color of his skin—as well as where his bodyguards were stationed. Gilmore asked, only half jokingly, if they were planning another hit, and he was told that the internal politics of Cuba were at the moment "stabilized" and it was hoped they would remain so for the time being. Anyway, they said—in turn only half joking—"the mob tried to kill him more than we ever did." It was a reference to mob boss Meyer Lansky's outrage over the loss of the corrupt Batista-sanctioned casinos and nightclubs after the revolution.

John McCosker continues his research at the California Academy of Sciences. Richard Fagen enjoys his retirement in Washington State and Dick Robins his in Kansas.

Several scientific papers in the United States and Cuba are being prepared for publication to describe new species found on the expedition. But at this writing, only one paper, by Dr. Tammy Frank on bioluminescence, has been published. Drs. Claro and Alcolado continue to study the coastal environment of Cuba with great dedication. I recently asked Alcolado if he would tell me what his expectations were on this expedition, and he said: "Very important for me was to exchange my experience with Shirley Pomponi, a very prestigious sponge specialist and a very kind person as well. It was a demonstration about how nice scientific and human relationships can exist between our countries and how fine is to work together in peace." Indeed, despite the concerns over compromised research, the fact remains that marine science that otherwise would have not been accomplished in Cuban waters took place. Cuban nationals and Americans did work together, and they did so very well.

At this writing, Fidel Castro remains a very alive El Comandante, and the U.S. embargo that prohibits Americans from trading with Cuba is still intact. Dr. Dario Guitart Manday, the keeper of Poey's original unpublished books, passed away on March 23, 2000, his dream of a shared ecological marine reserve with the United States unrealized.

The sea and the animals that live in it continue to wash freely between Cuba and the United States, unhindered by the conceits of laws and boundaries and other human-declared prohibitions.

BIBLIOGRAPHY

Adams, Chuck. 1994. "The Commercial Fishing Industry of Cuba: The Times They Are A-Changin'." *Fathom.* Gainesville, Fla.: Florida Sea Grant Program. Summer.

Albrecht, Andreas, et al. 1977. Unedited letter to the editor of the *New York Times* regarding denial of attendance of Cuban chemists at the U.S./Latin American Workshop in Quantum Chemistry at the University of Florida. March 13.

Alcolado, Pedro, Instituto de Oceanología, Academia de Ciencias de Cuba. Personal communication with the author (numerous 1999–2000).

"Alleged Castro Plot Tied to Exile." 1997. Associated Press. April 2.

Annual Report. 1996. Harbor Branch Oceanographic Institution. Fort Pierce, Fla.

Annual Report. 1997. Center for Marine Conservation. Washington, D.C.

Aquaculture Center for Training, Education, and Demonstration. 2000. Course Catalog. Fort Pierce, Fla.: Harbor Branch Oceanographic Institution.

Baker, Christopher P. 1997. *Cuba Handbook.* Moon Travel Handbooks. Chico, Calif.: Moon Publications. November.

Barbour, Thomas. 1946. *A Naturalist in Cuba.* Boston: Little, Brown and Company.

Bauza, Vanessa. 2001. "Cuba Prospecting for Oil in Gulf of Mexico." *South Florida Sun-Sentinel.* July 26.

Bell, Maya, and Deborah Ramirez. 1998. "Cubans Hear New Message: Bring Religion to Your Families and to Your Schools, the Pope Said during His First Mass in Cuba." *Orlando (Fla.) Sentinel.* January 23

Belleville, Bill. 1997. HBOI Personal Dive Log. Cuba '97. R/V *Seward Johnson.* December.

Blow, Michael. 1992. *A Ship to Remember.* New York: William Morrow and Company.

Bouma, Katherine. 1997. "Scientists Look for New Life in Ocean's Last Frontier: Biologists Are Investigating the Unspoiled, Unexplored Waters off Cuba's Coast." *Orlando Sentinel.* December 5.

Broad, William. 1997. *The Universe Below: Discovering the Secrets of the Deep Sea.* New York: Simon and Schuster.

Bustamante, Georgina, The Nature Conservancy. Personal communication with the author. November 18, 1999.

Campbell, Joseph. 1988. *The Power of Myth.* New York: Doubleday.

"Capacity-building in MPAs: Practitioners Face Challenges, View Opportunities." 2000. *MPA News* (International News and Analysis on Marine Protected Areas). Seattle, Wash.: School of Marine Affairs, University of Washington. March.

Carr, Archie. 1979 (1955). *The Windward Road.* Gainesville, Fla.: University Presses of Florida.

Castañeda, Rolando. 1996. "Cuban Economic Policy: Misguided Economic Reforms." New York: SUNY Report, Inter-American Development Bank.

"Castro Enjoys Visit by Illinois Governor." 1999. Associated Press. October 24.

"Castro Visits U.S. Ship in Havana Port." 1998. Reuters. January 3.

Centeno, Miguel Angel. 1995. "Domination, Contract, and Trust in the Cuban Transition." Conference paper for "Toward a New Cuba? Legacies of Revolution." Princeton: Princeton University. March 15.

Centeno, Miguel Angel, and Mauricio Font, eds. "The Invisible Crisis: The Exhaustion of Politics in 1990's Cuba." New York: SUNY Report, Cuba in Perspective.

Cernetig, Miro. 1977. "Thank You, Fidel, May I Have Another Gold Ingot?" *Outside Magazine.* May.

Charles, Simon. 1997. *The Cruising Guide to Cuba.* Dunedin, Fla.: Cruising Guide Publications.

Claro, Rodolfo. Correspondence to R. Grant Gilmore Jr. regarding Dario Guitart Manday. July 2000.

Claro, Rodolfo, ed. 1994. *Ecología de los Peces Marinos de Cuba*. Havana, Cuba: Academia de Ciencias de Cuba.

———. 2002 [in press]. *Ecology of the Marine Fishes of Cuba*. Washington, D.C.: Smithsonian Institution Press.

Collis, David S. 1995. "Cuba Briefing Paper Series: Environmental Implications of Cuba's Economic Crisis." The Cuba Project, Center for Latin American Studies. Georgetown University. No. 8. July.

Collis, David S., ed. 1995. "The Caribbean Environment: Issues of Mutual Concern." Washington, D.C.: Georgetown University Caribbean Environmental Conference Summary. December 5–6.

Colonization and Trade in the New World (Map). 1977. *National Geographic Magazine*. Washington, D.C.: National Geographic Society. December.

Conte, Andrew. 1998. "Castro, Cuba Sea Life Impress Scientists." *The Port St. Lucie (Fla.) News*. January 7.

Cousteau, Jacques-Yves, with James Dugan. 1963. *The Living Sea*. New York: Harper and Row.

Cowern, Christine. 1999. "Natural History vs. the Environment." *Natural History* magazine.

Cuba: Consular Information Sheet. 1997. Washington, D.C.: U.S. State Department. July 22.

"Cuba: Forbidden Depths." 1999. 120-minute broadcast documentary. Discovery Communications. June 6.

"Cuba Turns Eco-Friendly." 2000. Associated Press. November 26.

Cuban Assets Control Regulations. 1995. *Federal Register*. Office of Foreign Assets Control. Department of the Treasury. October 20.

"Cuba's Nuclear-plant Construction Unsettles U.S." 1997. Hearst Newspapers. August 31.

Daly, Sean. 1999. "Eight Arms and the Man." *Washington City Paper*. November 19–25.

Darwin, Charles. 1989 (1839). *The Voyage of the Beagle*. New York: Penguin Classics.

Davalos, Fernando. 1984. "Viaje al Cosmos Subacuático de Cuba." Havana, Cuba: Bohemia. February.

DePalma, Anthony. 2000. "Finding Ways to Dabble in Cuba, Legally." *New York Times*. March 5.

"Did U.S. Infest Cuba with Bugs?" 1997. Associated Press. August 28.

"Discussion Points in Santiago." 1997. Communication Memo from Al Giddings and Jim Lipscomb aboard the R/V *Seward Johnson*. December 8.

"Dissidents Draw Castro's Wrath." 1999. Associated Press. November 3.

Eager, Walter. 1998. "Harbor Branch's Cuban Expedition Proves Success." *(Vero, Fla.) Press Journal*. May 31.

Earle, Sylvia A. 1995. *Sea Change: A Message of the Oceans*. New York: G. P. Putnam's Sons.

EarthTrends (http://earthtrends.wri.org/). 2001. Coastal and Marine Ecosystems: Country Profiles: Cuba. Biodiversity and Protected Areas: Country Profiles: Cuba. World Resources Institute. Last accessed December 3, 2001.

Ecott, Tim. 2001. *Neutral Buoyancy: Adventures in a Liquid World*. New York: Atlantic Monthly Press.

Ellis, Keith. 1985 (1983). *Cuba's Nicolás Guillén: Poetry and Ideology*. Toronto: University of Toronto Press.

Ellis, Richard, and John E. McCosker. 1991. *Great White Shark: The Definitive Look at the Most Terrifying Creature of the Ocean*. Stanford: Stanford University Press.

"Estefan Feels Pain of Cuban Outrage." 1997. Associated Press. October 9.

"Exiles Directed, Financed Cuba Bombing, Paper Says." 1997. *Miami Herald*. November 16.

"Exile's Laser Does Little Good over Cuba." 1997. Reuters. November 2.

"Expedition Members—Forbidden Waters: Final Crew List." 1997. December.

Fagen, Richard. 1990. *Closer to Houston*. Santa Barbara, Calif.: John Daniel.

Fagen, Richard R., and Patricia N. Fagen. 1970. "Revolution for Cuba's Lobster Industry." *Geographical Magazine*. September. London.

Fagen, Richard, with Roger Dooley. 1997. Hand-drawn underwater map of Sambo Head. December 19.

"Farmers See Cuba As a Future Threat." 2000. *Tampa Tribune*. November 24.

Flannery, Mary Ellen. 1998. "Castro's Visit Not Only Surprise for Researchers: Real Excitement Is Discovering Four Species of Fish." *Palm Beach Post*. January 6.

Font, Mauricio A. 1995–96. "Shift in U.S. Policy Toward Cuba." New York: Queens College.

Frank, Tamara M. 1999. "Comparative Study of Temporal Resolution in the Visual Systems of Mesopelagic Crustaceans." *Biological Bulletin* 196 (April). Woods Hole, Mass.: Maine Biological Laboratory.

Franklin, Jane. 1997. *Cuba and the United States: A Chronological History*. Hoboken, N.J.: Ocean Press.

Fuentes, Norberto. 1984. *Hemingway in Cuba*. New York: Carol Publishing Group.

George, Terry. 1996. "Back to Havana." *Travel Holiday.* March.

Gibbs, W. Wayt. 1996. "A New Way to Spell Relief: V-e-n-o-m: A Toxin from Killer Sea Snails Promises a Better Painkiller." *Scientific American.* February.

Giddings, Al, and Roger Dooley. 1997. "Dive Sites and Route of the Discovery Expedition." December.

Gilmore, R. Grant, Jr. 1997. "Cuban Mangroves—Seagrass Meadows." Communication memo to Al Giddings and Jim Lipscomb aboard the R/V *Seward Johnson.* December 16.

———. 1998. "Final Cruise Summary: Cruise No. 97-035." Fort Pierce, Fla.: Harbor Branch Oceanographic Institution.

———. 1997. "Lipogramma Robinsi, a New Basslet from the Tropical Western Atlantic." *Bulletin of Marine Science.* Miami: Rosenstiel School of Marine and Atmospheric Science of the University of Miami.

———. 1997. "Specific Research Objectives" (Pre-cruise scientific summary).

———. 1998. "Preliminary Cruise Report for R/V *Seward Johnson* Cruise No. 97-035 [to U.S. Department of State]." Harbor Branch Oceanographic Institution. February 5.

———. 1997. Personal pre-trip correspondence to John McCosker regarding scientific techniques and tools relevant to the Cuba Expedition. November 21.

Gilmore, R. Grant, Jr., and Robert S. Jones. 1992. "Color Variation and Associated Behavior in the Epinepheline Groupers, *Mycteroperca Microlepis* (Goode and Bean) and *M. Phenax* Jordan and Swain." *Bulletin of Marine Science.* Miami: Rosenstiel School of Marine and Atmospheric Science of the University of Miami.

Goering, Laurie. 1999. "Havana's Showcase Summit Ends with Castro in Sour Mood." *Chicago Tribune.* November 17.

Goetzman, Keith. 1997. "Return of the Mambo Kings." *Utne Reader.* Minneapolis, Minn. November/December.

Graulich, Heather. 1998. Exploring Cuba's Forbidden Waters. *Palm Beach Post.* West Palm Beach, Fla. January 13.

Guillén, Nicolás. 1974. *Tengo.* Broadside Press.

Hagstrom, Suzy. 1998. "Curious Castro Boards U.S. Ship." *Orlando (Fla.) Sentinel.* January 4.

Harbor Branch Profiles. 1998 (With 1997 *Annual Report*). Fort Pierce, Fla.: Harbor Branch Oceanographic Institution.

"Hassler Expedition 1871–1872." 2001. See http://www.mcz.harvard.edu/fish/hassler.htm. Last accessed December 3, 2001.

"Havana Says Policies Help Its Forests Thrive." 1999. Associated Press. August 11.

Hemingway, Ernest. 1977 (1970). *Islands in the Stream*. New York: Scribners.

————. 1996 (1937). *To Have and Have Not*. New York: Scribners.

"History of Work in Cuba." 1997. Center for Marine Conservation Briefing Paper. Washington, D.C.

Hoover, Pierce. 1999. "Treasures of Cuba." *Sport Diver*. Winter Park, Fla.: World Publications. December.

Humann, Paul (edited by Ned DeLoach). 1996. *Reef Coral Identification: Florida, Caribbean, Bahamas*. Jacksonville, Fla.: New World Publications.

———— (edited by Ned DeLoach). 1996. *Reef Fish Identification: Florida, Caribbean, Bahamas*. Jacksonville, Fla.: New World Publications.

———— (edited by Ned DeLoach). 1996. *Reef Creature Identification: Florida, Caribbean, Bahamas*. Jacksonville, Fla.: New World Publications.

Hylton, Wil S. 1997. "Island of Forbidden Delights." *Outside* magazine. November.

Johnson, Paul. 1994. "Coastal Development May Benefit from Florida's Experience." *Fathom*. Gainesville, Fla.: Florida Sea Grant Program. Summer.

Journals and Other Documents on the Life and Voyages of Christopher Columbus. 1963. Avon, Conn.: Heritage Press.

Kennedy, Robert F., Jr. 1996. "Energy: Mission to Cuba Journal." Natural Resources Defense Council. New York City. February.

Klingel, Gilbert C. 1997 (1940). *Inagua: An Island Sojourn*. New York: Lyons and Burford.

Kofoed, Jack. 1960. *The Florida Story*. Garden City, N.Y.: Doubleday.

Kolata, Gina. 1996. "Deadly Snails Take Pinpoint Aim." *New York Times*. August 6.

Koppes, Steven N. 1999. "A River Runs to It: Can Georgia Estuaries Survive Impending Coastal Development?" *Research Reporter*. Athens: University of Georgia. September.

Kreeger, Karen Young. 1996. "U.S. and Cuban Collaborators Undeterred by Economic Embargo, Ideological Standoff." *The Scientist*. Philadelphia. April 15.

Lampf, Gregg, Martek Biosciences. Personal communication with the author. September 1, 1998.

Lee, Alfonso Silva. 1996. *Natural Cuba*. St. Paul, Minn.: Pangaea.

Levinson, Sandra. 1997. "Cuba Update." New York: The Center for Cuban Studies. September–December.

Lipscomb, James. 1997. Abbreviated treatment for "Forbidden Waters." September 2.

Little, Jane Braxton. 2000. "Management by Poison." *Forest Magazine*. Eugene, Ore.: Forest Service Employees for Environmental Ethics. March–April.

Long, Phil. 1998. "Cuban Fish Tale Makes History." *Miami Herald*. January 12.

Lunan, Charles. 1993. "Cuban Tourism in Limbo." *Fort Lauderdale Sun-Sentinel*. October 10.

Mapa Turístico General de Cuba. Ediciones Caribbean's Color S.A. Havana, Cuba.

Marine Statistics for Cuba: Marine Protected Areas of Cuba. Cambridge, U.K.: World Conservation Monitoring Centre.

Marwick, Charles. 1998. "Nature's Agents Help Heal Humans—Some Now Take Steps to Reciprocate." *JAMA: The Journal of the American Medical Association*. June 3.

Masefield, John. 1923. *The Collected Poems of John Masefield*. London: Heinemann.

Matthiessen, Peter. 1997 (1971). *Blue Meridian: The Search for the Great White Shark*. New York: Penguin Nature Classics.

McCosker, John E. 1977. "Flashlight Fishes." *Scientific American*. San Francisco. March.

McCosker, John. 1978. "Fish That Flash." *Outside*. September–October.

McMurray, Kevin. 1995. "Forbidden Cuba: Diving's Last Taboo." *Sub-Aqua* magazine.

Mendelsohn, Jack. 1996. "Nuclear Plant Shows Danger of Isolation." *Orlando (Fla.) Sentinel*. February 25.

Miller, James J. 1998. "An Environmental History of Northeast Florida." Gainesville: Florida Museum of Natural History.

Miller, Tom. 1992. *Trading with the Enemy: A Yankee Travels through Castro's Cuba*. Basic Books (HarperCollins).

Museum of Comparative Zoology at Harvard University. Harvard University web site, http://www.mcz.harvard.edu/fish/history.htm. Last accessed December 3, 2001.

"New Trend: Retiring Overseas: Trend Spotters Say Cuba and Other Latin American Countries Will Become Retirement Destinations." 1996. *Miami Herald*. August 14.

"Next Frontier: The Ocean Floor." 1997. Knight Ridder Washington Bureau. October 5.

"Odd Creatures Thrive on Sea Floor." 2000. Knight Ridder Newspapers. January 2.

Onslow, Will. 1997. "Havana on the Verge." *Esquire*. June.

Oro, Jose. 1994. "Cuba Struggles without American Markets." *Fathom*. Gainesville: Florida Sea Grant Program. Summer.

O'Rourke, P. J. 1996. "Cubanomics: In Fidel Castro's Crumbling Socialist Paradise, the Rum Is Older than the Whores, the Currency Is Worthless, and Everybody's Working for the Yankee Dollars." *Rolling Stone*. July 11–25.

Palumbi, Stephen. 2001. MPA Perspective: Genetics, Marine Dispersal Distances, and the Design of Marine Reserve Networks. *MPA News*. Seattle: School of Marine Affairs, University of Washington. March.

Parsa, T. Z. "Cuba Red." 1997. *New York Magazine*. November 17.

Pattullo, Polly. 1996. *Last Resorts: The Cost of Tourism in the Caribbean*. London, U.K.: Cassell.

Payne, Douglas W. 1996. "Life in Castro's Mafia State." *Society*. January/February.

Perez, Louis A., Jr. 1996/97. "What You Can and Cannot Say about Cuba in Florida." *Forum*. Tampa: The Florida Humanities Council. Winter.

Perrottet, Tony, and Joann Biondi, eds. 1995. *Insight Guides: Cuba*. New York: Houghton Mifflin.

Poore, Charles, ed. 1953. *The Enduring Hemingway: An Anthology of a Lifetime in Literature*. New York: Charles Scribner's Sons.

Putman, John J. 1999. "Evolution in the Revolution: Cuba." *National Geographic Magazine*. Washington, D.C. June.

República de Cuba: Departamento de Capitanías de Puerto. Permiso Especial de Navegación. Permiso No. 270. December 1997.

Ripley, C. Peter. 2000. *Conversations with Cuba*. Athens: University of Georgia Press.

Rohter, Larry. 1997. "Cancún It's Not, but Cuba Welcomes More Visitors." *New York Times*. September 30.

Rossier, Robert. 1995. "Rebreathers." *Alert Diver: The Magazine of Divers Alert Network*. Durham, N.C. January/February.

Rouse, Irving. 1992. *The Tainos: Rise and Decline of the People Who Greeted Columbus*. New Haven, Conn.: Yale University Press.

Ryan, Alan, and Christa Malone, eds. 1997. *The Cuba Reader*. New York: Harvest Books.

Sanderlin, George, ed. and trans. 1971. *Bartolomé de Las Casas: A Selection of His Writings*. New York: Knopf.

"Saving Sea Turtles, But at What Cost?" 1999. Associated Press. February 14.

"Scientific Consensus Statement on Marine Reserves and Marine Protected Areas."

2001. Annual Meeting of the American Association for the Advancement of Science, National Center for Ecological Analysis and Synthesis. University of California, Santa Barbara. February 17.

Sedaghatkish, Gina, and Ellen Roca, eds. 1999. Rapid Ecological Assessment: U.S. Naval Station, Guantánamo Bay, Cuba. Arlington, Va.: Conservation Science Department, Latin American and Caribbean Region, The Nature Conservancy. February.

Sheth, Priyanka. 1998. "Researchers Return from Cuban Waters." *Fort Pierce (Fla.) Tribune.* January 6.

Smith, Allan H., and Tom van't Hof. 1991. Coral Reef Monitoring for Management of Marine Parks: Cases from the Insular Caribbean. Caribbean Natural Resources Institute. St. Lucia, West Indies.

Smith, Michael L. 1997. "Scientists Discover New Life Forms during Caribbean Expeditions!" *Marine Conservation News* 9, no. 3. Washington, D.C.: Center for Marine Conservation.

Smith, Michael L. 1995. "The Environment in U.S.-Cuban Relations: Opportunities for Cooperation." Inter-American Dialogue Conference Report. April.

Smith, Michael L., Center for Marine Conservation. Personal communication with the author. Nov. 21, 1997.

Snow, Anita. 2001. "Tourism Replaces Sugar as Cuba's Top Industry." Associated Press. June 10.

Steneck, Robert S., Judith C. Lang, Philip A. Kramer, and Robert N. Ginsburg. 1997. Atlantic and Gulf Reef Assessment: Rapid Assessment Protocol. Report. October.

Taviani, Paolo Emilio. 1991. *Columbus, the Great Adventure: His Life, His Times and His Voyages.* London: Orion Books.

The Caribbean Scientific Initiative: A New RARE Center Program. 1993. *Rare Center News.* Philadelphia, Penn.: RARE Center for Tropical Conservation. Fall.

Thomas, Bella. 1996. "For Europeans, Cuba Hasn't Lost Its Magic." *New York Times.* June 28.

Thomas, Jo. 1993. "By Choking Cuba, Cradling Castro?" *New York Times.* March 14.

Tourism and Cruise Passenger Arrivals in 1999. 1999. Caribbean Tourism Organization. New York. November.

Treasures of the World Lost and Found. 2001. National Geographic Maps. Washington, D.C. July.

"Two Face Trial in Deaths of Cubans Trying to Flee." 1999. Associated Press. October 24.

UNESCO Programme on Man and the Biosphere (pamphlet). 1996. New York: UNESCO.

Viders, Hillary. 2000. "Dr. Bill Hamilton: Getting Up to Speed with the 'Mix Master.'" *Alert Diver: The Magazine of Divers Alert Network.* Durham, N.C. May/June.

Villar, Arturo. 1994. "Tourism Offers Economic Hope for Cuba." *Fathom.* Gainesville, Fla.: Florida Sea Grant Program. Summer.

"Void in Cuban-American Leadership Deepens." 1999. *New York Times.* September 12.

Weiner, Tim. 1997. "The Trouble with Assassinations." *New York Times.* November 23.

West Indies (map). 1997. *National Geographic* 172, no. 5, p. 644A. Washington, D.C.: National Geographic Society. November.

"When Canadian Divers Explore off Cuba, They Come Up with Riches." 2000. Reuters. November 20.

Widder, Edith. 2000. "Glowing Jellyfish Have a Lot to Say." *National Geographic* 198, no. 1. Washington, D.C.: National Geographic Society. July.

Widder, Edith; illus. by Charissa Baker. 1998 [in press]. *The Bioluminescence Coloring Book.* Fort Pierce, Fla.: Harbor Branch Oceanographic Institution.

Wider Caribbean Sea Turtles ID. Wider Caribbean Sea Turtle Conservation Network. United Nations Environmental Programme.

Williams, Diana. 1999. *Lonely Planet: Diving and Snorkeling Cuba.* Victoria, Australia: Lonely Planet Publications.

Wilson, Edward O. 1992. *The Diversity of Life.* Cambridge, Mass.: The Belknap Press of Harvard University Press.

"The World Heritage List: Old Havana and Its Fortifications." World Heritage Information Network. New York: UNESCO.

Zuckerman, Mortimer B. (Editorial). 1995. "Let's Start Talking to Castro." *U.S. News and World Report.* May 15.

INDEX

Claro Madruga, Rodolfo, 27, 54, 84, 87, 158, 242, 251; book by, 122–23, 125; Castro and, 234; in Cayman Trench, 56; and Cayo Rosario, 142; at Chivirico, 66; at Corrientes, 204; in documentary, 32, 57, 72, 106, 189; as ecologist, 32, 107, 120–21, 172; fish identification by, 101–2; in Florida, 19, 123–24; in Guacanayabo, 74, 76, 81; in Guanahacabibes, 202; in Havana, 230–31; and Instituto de Oceanología, 27, 227–28; in JSL, 64; on Seward, 40

Cnidaria, 77, 154

Cocodrilo, 175, 176–82

coelacanth, 129

Cold War, 8

Coloma (boat), 191–93

Colony, The (hotel), 184, 186, 187–88

Columbus, Christopher, 75, 95; landings of, 36–37, 184; and Taino Indians, 76, 118, 204–5

Conan, Neil, 119–21

conch (Strombus gigas), 135–36

Conda, Mike, 60, 74, 76–77, 134, 138, 176

coney, 134–35

coral reefs: on Banco Jagua, 112; Cousteau's description of, 207; of Ensenada de Corrientes, 201, 205–8; in Guacanayabo, 74, 76; of Sambo Head, 160–64; in seamounts, 68, 106, 112; spur-and-groove, 135; threats to, 155, 205–6

corals: black, 89; on Colón shipwreck, 63; fire, 72; growth rate of, 12; sea whip, 115

Corrientes bay, 201, 205–8

Costello, Glenn, 131

Cousteau, Jacques-Yves, 5–6, 207

crabs: arrow, 133; land, 202

crinoid (feather star), 113–14

Cristóbal Colón (warship), 59–64, 237, 238

crocodile, Cuban (Crocodilus rhombifer), 80, 138, 171

Cruising Guide to Cuba, The (Charles), 66, 211–12

Cruza de la Parra, 37

ctenophores, 154

Cuba: approval of expedition by, 27–28; under Castro, 183–84; ecological importance of, 28, 29; entry into, 39–40; European settlers in, 76, 78, 143–44, 203; Florida and, 29–30; "Forbidden Zones" in, 32; historic role of, 16; origins of, 43; people of, 44, 179; prehistory of, 43, 67–68, 75; Soviet Union and, 39; trade with, 8, 11; United States and, 8–11, 28, 48–50, 183, 221, 249, 251

"Cuba: Forbidden Depths": Castro controversy in, 249; Cuban scientists in, 32, 57, 72, 106; as documentary title, 11, 24–25; Fagen's concerns about, 168, 210–11; sense of place in, 108. See also documentary of Cuba expedition, filming of

Cubanacan dive outfitters, 89

Cuban Revolution, 42, 66, 73, 119, 183

Customs and Immigration in Cuba, 39–40

Darío, Rubén, 11

Darwin, Charles, 3, 153

Day, Ray, 39, 132

decompression sickness ("the bends"), 34

Deep, The (movie), 162–63

development-related impacts, 15, 85, 116, 203

dinosaurs, in Cuban prehistory, 43

Discodermolide, 17

Discovery Channel: Castro controversy and, 249; Ecuador expedition for, 27;

flashlight fish (*Kryptophanaron alfredi*), 195, 196–97, 201
Florida, Cuba's influence on, 29–30
Florida Keys, 228
Florida Story, The (Kofoed), 9–10
Flower Garden Banks, 68
flying fish, 46
"Forbidden Zones," 32
four-eyed butterfly fish, 112
Fowler, Henry, 102
Frank, Tammy, 17, 94, 100, 154, 251
Frente group, 118
Fuentes, Norberto, 223, 225

"Galápagos: Beyond Darwin" (film), 26, 107
Galápagos expedition, for Discovery Channel, 26, 28, 107
garbage, in Guantánamo Bay, 50
Gardens of the Queen, 74, 92, 94
geology, of Cuba, 43, 48, 50, 67–68, 75, 127–28
Giddings, Al, 15–16, 29, 250; in Bahamas, 26; on Banco Jagua dive, 111, 116, 117; on Cabo Francés dive, 194, 195, 197, 200; Castro and, 29, 33, 210, 223, 234–38, 240–42; in Cayman Trench, 51, 52; on Cayo Rosario dive, 134–35; and Cayos Aguardientes dive, 151; on Chivirico seamount dive, 69, 70; at Cocodrilo, 176–77; on *Colón* dive, 60, 61, 62; on Corrientes dive, 204, 208; and Fagen, 71, 168, 169; filming ship's aquarium, 56–57, 132; and *jutia*, 92–93; at Laberinto de las Doce Leguas, 93; on lobster boat, 193; and mangroves, 85, 86; personality of, 18–19, 71; on Punta Francés dive, 184; on Tortuga Hotel, 95; underwater films of, 18, 53, 162–63, 237

Gilmore, Grant, 16, 22, 28–29, 32, 48, 79; on Banco Jagua dive, 109, 115, 117; and Bay of Pigs, 118; and Castro, 234, 237, 251; in Cayman Trench, 56; at Cayo Rosario, 129, 138–45; at Cayos de las Doce Leguas, 101, 105; and Cuban fish collection, 103; and deepwater fish, 103, 107–8; and disappointment with documentary, 250; and expedition retrospective, 243; fish drawings by, 102; fishing, 45, 96, 138–45, 167, 187; and fish songs, 79; fish studies by, 109–10, 131, 133; in Guacanayabo, 74, 76, 81; and Guitart, 229; in Havana, 219, 222; and HBOI, 57–58, 250–51; at Instituto de Oceanología, 227; and mangroves, 84, 85–86, 92; at press conference, 248–49; Robins and, 140; on Sambo Head dive, 167; on Tortuga Hotel, 92; and *Verilus* hunt, 103, 107, 165, 166, 234
"Gitmo" (Guantánamo), 47, 48–50
glassy sweepers, 63
gobies, 131
Golfo de Batabanó, 32, 74, 118, 122–23, 125, 190
González, Diógenes, 38, 45
Granma (boat), 66, 73
Grant, Jay, 25, 45, 74, 93, 126–27, 188, 241
green flash, 58
green moray, 162
green sea turtle, 178
grouper: color changes in, 80, 110; coney, 134–35; misty (*Epinephelus mystacinus*), 167; Nassau (*Epinephelus striatus*), 108, 109, 114–15; overharvesting of, 67, 110–11; red hind, 68; scamp (*Mycteroperca phenax*), 80, 110; sex

Cuban embargo by, 8–11, 221, 251;
fish overharvesting in, 67, 229; in
Guantánamo, 48–50
Uvero, El, 59–64

Varadero, 74, 126
Vedado district, of Havana, 217, 219
Velázquez, Diego, 78
veriles, 206–7
Verilus (spiny ray fish), 103, 107, 132,
165–66, 229, 234, 243
Viscaya shipwreck, 66

warblers, 49
War of Cuban Independence. *See*
Spanish-American War
Weiner, Jonathan, 132

wet-lab aquarium, 56–57, 72, 132–33, 135
Widder, Edie, 17, 94, 100, 149–50,
152–60, 235
Wilson, Edward O., 203
Wimberg, Randy, 132, 186; on Banco Jagua
dive, 112, 114; in Cayman Trench, 56;
on *Colón* dive, 61, 62; on Isla de la
Juventud dive, 175
Windward Passage, 31–34
woodpecker, Cuban ivory-billed, 36
Woods Hole Oceanographic Institution, 3
wrasse, 133

yellowhead jawfish (*Opistognathus
aurifrons*), 136

Zapata Peninsula, 123–24